Cisco Unified Presence Fundamentals

Brian Morgan, CCIE No. 4865

Shane Lisenbea

Michael C. Popovich III, CCIE No. 9599

D0902603

Cisco Press

800 East 96th Street

Indianapolis, IN 46240

Cisco Unified Presence Fundamentals

Brian Morgan, CCIE No. 4865

Shane Lisenbea

Michael C. Popovich III, CCIE No. 9599

Copyright© 2010 Cisco Systems, Inc.

Published by:
Cisco Press
800 East 96th Street
Indianapolis, IN 46240 USA

Printed in the United States of America

First Printing June 2010

Library of Congress Cataloging-in-Publication Data:
Morgan, Brian (Brian Edward)
    Cisco Unified Presence fundamentals / Brian Morgan, Shane Lisenbea, Michael Popovich III.
        p. cm.
    ISBN 978-1-58714-044-0 (pbk.)
  1. Telecommunication—Message processing.   2. Internet telephony.   3. Multimedia communications.
I. Lisenbea, Shane, 1970–   II. Popovich, Michael, 1973–   III. Cisco Systems, Inc.   IV. Title.

    TK5102.5.M654   2010
    006.7—dc22

2010019260

ISBN-13: 978-1-58714-044-0

ISBN-10: 1-58714-044-6

Warning and Disclaimer

This book is designed to provide information about Cisco Unified Presence. Every effort has been made to make this book as complete and as accurate as possible, but no warranty or fitness is implied.

The information is provided on an "as is" basis. The authors, Cisco Press, and Cisco Systems, Inc. shall have neither liability nor responsibility to any person or entity with respect to any loss or damages arising from the information contained in this book or from the use of the discs or programs that may accompany it.

The opinions expressed in this book belong to the author and are not necessarily those of Cisco Systems, Inc.

Trademark Acknowledgments

All terms mentioned in this book that are known to be trademarks or service marks have been appropriately capitalized. Cisco Press or Cisco Systems, Inc., cannot attest to the accuracy of this information. Use of a term in this book should not be regarded as affecting the validity of any trademark or service mark.

Corporate and Government Sales

The publisher offers excellent discounts on this book when ordered in quantity for bulk purchases or special sales, which may include electronic versions and/or custom covers and content particular to your business, training goals, marketing focus, and branding interests. For more information, please contact: **U.S. Corporate and Government Sales**   1-800-382-3419   corpsales@pearsontechgroup.com

For sales outside the United States, please contact: **International Sales**   international@pearsoned.com

Feedback Information

At Cisco Press, our goal is to create in-depth technical books of the highest quality and value. Each book is crafted with care and precision, undergoing rigorous development that involves the unique expertise of members from the professional technical community.

Readers' feedback is a natural continuation of this process. If you have any comments regarding how we could improve the quality of this book, or otherwise alter it to better suit your needs, you can contact us through e-mail at feedback@ciscopress.com. Please make sure to include the book title and ISBN in your message.

We greatly appreciate your assistance.

Publisher: Paul Boger	**Manager Global Certification:** Erik Ullanderson
Associate Publisher: Dave Dusthimer	**Business Operation Manager, Cisco Press:** Anand Sundaram
Executive Editor: Mary Beth Ray	**Technical Editors:** Kevin Hogan and Ben G. Martin
Managing Editor: Sandra Schroeder	**Copy Editor:** Apostrophe Editing Services
Senior Development Editor: Chris Cleveland	**Proofreader:** Sheri Cain
Senior Project Editor: Tonya Simpson	**Editorial Assistant:** Vanessa Evans
Book Designer: Louisa Adair	**Cover Designer:** Sandra Schroeder
Composition: Mark Shirar	**Indexer:** Tim Wright

Americas Headquarters	Asia Pacific Headquarters	Europe Headquarters
Cisco Systems, Inc.	Cisco Systems (USA) Pte. Ltd.	Cisco Systems International BV
San Jose, CA	Singapore	Amsterdam, The Netherlands

Cisco has more than 200 offices worldwide. Addresses, phone numbers, and fax numbers are listed on the Cisco Website at **www.cisco.com/go/offices.**

CCDE, CCENT, Cisco Eos, Cisco HealthPresence, the Cisco logo, Cisco Lumin, Cisco Nexus, Cisco StadiumVision, Cisco TelePresence, Cisco WebEx, DCE, and Welcome to the Human Network are trademarks; Changing the Way We Work, Live, Play, and Learn and Cisco Store are service marks; and Access Registrar, Aironet, AsyncOS, Bringing the Meeting To You, Catalyst, CCDA, CCDP, CCIE, CCIP, CCNA, CCNP, CCSP, CCVP, Cisco, the Cisco Certified Internetwork Expert logo, Cisco IOS, Cisco Press, Cisco Systems, Cisco Systems Capital, the Cisco Systems logo, Cisco Unity, Collaboration Without Limitation, EtherFast, EtherSwitch, Event Center, Fast Step, Follow Me Browsing, FormShare, GigaDrive, HomeLink, Internet Quotient, IOS, iPhone, iQuick Study, IronPort, the IronPort logo, LightStream, Linksys, MediaTone, MeetingPlace, MeetingPlace Chime Sound, MGX, Networkers, Networking Academy, Network Registrar, PCNow, PIX, PowerPanels, ProConnect, ScriptShare, SenderBase, SMARTnet, Spectrum Expert, StackWise, The Fastest Way to Increase Your Internet Quotient, TransPath, WebEx, and the WebEx logo are registered trademarks of Cisco Systems, Inc. and/or its affiliates in the United States and certain other countries.

All other trademarks mentioned in this document or website are the property of their respective owners. The use of the word partner does not imply a partnership relationship between Cisco and any other company. (0812R)

About the Authors

Brian Morgan, CCIE No. 4865, is a consulting systems engineer with Cisco specializing in Unified Communications and Collaboration technologies. In 20 years in the networking industry, he has performed in a number of roles, including network consultant, Certified Cisco Systems Instructor, and engineering director for a telecommunications company. When he's not spending time with the family, Brian enjoys working with local high school and college students enrolled in local Cisco Network Academy programs in North Texas.

Shane Lisenbea is a product sales specialist for Unified Communications. With 20 years of telephony experience, he started at the ground level of pulling wire to where he is today. During that path, Shane held many positions that include lead technician, supervisor, technical marketing engineer, and consulting system engineer. When Shane is not at work, he is still at work with several projects going all the time.

Michael C. Popovich III, CCIE No. 9599, is a consulting systems engineer with Cisco specializing in Unified Communications and Enterprise Social Software technologies. With 12 years in networking, he has spent most of that time in consulting roles with Cisco partners and Cisco working mainly with routing/switching and Unified Communication technologies. In the pursuit of a good work/life balance, Michael spends his spare time diving, riding motorcycles, and enjoying the outdoors when possible.

About the Technical Reviewers

Kevin Hogan, CCIE No. 24472, attended the University of Iowa where he graduated with a BBA degree in management information systems. Kevin worked for four years at a technology value-added reseller where he was responsible for deployment and maintenance of customer voice and data infrastructures before joining Cisco in 2006. He has spent the majority of his time at Cisco as a consulting systems engineer for Cisco Unified Communications and collaboration products focusing on large accounts across the Midwestern United States. Kevin currently resides in Urbandale, Iowa with his wife, daughter, and Labrador.

Ben G. Martin attended Oklahoma State University, where he majored in electrical engineering technology. Upon his graduation from Oklahoma State, he was hired by Cisco. He has spent the last six years working as a systems engineer specializing in Unified Communications. Ben has worked extensively with customers in the Kansas City metro area, focusing mainly on the design of data and voice networks. Ben holds his CCNP, CCDP, CCVP, CCSP, CISSP, and CWNP certifications and always seeks to learn more about new technologies. Ben lives with his wife in Olathe, Kansas.

Dedications

From Brian:

This book is dedicated to my lovely, and exceedingly patient, wife Beth. I'd also like to include my twin daughters, Amanda and Emma, who will be driving by the time this book is on the shelf. Be afraid.

From Shane:

I would like to dedicate this book to my father and my son. They both inspire me to do my best even when I feel I am not equal to the task.

Acknowledgments

From Brian Morgan:

I'd like to take a moment to specifically recognize two key contributors to this book: Kevin Hogan and Ben Martin. More than simply technical editors, Kevin and Ben were instrumental in making the book more complete. Without their involvement, there would be significant gaps in the coverage of this topic.

I'd also like to recognize John C. Bellamy, a man I've only met on a couple of occasions, but who has had an enormous impact on my career through the knowledge he has shared. Thank you for your contribution to our industry and my career.

A big thank-you goes out to the production team for this book. Mary Beth Ray and Christopher Cleveland are amazing people and a pleasure to work with. They took a chance in moving forward with this project. It is my sincere hope to work with them again in the near future.

Finally, I want to thank my co-authors, Shane and Michael. We've all worked together off and on for the past few years. This is the first project on which we've really had to be in each others' faces regularly, sometimes to the point of frustration. Timelines, travel schedules, customer meetings, and other issues constantly jump up and down demanding attention. Thank you both for helping me stay on task as I hope I've helped you. May this book be everything you hoped it would be.

From Shane Lisenbea:

I would like to thank Kevin and Ben for their part in getting this project done. The production team has been stellar in their efforts and are real professionals on getting everything just right.

To the co-authors, Michael and Brian, it has been a pleasure to work with you both on a project like this. Thank you for everything you guys do. It's a pleasure to work with folks that are just go getters.

This last acknowledgment is to the folks who taught me the foundations of telecommunications. Scott Miller, Russell Huckaby, Howard Hayne, and Greg Whittington together taught me lessons that I live off of today. Without them, I wouldn't be where I am today.

From Michael C. Popovich III:

I would like to thank Mary Beth Ray and Christopher Cleveland for the constant support on this book and helping us maintain timelines. And thanks to the technical reviewers, Kevin Hogan and Ben Martin, for the valuable feedback to ensure the book's relevance to our target readers.

Contents at a Glance

Contents

Icons Used in This Book

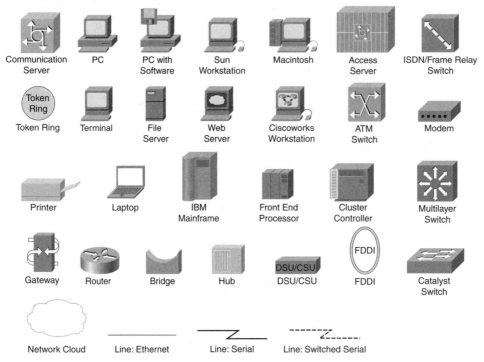

Command Syntax Conventions

The conventions used to present command syntax in this book are the same conventions used in the IOS Command Reference. The Command Reference describes these conventions as follows:

- **Boldface** indicates commands and keywords that are entered literally as shown. In actual configuration examples and output (not general command syntax), boldface indicates commands that are manually input by the user (such as a **show** command).

- *Italic* indicates arguments for which you supply actual values.

- Vertical bars (|) separate alternative, mutually exclusive elements.

- Square brackets ([ ]) indicate an optional element.

- Braces ({ }) indicate a required choice.

- Braces within brackets ([{ }]) indicate a required choice within an optional element.

Introduction

Unified Communications and Collaboration is on the so-called "Hot List" in any forum wherein people are discussing communications and ways to better stay in touch. This book is aimed at explaining the concepts, ideas, and capabilities behind Presence, which is likely one of the least understood and most underestimated features in a Unified Communications solution. It has the power to end phone-tag before the game even begins. It has the power to ensure that you reach the right resource by the right means and on the first attempt.

Goals and Methods

The most important and somewhat obvious goal of this book is to explain not only the concepts behind Presence but also the technologies involved, their interdependencies, and how to troubleshoot them. It is understood that knowing a concept is not sufficient in and of itself. There must be comprehension and direction; a primer of sorts. With that in mind, some discussion of practical applications of Presence as a technology has also been addressed herein.

The book has been organized such that you might begin with little or no knowledge of Presence as a concept. The ideas behind it, installation and deployment of the technologies, and some possible applications are discussed to show some basic capabilities. It is largely up to you to decide how to best utilize these technologies within your organization; However, we assist in getting things moving in the right direction.

Who Should Read This Book?

This book is not designed to be a general networking topics book, although it can be used for that purpose. It is meant to be a reference before, during, and after the implementation of Cisco Unified Presence. It is both a guide and a reference resource. This book is intended to assist in understanding, installing, deploying, and troubleshooting numerous aspects of Cisco Unified Presence. In being so, it will be quite specific in those places where it is most important. With the installation out of the way, much of the level of specificity herein will disappear. This is due to the authors' desire to avoid placing impediments to imagination. Unified Communications and Collaboration solutions are intended to be customized to fit a particular environment, solve business needs, and transform the way in which business is done. As you read this book, you can apply the information to your own environment and shape it into your own solution to meet your needs and that of your business.

How This Book Is Organized

As mentioned, this book is both a reference and a guide. It walks you through the installation process and detail interdependencies between various systems within a Cisco Unified Communications environment. So it might be of most benefit to read the book cover-to-cover prior to stepping into an installation effort. You can likely learn things in the troubleshooting chapter that can save you some pain in the installation phase, for example. The outline of the book is as follows:

- **Chapter 1, "What Is Unified Communications?"**—This chapter provides a high-level tour of Unified Communications components. The purpose of doing so is to provide a base upon which a solid understanding of Presence and its uses can be built.

- **Chapter 2, "Cisco Unified Presence Overview"**—This chapter provides an introduction to Presence as a concept before getting deeper into Presence features and functionality. This provides a better understanding of the concepts discussed in the remainder of the book surrounding both the Presence Server and Presence clients.

- **Chapter 3, "Installing Cisco Unified Presence Server 7"**—This chapters provides a step-by-step guide to installing Cisco Unified Presence Server 7.x. It also discusses in detail the interdependencies between the Cisco Unified Presence Server and the Cisco Unified Communications Manager, as well as the configuration of those interdependencies.

- **Chapter 4, "Cisco Unified Presence Integration with Cisco Unified Communications Manager"**—This chapter provides a deeper view of the combined functional capabilities of Cisco Unified Presence and Cisco Unified Communications Manager. It covers LDAP integration and configuration along with user and phone feature association.

- **Chapter 5, "Cisco Unified Personal Communicator"**—This chapter covers the installation and configuration of the Cisco Unified Personal Communicator. Aside from simply installing the client, this chapter discusses the interdependencies between user, desk phone, and CUPC client as they relate to one another. The configuration includes not only the Cisco Unified Presence Server dependencies, but also those within the Cisco Unified Communications Manager.

- **Chapter 6, "Cisco Unified Presence Practical Applications"**—This chapter provides some general use cases for Presence as a feature. It looks into how Presence might be used by a varied user base with varied needs and provides some high-level case studies of features that different types of users might utilize.

- **Chapter 7, "Cisco Unified Presence Federation"**—This chapter discusses needs and configuration of both intradomain federation and intradomain federation with Cisco Unified Presence Server clusters. It also goes into the basics of interdomain federation with Microsoft OCS.

- **Chapter 8, "Leveraging Cisco Unified Presence in Vertical Markets"**—This chapter provides a use-case overview of how varying types of businesses might utilize the feature set provided by Cisco Unified Presence.

- **Chapter 9, "Troubleshooting Cisco Unified Presence"**—This chapter covers the troubleshooting aspect of Cisco Unified Presence. This includes troubleshooting the Cisco Unified Presence Server, Cisco Unified Personal Communicator, and Cisco Unified Communications Manager and the interdependencies between all these elements.

Chapter 1

What Is Unified Communications?

The intent of this chapter is to provide a high-level overview of Cisco Unified Communications (UC) as a collaborative solution that enables its users to perform their job functions more efficiently. Increasing efficiency decreases the amount of time required to perform the same job function. Depending on circumstances, these decreases can be dramatic.

The definition of Unified Communications is different based upon the vendor's solution being defined and how it is implemented. This type of definition is unique and can confuse the topic because each vendor can have their own nomenclatures, so industry terms and definitions are necessary. The industry's definition of Unified Communications follows:

> *Unified communications (UC)* is the integration of nonreal-time communication services such as unified messaging (integrated voicemail, e-mail, short message service [SMS], and fax) with real-time communication services such as instant messaging (chat), presence information, IP telephony, video conferencing, call control, and speech control. UC is not a single product but a set of products that provides a consistent unified user interface and user experience across multiple devices and media types.

The root of the preceding definition is that a UC solution is a convergence of real-time and nonreal-time services that are equally usable across multiple means of access.

This chapter briefly covers some basic background information regarding the following:

- Telephony history

- Private Branch eXchange (PBX) architecture

- IP-based call control

Some discussion then follows regarding the user experience as it pertains to legacy telephony technologies then and Cisco UC now and how Cisco is simplifying the means by which companies deploy the various technologies available on a user-by-user basis. By basing the licensing model on the users and their chosen workspace, a more efficient, fluid deployment model can emerge.

Cisco UC is far from simply dial tone. The Time Division Multiplexing (TDM) technologies of past decades are quickly becoming architectural fossils. Many of the traditional TDM vendors have made attempts to seize a part of the UC market, but their successes are largely contained to their so-called loyal-at-all-costs clientele.

Before any discussion of UC can really take place, a frame of reference must be established. To accomplish this, a discussion regarding past and present communications is in order.

Telephony History

Telephony as we know it goes back quite a while. In fact, it goes back farther than most people care to explore. Was Alexander Graham Bell the first to produce the telephone in 1876? Or the more pertinent question, was he the first to file the patent? Much controversy surrounded Bell's invention. One Elisha Gray might have been very much in favor of Bell meeting with some misfortune. But, alas, it was not to happen. Although Elisha Gray's patent for the telephone might have proved a workable solution, Bell had one critical element that Gray did not possess. The simple knowledge of speech and linguistics. Bell's mother was hearing impaired. His grandfather, father, and brother were all noted teachers of elocution and speech (what we know today as the study of linguistics). Bell and his father were largely responsible for what would become the International Phonetic Alphabet. Bell understood what it took to not only speak but to also make speech. Speech and speaking were the core of the family business.

Interestingly, Gray wasn't the only one who wished Bell ill. Thomas Edison was actually hired to take Bell down by any means necessary. Edison made a number of motions toward that goal, but we ended up with inventions such as the microphone due to his efforts.

History as it was and as we know it are likely two quite different things. For a pointed example of this, spend a few minutes exploring who actually invented the telegraph years before Morse entered the picture.

Suffice to say that Bell, et al, gave us the analog telephony technologies that were lacking to that point. Where did the digital side come in? In 1924, a gentleman by the name of Harry Nyquist, of Bell Labs, was one of two men who developed the first publicly available fax machines. In 1927, he taught us that the number of pulses that could be put through a telegraph channel per unit time is limited to twice the bandwidth of the channel. This would later be adapted into the Nyquist-Shannon theorem that is the basis of nearly all telecommunications. A range of 0–4000 Hz would be sampled 8000 times per second in each channel. Each sample is 8 bits in size. The result of 8000 samples at 8 bits each comes out to 64,000 bps or what we know as a DS0.

The digital hierarchy of T1/E1 is well out of scope for this discussion, but it is relevant because it is still widely used today. These bandwidth rates were set in excess of 80 years ago, and we still know that one timeslot has a bandwidth of 64 kbps. We know that 24 timeslots create a DS1. We know that 30 timeslots create an E1. These are transmitted utilizing a TDM algorithm such that they are all processed in tandem.

Why is history so important? That's such a clichèd question and it appropriately has a clichèd answer. Those who don't know history are doomed to repeat it. This isn't always a bad thing, but it is usually an inefficient thing. The technologies that got us to this point were amazing in their time. They are time tested and highly dependable. But time goes on and technology advances.

Why hasn't this technology advanced in more than 80 years? The short answer is a resounding, "IT HAS!" It took a forward-thinking company whose comfort zone is the so-called bleeding-edge of technology to bring all the pieces together into a new way of looking at telephony. This book is a discussion of one facet of those advances.

PBX Architecture and Call Control Basics

With the all-too-brief history lesson aside, some discussion of the technologies that got us to this point is in order. The concept of call control refers to the software and logic involved in providing telephony features including, but not limited to, call setup, call teardown, and the various features we've all come to associate with telephony systems (hold, transfer, park, and so on). TDM technologies are still in widespread use throughout the planet. Many have been in production for 15 years or more. The majority of traditional Private Branch eXchange (PBX) switches share the common underlying architecture illustrated in Figure 1-1.

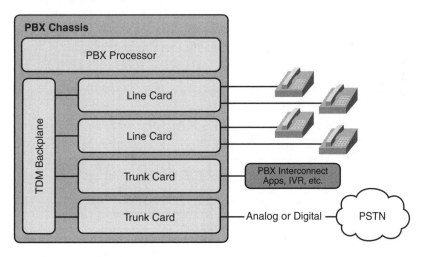

Figure 1-1   *General PBX Architecture*

As seen in the figure, the essential components of the PBX include

■ **Backplane:** The central infrastructure that interconnects the telephony components of the PBX

■ **Processor:** A collective term referring to the switching fabric, path selection algorithms, and other components related to call routing.

■   **Line cards:** Mission-specific interfaces for digital and analog phones or other end-points (faxes, modems, and so on)

■   **Trunk cards:** Mission specific interface for PSTN, applications, interactive voice response (IVR), PBX interconnection (also known as *tie lines*), and related connectivity

All these components play their part in the overall telephony picture.

Inbound calls enter via trunk lines, whether analog or digital. The manner of entry makes little difference to this general overview. The call signaling is transmitted across the backplane to the processor for path selection. The PBX is simply another type of switch capable of much the same process as a LAN switch or a router. The underlying process is similar. Information enters through an ingress port. This information carries unique identifiers for both the source and destination. Based on the destination information, a route lookup is performed and path selection is made resulting in the selection of an egress port. At that point, a path switch is performed, and the relevant information or portion thereof is sent out the selected port. The processes are somewhat similar, at least in concept, in both the voice and data realms.

The PBX processor makes the pathing decision for the call based on the Called Party Number (CdPN). The Calling Party Number (CgPN), while included in the signaling information, is not utilized for path selection. At this point, the call will be forwarded on to the egress port, be it another trunk port (if the CdPN exists as an extension of another PBX) or to a line card associated with a specific phone that owns the CdPN (resulting in ringing). When the CdPN phone is answered, the voice path is established and the call is active. Figure 1-2 illustrates the path of both the signaling and the voice.

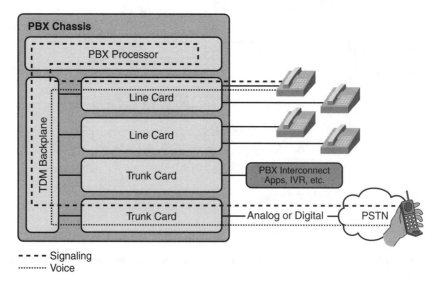

Figure 1-2   *Signaling and Voice Path Through the PBX*

The essential purpose of a PBX is to provide dial tone and essential call features such as transfer, hold, and so on. After it has provided these base services, the capability of the PBX to expand functionality can rapidly hit a brick wall, so to speak.

IP-Based Call Control

In the past 15 years, a movement away from TDM and toward IP has erupted within the voice networking realm. This move has not been accepted easily by everyone. Some still hold out in their blatant refusal to adopt the future of communications.

The first real application of the idea of sending voice traffic across an IP network came in the form of IP Trunking. That is, the IP network provided a mechanism that made it possible for traditional PBX network administrators to eliminate point-to-point tie lines and utilize the data infrastructure in passing voice traffic between PBXs within the enterprise. Voice traffic would be passed to the IP network via voice gateways (typically H.323 gateways). These gateways are simply routers with additional code built into their operating systems that enable the recognition and routing of voice traffic through the use of statically configured dial peers.

IP Telephony (IPT), as an independent call control capability, began simply as an IP-based PBX. Its initial aim was to provide a means of replicating the services offered by a TDM PBX but on an IP-capable platform. The removal of the TDM backplane from the architecture didn't change the need for the core components discussed in the previous section. They are still necessary. Obviously, they present themselves in different forms than previously described.

Each component is illustrated in Figure 1-3 as it relates to both the previous discussion and the IPT architecture.

In the simplest possible terms, voice has become another application traversing the data network. That is not to say that it can be treated as simply another application. It still remains highly sensitive to latency and jitter. It must be protected throughout the network as a critical traffic type. The same is true for video traffic, which will be discussed briefly later in this chapter.

The Network Is the Platform

As shown in Figure 1-3, the core components of the traditional PBX architecture are still in existence. What has changed is the way in which these services are offered. The network is the platform that enables all the applications seen as mission-critical. It is now the platform that enables voice, video, and collaborative technologies of which the PBX could only dream.

As an IP-based entity, the voice network now has all the layers of redundancy and protection afforded to data traffic. This includes convergence capabilities, quality of service (QoS) capabilities, traffic engineering, and more. One of the single largest benefits of an IPT infrastructure is the reduction in overall resources necessary to provide like-for-like services. No longer are tie lines necessary as the network provides dynamic routing capabilities in reaching site-to-site. The entire legacy voice network can be decommissioned and the associated costs reclaimed.

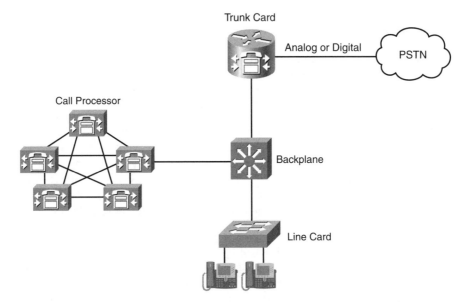

Figure 1-3   *IPT Architectural Overview*

Referring to Figure 1-3, one detail of note is that the trunk and line cards are no longer dedicated resources in a PBX cabinet. They are voice-capable routers and LAN switches, respectively. These devices are not mission-specific to voice. The voice-capable router, for example, is known as an Integrated Services Router (ISR), which also has virtual private networking (VPN), firewall capabilities, voice, IP routing, and more built into it. The ISR can be a fully self-contained, secure system for remote offices. Furthermore, the ISR can provide LAN switch ports with Power over Ethernet (PoE), call control, VPN connectivity (for both clients and point-to-point connections), firewall services, and more all in a single chassis.

The LAN switches are now largely Layer 3-aware and capable of intelligently providing power to various endpoints as needed based on their requirements. The network as the platform has extended not only reachability but also capability of the typical network device. Figure 1-4 illustrates the signaling and voice media pathways in an IPT deployment.

Cisco Unified Communications is centered on the concept of Services Oriented Network Architecture (SONA). This enables the intelligence to be placed into and leveraged from the network.

The intelligence leveraged can be accessed through more than just traditional means, that enables a user of a UC-enabled system direct access to information previously restricted to less than mobile components. The services are composed of call control, Presence, voicemail, video, Instant Messaging (IM), and web collaboration.

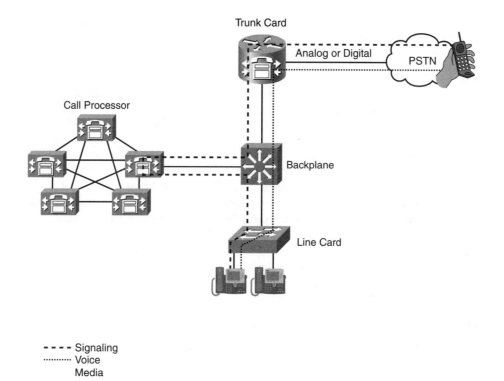

Figure 1-4   *Signaling and Media with IP Telephony*

Cisco Unified Communications Manager

Call control is the body and soul of Unified Communications. Unified Communications Manager performs the Cisco call control functions that enable through signaling and discovery protocols the processing and management of gateways and dial plan, directory, directory integration, application integration, and desperate PBX integration.

From the beginning, the phone system inspired the need to know whom or what might be available or busy. Some phone systems (key systems) took a squared approach that would have a line key that would indicate busy or idle. A Busy Lamp Field (BLF) also translated this function to individual users to show availability. The same BLF indicators were further enhanced to provide speed dial calls to the number it was programmed to.

The BLF, along with the entrance of call centers, initiated the need for presence or the ability to see who is available, when, and on what device.

Cisco Unified Communications Manager (CUCM) is the evolution of Cisco IP-based call control. In relation to the traditional PBX, CUCM provides the processor function. It started its existence in the late 1990s as CallManager. The change to Communications Manager is relatively recent and coincided with the release of CUCM version 6.0 in the latter half of 2007. There have been significant additional changes as well. CallManager has traditionally been a Microsoft Windows-based call control element. CallManager version 5.0 was essentially a reengineering of the product resulting in its conversion to a Linux-based appliance.

Note   CallManager version 4.3(2) is the final release of a Windows Server–based call control solution. All future development and releases of the CallManager/Communications Manager will be on the Linux platform.

Like its predecessor, CallManager, the Communications Manager functions in a clustered architecture. This clustered appliance architecture enables the call control functionality to be spread geographically. Each appliance in the cluster is capable of running call control on its own for a varied number of phones if connectivity is lost between the cluster members. The number of phones supported varies by appliance platform (that is, Media Convergence Server [MCS] Server Model). Table 1-1 shows the MCS server options and number of phones supported per server. You need to understand that these are maximum endpoint counts and that the total number can be reduced based on configuration variables such as Computer Telephony Interface (CTI) Ports, voicemail ports, gateways, and various other possibilities.

Table 1-1   *Maximum Devices per Server Platform*

MCS Server Model	Number of Supported Endpoints
MCS-7815	300
MCS-7816	500
MCS-7825	1000
MCS-7835	2500
MCS-7845	7500

Far from providing simple dial tone, CUCM provides services for voice, video, mobility and presence for up to 30,000 users on a single cluster (assuming the use of MCS-7845 platforms). Chapter 2, "Cisco Unified Presence Overview," discusses these features in more detail.

Endpoint Network Access

An endpoint is considered to be any device that makes use of the infrastructure to place or receive IP-based calls whether they are audio, video, or a combination of the two. Endpoints making use of the Cisco Skinny Client Control Protocol (SCCP) will be registered to the CUCM for all call control functions. SCCP endpoints are not the only endpoints that CUCM is capable of controlling. As an open system, the CUCM supports

Session Initiation Protocol (SIP)-based phones. This includes Cisco IP Phones running SIP loads and third-party SIP-based phones. Additionally, H.323 endpoints are fully compatible with the architecture; however, they might require the installation of an H.323 Gatekeeper to route calls to/from them, but they will easily integrate.

As a bit of internetworking technology review, following are three layers of basic architecture when designing networks:

- **Core layer:** The heart of the network where most services and applications will be hosted.

- **Distribution layer:** Provides redundant paths to and from the Core from multiple points within the network.

- **Access layer:** Houses the LAN switches into which user computers and phones will connect. No user equipment should connect to any other layer.

The aforementioned telephony endpoints can make use of the access layer devices in the network infrastructure, which might include LAN switches, wireless access points, and others where applicable. The end result of this is that the access layer devices are essentially fulfilling the role of the line cards in the traditional PBX model. They provide the phone access to the network resources it requires to place and receive voice and video calls.

Integrated Services Routers

The Cisco core business has always been routing and switching. If routing and switching can be considered the Cisco central nervous system, the gateways are the mouth, eyes, and ears that allow information in and out.

Gateways open up communications between systems via data, voice, and video. With the continued use of industry protocols, such as H.323 and Session Initiation Protocol (SIP) and their capabilities, additional information (such as Presence, IP Phone Applications/Services, and so forth) is now being passed along or is capable of being passed along that further enriches a UC environment.

Before Unified Communications came to be known as an industry term, the roads to the UC path were already being paved.

Phone systems could share calls or call paths through trunking capabilities as with TIE trunks. Networking phone systems began to allow multiple vendor solutions to work together. Networking with voicemail and other applications solutions became necessary. This all points to the early need to federate (that is, translate and exchange) information or share information across multiple entities in a company or across multiple companies.

Call control and messaging marked the beginning of the shift from traditional (or TDM) services to what would become Unified Communications. Software, services, and other applications began a steady migration into the network as the natural side effect of the versatility offered by an IP network.

Microsoft and IBM, along with a few other companies, made or helped create popular e-mail and instant messaging through their suite of desktop software. With e-mail and IM, the top two means of nontelephone-based communication, networking, or communications between multiple companies and vendor solutions became and still is a required way of doing business as the proficiencies gained were too large to ignore.

UC's second path was solidified when IM clients brought into being the centerpiece of UC that is Presence. The ability to change one's availability dynamically based on time, schedule, or simple preference caught on and spread quickly.

Gateways have supplied the roads in which UC travel across as they supply the interfaces and protocols that allow for communications and information exchange to happen.

Several gateways can be used for these types of solutions and Cisco has several, but the most common in Cisco are referred to as Integrated Services Routers (ISR).

ISRs and the newly announced ISR G2 routers are multipurpose routers. The ISR routers include 2800 and 3800 model routers in which the ISR G2 routers include 2900 and 3900 router models. They provide the capability to optimize multiple services into a single platform to deliver a consistent user experience. The consolidation of services into a single chassis reduces the overall footprint of the devices traditionally necessary to provide those same services. Services in the ISR platform include

- **Routing:** Traditional internetwork routing capabilities.

- **Switching:** LAN switching blades and modules.

- **Unified Communications:** Fully self-contained or Survivable Call Control. That is, the ISR can stand on its own as a primary call control entity, or it can provide resiliency services to phones that exist in the site where it is located. If connectivity to the primary call control entities is lost, specific code can be invoked on the router that enables the local phones to utilize it for call control purposes until connectivity is restored.

- **Integrated security:** Full firewall and VPN connectivity.

- **Application performance:** Bandwidth/WAN optimization and acceleration.

- **Management:** GUI administration and configuration toolset.

- **Mobility:** Integrated wireless services including 802.11a/b/g and 3G capabilities.

Obviously, for the purposes of this book, the focus is on the UC portion of the functionality. An ISR can provide full call control functionality to a number of phones ranging from 25 to 300 depending on the ISR platform in question. This is particularly useful in branch deployments where each branch or remote site is an island and maintains its own dial plan. The call control functionality can be configured via IOS command line or via web GUI.

If this is not the desired topology, the same ISR platform can undergo a simple configuration change to become a Survivable Remote Site Telephony (SRST)–capable device. That is, it becomes the local call control device if connectivity is lost to the CUCM cluster. In this role, basic call control capabilities are provided for up to 1200 phones, depending on the router model.

The ISR can fulfill the role of the trunk card in the traditional PBX architecture. Both analog and digital voice connections to the ISR can be accomplished in a number of ways. The same interfaces are used regardless of whether the connection will be made to the PSTN or to a legacy TDM PBX. Digital T1/E1 cards and Digital Signal Processor (DSP) resources can be installed into the router to provide digital connectivity. The DSPs are the *call handlers*, the basic function of which is to convert the call between TDM and IP. If analog connectivity is wanted, the use of Foreign Exchange Office (FXO) ports enable connection to the PSTN or PBX, whereas Foreign Exchange Station (FXS) ports can function as analog phone/fax/modem connections and Direct-Inward-Dial ports.

Applications

Applications embody the intelligence of a UC solution. They are sometimes canned, off-the-shelf applications and other times they're custom applications developed with a purpose in mind. Applications make the solution into more than just a phone system.

The applications that make up the UC solution are as follows:

- Application Extension Platform (AXP)
- Cisco Unified Application Environment (CUAE)
- Conferencing
- Unified Communications Mobility
- Voice messaging
- Unified Presence

Application Extension Platform

Cisco AXP is an application services hosting platform that uses the Cisco ISR as the physical platform. Leveraging the modularity of the ISR and ISR G2, a number of different physical configurations of this module have been made available based on size and scope of processing demands to be made on the developed applications. Smaller versions would suffice for smaller footprints and embedded applications where high-end versions are specifically designed for applications requiring extensive processing capabilities and additional memory, high availability, and so on.

The Cisco AXP provides a service platform on which applications can run. The Cisco AXP ships with a virtualized hosting environment and a host of monitoring and configuration application programming interfaces (API) available to the applications running on the module.

The product also offers a software development kit (SDK) that enables functions and a management interface that allows for a centralized management environment. The SDK provides all the tools needed in packaging, hosting, and integrating applications into the router. This includes the ability to utilize third-party applications, Linux .rpm packages, and application troubleshooting. A CLI extension API provides tools needed in extending the AXP CLI with custom commands. The SDK also includes a number of examples of source code illustrating the usage of APIs.

The Cisco AXP bridges application systems with network systems. At an architectural level, the capability to combine two loosely coupled systems into an integrated solution has numerous advantages. Applications such as desktop/server management solutions, branch-embedded call recording for banks, secure healthcare records solutions, bill payment engines, fax over IP, and more help overcome business obstacles by meeting specific needs of an industry or vertical. These enhancements contribute directly to tighter business processes and models that keep the customer competitive.

CUAE

The Cisco Unified Application Environment (CUAE) provides a ready-to-use application suite and custom development tools that enable you to integrate UC into other applications or create your own specific applications.

A few applications are available today, with more being added on an ongoing basis.

The CUAE is composed of the following:

- **Cisco Unified Application Designer (CUAD):** A visual integrated development environment (IDE) that makes creating your own applications easy through an interface that doesn't require previous development experience

- **Cisco Unified Application Server (CUAS):** An application server for converged applications that simplifies telephony protocols, provides reliability by mediating between the application and Communications Manager, and provides standard management for applications

- **Cisco Unified Media Engine (CUME):** A software-only media server that provides off-the-shelf and media processing for all applications built with CUAD

Conferencing

Cisco Unified MeetingPlace is a collaboration tool that brings together voice, video, and web for Cisco UC. Cisco Unified MeetingPlace supports organizations by providing an effective means of communication enabling people to meet at any time from anywhere. The solution is deployed on-premises over a customer IP network.

Cisco Unified MeetingPlace also works as an audio bridge for WebEx, by keeping audio conferencing on-premise. WebEx, like MeetingPlace, provides a platform for audio and web collaboration, with the difference being that WebEx is software as a service application, or what some refer to as a *cloud service*.

The Cisco portfolio in audio and web collaboration is now robust as both MeetingPlace and WebEx can augment each other's capabilities as a single product.

UC Mobility

The progression of telecommunications to the point where it is today shows the evolutionary growth where UC came from and where improvements can be made for the next version or generation of communications. Early telecommunications devices have evolved from rather large and awkward devices to the sleek, stylish, and highly portable smart devices we use today. In most cases, the use of both static and mobile devices is commonly used today; however, the communication habits of the next generation of information workers will continue to change.

The trend to not leverage devices such as desktop phones, which force users to be in a static location, has been a key driver for the transition into a user requesting and sometimes demanding the flexibility of being connected anywhere, anyplace, or anytime.

Hard phones, wireless-capable devices, cellular networks, and smart phones have literally unleashed a new work force for today and in the future. The *traditional* "workplace" restricted workers to a desk—the *now* "workspace" happens anywhere and anytime the request is made and in moments in time depending on where the worker is currently located. These architectural enhancements now reduce the process time by increasing the overall capabilities and availability, which is the importance of UC.

Accomplishing anytime, anywhere access through mobility required that the capabilities and functionality offered with the traditional workplace communications was critical for mobile communications to be successful. The cell phone and its capabilities began to expand into other areas such as texting, multimedia messages, and so on. PDAs such as the iPAC from HP or Palm Pilots started the mobile application creation that affected many business verticals such as healthcare, transportation such as UPS or FedEx, among many others.

The cell phone, smart phone, PDAs, and other attached devices converged together to give a users an easy-to-carry application platform that has fostered the business transformation on when, where, and how a user performs their roles.

Voice Messaging

Voice messaging is one of the older applications that has been incorporated into the UC product suite.

The ability to communicate obviously is important, but where messaging shines is that it enables multiple means of communication from a caller to the intended recipient. This type of communication was huge because it allowed for a more mobile workforce and began to unlock users from their static cubicles. Not having to answer every call so there were no gaps in the communication chain added productivity benefits that were hard to ignore. Because this was a game changer, it quickly caught the attention of companies, which is what eventually took an answering machine to the heights of Unified Messaging.

Increasingly, users demanded more functionality to be available to further enable users to be multimodal. This ushered in features such as the following:

- **Dropped call recovery:** The capability to be placed back in the same point of the conversation where it was interrupted

- **Message monitor:** The capability to listen to a message being left and then choose to take the call or let the caller leave a message

- **Notification:** The capability to be notified of a message that was left for the user by Message Waiting Indicator (MWI), Alpha Numeric Paging, Short Message Service (SMS), or Simple Mail Transfer Protocol (SMTP)

Knowing you could be away from the desk empowered the workforce to multitask in new ways. Users becoming increasingly more mobile meant that the tools that were used needed to be more flexible and friendly to devices that fostered a decoupling of the user from the desk. Voice messaging took the natural evolution to incorporate itself in the corporate infrastructure so as to reduce administration and take advantage of the network and its components.

Unified Messaging simplified the capability to manage multiple means of communications such as e-mail, voicemail, and fax messages by taking multiple directories and using just one, taking multiple message stores and making them one, increasing the access and availability to messages and leveraged security, and authentication to reduce the complexity while still offering a secure means of access to better the user experience.

Unified Presence

Presence is the aggregation point of availability represented by a single or multiple devices associated with a user account that can be monitored by others.

Presence is the glue that uniquely folds together real time and nonreal-time communications by incorporating capabilities that in themselves are not new but can be leveraged in new ways.

Although mobility drove the release of users from their desks, it created new challenges to address, such as how best to reach a resource or what form of communication to use.

Presence was the answer to this by first leveraging a directory for contact information. Having a single source of the available users gives the user access to the entire workforce for all potential resources. This scales the addressable potential for a quicker means of resolution.

Presence preference capabilities provide the means of what device a particular user prefers to be communicated with. Knowing how each user wants to be communicated with takes out the guesswork of what will be the fastest means to communicate with a user.

Availability shows the status of the user whether they are online, offline, idle, busy, or away. Availability increases the time to resolution by enabling the user to reach out to a source that is available. It also helps to ensure that interruptions don't stall other work by users that are currently engaged.

The capability to quickly see who is or isn't available and on what device increases productivity, scales an organization's resources, and speeds resolution by reaching out to the right user at the right time with the device that is best for both ends to accomplish the task at hand.

User Experience

So, where has all this discussion of history and technology gotten us? We understand now that things are changing with the times and that phones are no longer just phones. They're network endpoints. The idea of having an office desk phone number, cell phone number, work phone number, voicemail phone number, and who knows how many others is simply reprehensible. It's inefficient for us as workers and for our colleagues when they need to reach us by trying each number in series. The next step is to expand the idea of what the "network" entails. The network is now an entity that is dynamic in nature. We access the network in a multitude of ways every day.

Every time you pick up your phone and tweet your status or update your Facebook page, you make use of the network. Your phone is, of course, a phone, but it is also your organizer, e-mail client, calendar, and who knows what else. It has become one of the primary means of accessing network resources. Shouldn't that experience be identical to the experience you'd have if you were sitting at your laptop or at your office desk? Therein lies the core idea of UC—one network experience regardless of means of access.

In a given day, you might use your cell phone, desk phone, home phone, softphone, and more. They should all be connected and aware of each other to some degree. I don't want multiple phone numbers and voicemail boxes to deal with. I want many devices, one phone number, and one voicemail box. I want to tell people how and where I want to be reached; that is, *if* I want to be reached at all. This *find me, follow me, hide me* capability is at the very core of Presence and therefore this book.

Presence is a real-time indicator of a person's willingness and availability to communicate. This is typically represented by status such as *Available*, *In Meeting*, *On the Phone*, *At Lunch*, or any other manner in which people might want to communicate their current status. Presence also includes details on users' preferred method of contact, be it IM, voice call, video call, or other.

However, UC doesn't stop there. It is all-encompassing with regard to means of communication. It includes integrations to phones, e-mail clients, calendars, and conferencing resources (including web, audio, and video conferencing). It includes IM and the capability to know how to reach someone the first time through the use of presence indicators that can be set manually or dynamically based on an Outlook schedule. It includes an integration to various models of cell phones enabling the use of the cell phone as if it were the desk phone. This includes contacts, call logs (received/missed/placed calls), and the ability to check the office voicemail box. The voice messages are presented in a list form so that they can be accessed in desired order and played via the cell phone. When played, the audio is streamed over the data channel so that no cellular airtime is utilized. All these features come together so that you have only a single voicemail box to administer, if so desired. When a call is made to your desk phone number, your cell phone rings simultaneously. If that call is not answered, it is taken back, and the caller is forwarded to your office voicemail. There's no longer a need to publish multiple phone numbers. This is called *Single Number Reach (SNR)*.

To further augment the SNR functionality, the user has the ability to move the call between phones at-will. For example, a call is answered on the desk phone but the conversation is taking longer than expected. With the push of a button on the desk phone, the call can be seamlessly transferred to the cell phone allowing the user the freedom to depart without missing any part of the call or having to reestablish the call. The opposite situation is also true. If a call made to the office phone number is answered on the cell phone, the call can be seamlessly transferred to the desk phone by simply hanging up the cell phone and picking up the desk phone handset.

In both cases, the call is passed seamlessly between the two phones.

Clients

Like any other solution, UC needs to have a front end or GUI that gives access to the services in a way that is operational without a lot of complexity. So being intuitive is a requirement; otherwise, the usefulness doesn't outweigh the cost benefits.

The clients in the Cisco Unified Communications solution consist of the following:

- Cisco IP Communicator (CIPC)
- Cisco Unified Communications Integration for Microsoft Office Communicator (CUCIMOC)
- Cisco Unified Mobile Communicator (CUMC)
- Cisco Unified Personal Communicator (CUPC)
- Cisco Unified Video Advantage

CIPC

Cisco IP Communicator (CIPC) is a Microsoft Windows application that delivers a software-based phone that supports the same capabilities as the desk phone through personal computers. This application enables computers with the functionality of IP Phones to provide voice calls on the road, in the office, or from wherever users have access to the corporate network.

The functionality of Cisco IP Communicator is designed for when users aren't just trying to take their office extension with them. Besides the capability to make and retrieve calls, users will also have access to the phone services they have in the office. This advantage boosts a business's capabilities for collaboration and responsiveness, and helps organizations keep pace with today's work needs by enabling the flow of business to happen whether the user is in the office or elsewhere.

CUCIMOC

Cisco UC Integration for Microsoft Office Communicator (CUCIMOC) is an application based on the Cisco Client Services Framework that provides access to Cisco Unified Communications services such as soft phone, mid-call control, messaging, conferencing, desk phone control, and phone presence directly from a tabbed interface in Microsoft Office Communicator.

Cisco UC Integration for MOC augments Microsoft Office Communicator's IM capabilities with call control and access to other applications supplied by CUC solution.

CUMC

Cisco Unified Mobile Communicator (CUMC) is an application applied to mobile handsets that extends enterprise communications capabilities and services to mobile phones and smart phones. By streamlining the communication experience, CUMC has enabled users with real-time collaboration across the enterprise regardless of whether they are in the office.

With CUMC, users benefit from being allowed to perform the following tasks:

- Place and receive calls

- Access company and personal directory information

- View busy or available status

- Securely send text messages

- Receive and play back voicemail messages

- View a list of messages and select the one they want to play back

- Conference and collaborate through integration with Cisco Unified MeetingPlace and WebEx

- Access recent call histories

CUPC

Cisco Unified Personal Communicator (CUPC) transparently integrates a wide set of applications and services into a single application whether on a PC or Mac. CUPC provides easy access from a single interface to communication services such as the following:

- Call control
- Video
- Instant messaging
- Web conferencing
- Voicemail

CUPC enables you to easily communicate with co-workers, partners, and customers from your office or on the go using the integrated soft phone or controlling the desktop phone and by sharing availability information and IMs inside or outside your business or between businesses.

Additionally, CUPC enables you to perform one-click escalations, which enable you to start with one form of communication and quickly incorporate other capabilities. For example, you could start with an IM and then one-click escalate to audio, audio with video, and then web collaboration with audio and video.

CUPC further enables the user with the ability to *Click-to-Dial* from other applications such as Microsoft's Outlook, Word, Live Meeting, Excel, Power Point, or from the web.

Click-to-Dial is an extension enabled to take advantage of call control and Presence while working in other applications, such as those in the preceding list.

Cisco Unified Video Advantage

Cisco Unified Video Advantage (CUVA) adds video to your environment by providing video telephony functionality to Cisco Unified IP Phones and Cisco IP Communicator soft phones. With CUVA, video telephony is incorporated into Cisco Communications Manager to be leveraged by being as easy as just making a phone call.

Because the Cisco solution is IP-based, enterprise organizations can take advantage of their existing networks to extend video to everyone in their organization. This also lends itself to a more rich communications environment for remote users.

User Workspace

When you walk into the office, wherever that might be (the definition varies greatly these days), and sit down at your desk, you're making use of your workspace. The workspace includes all the tools you use day to day in the course of accomplishing your job goals. It includes your computer with client software, IM, e-mail, calendaring, and so on. It includes both your desk phone and cell phone. It includes your voice messaging as well.

This is the concept behind the idea of the User Workspace License (UWL). The workspace is treated as an entity in and of itself when under licensing consideration. The desk phone, softphone, Presence, IM, voice messaging, cell phone client, web/audio conferencing, calendar integration, and even contact center agent licensing are assembled as a unit. These features can be enabled/disabled at will, but they're all part of the overall workspace and the user experience. This simplifies the budgetary calculations associated with each user by fixing the per-user cost based on desired feature-set.

The Cisco UWL comes in four flavors:

■ **Business Edition (CUCM Business Edition):** Includes call control, voice messaging, unified clients, mobility, and Presence

■ **Entry (CUCM):** Includes call control for one phone and mobility licensing

■ **Standard (CUCM):** Includes call control, voice messaging, unified clients, mobility, and Presence licensing

■ **Professional (CUCM):** Includes call control for unlimited phones per user, voice messaging, unified clients, mobility, Presence, mobile communicator client, web/audio/video conferencing, and contact center licensing

The workspace license is a highly simplified means of implementing advanced features at significantly lower cost.

Summary

Cisco Unified Communications encompasses a wide array of products and technologies. All these interact to provide features and functionality well beyond the confines of simple dial tone. No longer is the reliance on 19th- and 20th-century technologies a requirement. PBX technologies have a long and distinguished history; however, they must evolve or fade into obsolescence.

The user experience for UC has demanded that business communication evolve internally and externally. Communication resources and applications are forced to keep up with the rapid changes that users are no longer willing to be without. The mantra moving forward is anytime, anywhere access. The user experience will evolve to include any device and any media. Network resources and applications will be utilized in the same manner regardless of whether a user is accessing those resources from the office directly, via VPN connection from a laptop, or from a handheld device (phone, netbook, or similar device).

The network must evolve to provide a stable, reliable platform for voice and video interaction in real time for all users. This includes the capability to seamlessly collaborate across a varying array of user platforms while delivering an identical experience to each user and endpoint.

The network is the only way to deliver the platform from which UC are accessed. This enables you to scale and control the reliability of the platform for which voice, video, call control, messaging, IM, Presence, and gateways interact in real time for all users. This includes the capability for seamless collaboration across a variety of user hardware while delivering an identical experience to all users. In support of this, Cisco has created an exceedingly simplified licensing model based on the idea that users can access the network in their chosen manner. The Cisco Unified Workspace License enables the users to choose their means and degree of collaborative interaction.

Chapter 2

Cisco Unified Presence Overview

This chapter provides a foundational overview of the Presence solution offered by Cisco. Cisco Unified Presence Server (CUP Server) is the core component to the Cisco Presence solution and focuses entirely on an enterprise-capable architecture that integrates directly into the Cisco Unified Communications Manager (CUCM) product as an extended application.

Presence is often a term used to describe the capability of users to communicate a set of activities or real-time status across multiple devices. These activities are often tied to applications such as Instant Messaging (IM), calendaring, and real-time communication devices, such as desk phones, mobile phones, and so on. As outlined in RFC 2778, the three basic components to a Presence solution follows:

- **Presence service:** The service that aggregates and distributes Presence information between clients.

- **Presentities:** Presence clients that provide presence information to the Presence service to be stored and delivered to other clients.

- **Watchers:** Presence clients that receive Presence information from the Presence service. Following are two basic kinds of watchers:

    - **Fetcher:** Retrieves current Presence information from the Presence service about a presentity, which is a presence enable entity. This is done only once upon the user request.

    - **Subscriber:** Retrieves current and future Presence information from the Presence service about a presentity. This provides an ongoing Presence subscription for that client to receive status updates.

Presence capabilities continue to develop and many RFCs outline specific features related to Presence and what it is supposed to provide. The idea is that any device or user can be defined in these basic terms helps provide consistent features and capabilities across multiple services. Presentities will publish their status to the Presence service using a

PUBLISH or REGISTER message and provide a directory number (DN) or a Session Initiation Protocol (SIP) uniform resource identifier (URI). This presentity can exist on the same communications cluster as the Presence service or on another communications platform. To provide interoperability between communications systems, SIP is the protocol leveraged. Enterprise Presence solutions need to provide for a uniform definition of the main communication services such as IM, voice, video, e-mail, web calendaring, and so on, while SIP delivers the necessary features.

Cisco Unified Presence Components

Cisco has several components that all work together to provide a robust enterprise Presence solution. The following are the components necessary to deliver a comprehensive Cisco solution:

- Cisco Unified Presence Server (CUP Server)

- Cisco Unified Communications Manager (CUCM)

- Cisco Unified Personal Communicator (CUPC)

- Cisco Unified MeetingPlace or MeetingPlace Express

- Cisco Unity or Unity Connection

- Cisco Unified Videoconferencing or Cisco Unified MeetingPlace Express VT

- Cisco Unified Contact Center Enterprise or Cisco Unified Contact Center Express

- Cisco Unified Customer Voice Portal

- Cisco Unified Mobile Communicator (CUMC)

- Cisco Unified IP Phones

- Lightweight Directory Access Protocol (LDAP) Server 3.0

- Third-party Presence server

Figure 2-1 illustrates the components listed.

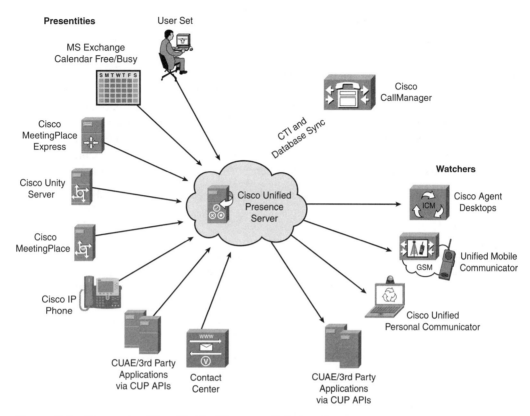

Figure 2-1   *Enterprise Cisco Unified Presence Solution Components*

CUCM Presence Capabilities

The beginning of this chapter defined three basic components involved in a Presence solution: Presence Service, Presentity, and Watcher. CUCM has the capability to deliver these three basic components in a standalone solution providing basic Presence services. The Cisco Unified IP Phone can be the presentity and the watcher with CUCM providing the Presence service function.

When an IP Phone sends a watcher request, the CUCM manages that request and sends a direct response if the presentity is colocated on the cluster. If the presentity is located on an external Presence service, such as another Unified CM cluster or CUP Server, and provided the SUBSCRIBE calling search space and Presence group allows for the watcher to monitor the requested presentity, the request is forwarded across the SIP trunk to the external Presence service. Presence response is received from the external presentity and current Presence status is updated to the watcher. This allows for basic Presence services to be provided within the CUCM cluster and is the cornerstone architecture to expand into the CUP Server solution. The Presence services currently provided natively with CUCM are Busy Lamp Field (BLF)/speed dials and call history logs.

CUCM Presence: BLF/Speed Dials

Presence-based speed dials offer the capability for a speed dial to have BLF functionality. This is an administrator-configured feature and the speed dial must be configured with a target directory number that is either on the CUCM cluster or a SIP trunk destination. The Presence status of a speed dial BLF provides visibility at a line level and not at the device level. The BLF will be active or inactive based on the line on-hook or off-hook only. Cisco IP Phones can be configured in CUCM as a Skinny Call Control Protocol (SCCP) or a SIP line-side device, and speed dial support is provided with both protocols. SIP line-side configured IP Phones are the only presentities that can be configured with a SIP URI instead of a target directory number.

Table 2-1 outlines the Cisco IP Phones that support speed dial BLF for SCCP and SIP.

Table 2-1   *Cisco Unified IP Phones Speed Dial BLF Support*

Cisco IP Phone	SCCP	SIP
7914G	Yes	No
7921G	Yes	No
7940G	Yes	No
7960G	Yes	No
7941G, 7941G-GE, 7942G, and 7945G	Yes	Yes
7961G, 7961G-GE, 7962G, and 7965G	Yes	Yes
7970G, 7971G-GE, and 7975G	Yes	Yes

*Cisco Unified IP Phones 7905, 7906, 7911, and 7912 do not support speed dial BLF.

Figure 2-2 shows the icon and LED appearance for the different Presences states.

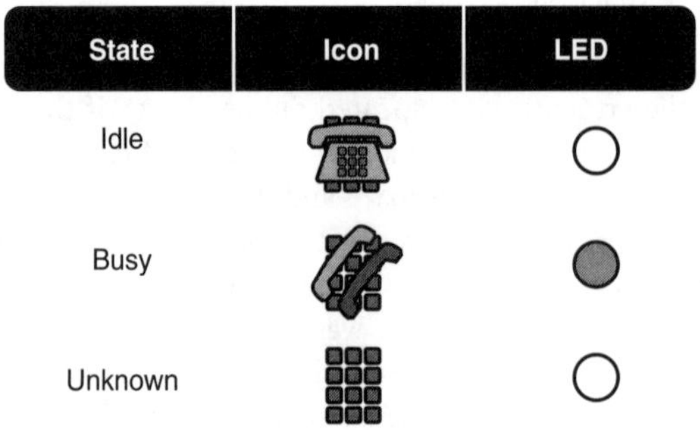

State	Icon	LED
Idle		○
Busy		●
Unknown		○

Figure 2-2   *Icons and LEDs Used for Different States with Speed Dial BLF*

CUCM Presence: Phone Directories

CUCM also provides Presence capabilities in the directories presented to the Unified IP phones. The BLF for Call Lists Enterprise Parameter controls this feature on a global basis and is available on supported phones using the Directories button. This feature applies to the Missed, Received, Placed Calls, and Personal and Corporate Directories.

Table 2-2 outlines the phone support for Presence-enabled phone directories.

Table 2-2   *Cisco Unified IP Phone Presence-Enabled Directories Support*

Cisco IP Phone	SCCP	SIP
7941G, 7941G-GE, 7942G, and 7945G	Yes	Yes
7961G, 7961G-GE, 7962G, and 7965G	Yes	Yes
7970G, 7971G-GE and, 7975G	Yes	Yes

*Cisco Unified IP Phones 7905G, 7906G, 7911G, 7912G, 7940G, and 7960G do not support Presence-enabled directories because of memory limitations on the platform.

Figure 2-3 shows the icon appearance for the different Presence states in the directories.

State	Icon
Idle	
Busy	
Unknown	

Figure 2-3   *Icons Used for Different States in CUCM Directories*

Cisco Unified Presence User

The central concept that must first be defined is a Presence user as it relates to the CUP Server. A user is configured in the CUCM 6.x and later server as an *end user*. This end user can be set up with a primary extension or associated to a line appearance. Cisco recommends that the end user is associated with the line appearance, and it is *required* when using the CUP PUBLISH Trunk service parameter. The line appearance association enables more aggregated information from the Presence service. End users can be configured for more than one line appearance, and each line appearance can have up to five end users.

SIP PUBLISH with CUP Server

When using the SUBSCRIBE/NOTIFY method, both CUCM and CUP Server must have a separate subscription dialog for each presentity being watched, and if a presentity is interested by two watchers, CUP Server sends two different SUBSCRIBE messages to the CUCM Trunk for the same number. Considering the behavior just outlined, this brings up concerns of scalability using the SUBSCRIBE/NOTIFY method. The CUP PUBLISH Trunk service parameter is recommended in Unified CM cluster 6.x and later because it leverages the SIP PUBLISH capabilities for event-state publication to the CUP Server. RFC 3903 outlines the framework for presentity event updates that provides for greater scalability than the SIP subscription mechanism used in Unified CM 5.x. The SIP trunk uses PUBLISH for presentity updates with the CUP Server, and the CUCM cluster acts as an Event Publication Agent (EPA) publishing Presence information of the defined presentities on the cluster. The CUP Server provides for the Event State Compositor (ESC) by receiving the updates, aggregating them, and updating all the subscribed watchers.

Figure 2-4 shows the relationship with the CUCM cluster, CUP Server, and IP Phones (presentities) using the SIP PUBLISH setup. The Unified CM cluster manages the IP Phones with SIP/SCCP protocols and then uses SIP PUBLISH to send updates to the CUP Server regarding the status of the IP Phones. The CUP Server has an HTTP connection with the IP Phones, so the CUP Server can update the phone screens and detect login/logout activities on the phones.

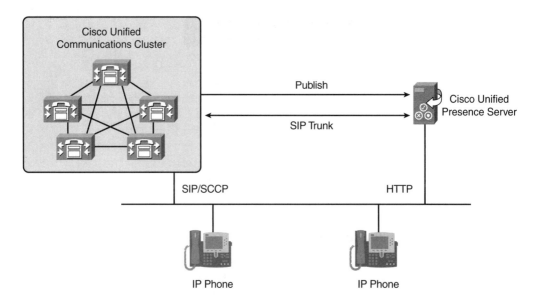

Figure 2-4   *How SIP PUBLISH Is Used with CUCM and CUP Server*

Chapter 4, "Cisco Unified Presence Integration with Cisco Unified Communications Manager," provides further details on SIP trunk configuration steps with the CUCM and CUP Server.

Deployment Models

When deploying Cisco Unified Presence, you need to consider a few things to determine the deployment model that is best suited:

- How many CUCM clusters are in the enterprise?

- Is high availability required?

- Is federation required?

- How many users?

> **Note**   Answers to these questions focus on determining the deployment model only and not what other features or requirements might need to be supported.

The CUP Server can be deployed in two main deployment models, each of which has several deployment options available:

- CUCM deployments:
    - Single cluster
    - Multicluster
- Federated (B2B) deployments:
    - Interdomain
    - Microsoft OCS

Cisco Unified Presence Cluster

The first thing to understand is how a CUP cluster is defined. A CUP Server cluster can have up to six servers in the cluster, and the basic architecture is similar to that of the CUCM cluster. One server in the cluster must be the publisher, and the other servers are subscribers. Within the cluster, you can have what a subcluster, which can have up to two servers in them; there can be up to three subclusters in a CUP Server cluster. Figure 2-5 shows the server architecture within a single CUP Server cluster without redundancy.

The CUP Server publisher uses a database connection with the CUCM publisher to synch user and device information. A CUP Server cluster can support only one CUCM cluster, so all users on a CUCM cluster must be defined on the corresponding CUP Server cluster. User assignment can be done automatically using the Synch Agent or manually. High availability within the cluster can be handled by the Synch Agent; Cisco recommends using the automatic feature of Synch Agent when setting up CUP Server.

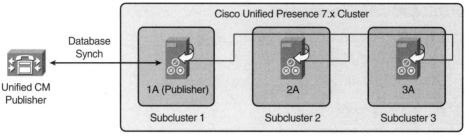

Figure 2-5   *Single CUP Server Cluster Architecture*

Synchronization times can vary in the initial CUCM integration with CUP Server and depends largely on the number of users in the CUCM cluster and how many subscribers are in the CUP Server cluster. Table 2-3 provides some guidance on how long synchronization should take with various user numbers and Cisco Media Convergence Server (MCS) platforms.

Table 2-3   *Synchronization Times for CUP Server Publisher*

Server Platform	Number of Users	Synchronization Time
Cisco MCS 7816	500	5 minutes
Cisco MCS 7825	1000	5 minutes
Cisco MCS 7835	1000	5 minutes
	10,000	25 minutes
Cisco MCS 7845	1000	5 minutes
	10,000	20 minutes
	30,000	70 minutes

*When doing initial database synchronization with a CUCM cluster, you need to plan for the times outlined in Table 2-4.

Synchronization takes a little more time when the CUCM is integrated with a CUP Server cluster and not a single node CUP Server Publisher. Table 2-4 outlines the amount of time that need to be allowed for full synchronization.

Caution   When CUP Server initially connects to Unified CM and starts the database synchronization, it is important that no administration tasks are done on the Unified CM cluster if the Synch Agent is still running.

Table 2-4   *Synchronization Time for CUP Server Publisher and Subscribers*

Server Platform	Number of Users	Synchronization Time
Cisco MCS 7816	500	5 minutes
Cisco MCS 7825	1000	10 minutes
Cisco MCS 7835	1000	10 minutes
	10,000	50 minutes
Cisco MCS 7845	1000	10 minutes
	10,000	40 minutes
	30,000	140 minutes

Cisco Unified Presence Redundancy

A topic that needs to be discussed before moving on to deployment models is redundancy compared to high availability. The terms are sometimes used synonymously, but for the sake of this book, they do not mean the same thing. Cisco Unified Presence specifically addresses the idea of redundancy and high availability, and there are deployment models that offer both. In this book, *redundancy* specifically talks about features and services within the Cisco Unified Presence cluster to have a backup or redundant server in case of failure. *High availability* is defined as a function that enables a multinode solution to provide higher scalability and limited enterprise service impact on a single node failure. More details about high availability are covered in a later section with specific deployment models.

CUP redundancy is offered in two configurations:

- **One to one (1:1):** For every primary subscriber, there is a backup subscriber.

- **Two to one (2:1):** For every two primary subscribers, there is one backup subscriber.

The CUP Server cluster can contain up to six servers and can have up to three subclusters to achieve high availability. The subcluster can have a primary subscriber and a backup subscriber to provide redundancy. Figure 2-6 shows the relationship between primary and backup subscribers in a subcluster.

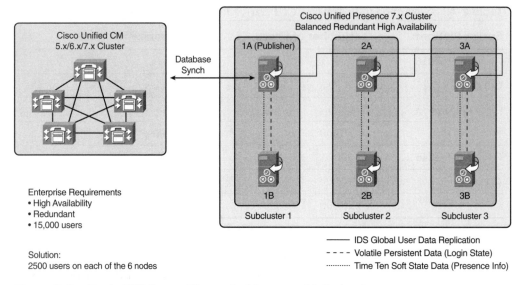

Figure 2-6 *Single CUP Server Cluster Architecture with Redundancy*

Users would be configured for the primary server and failover to the backup server if a failure occurs. Connections between the primary and backup servers constantly maintain login and Presence state, so upon a failure, the users are failed over in near real time for greater performance. It is important to understand the amount of users needed to be supported so that the CUP Server cluster can be configured correctly so that no one server is oversubscribed. This is one reason why Cisco recommends that all servers in the cluster use the same hardware platform because it is important that if a failure occurs, the backup subscriber can handle the users and services required.

Cisco Unified Presence Platform Scalability

The CUP Server can be deployed in a single server and multiserver cluster. Table 2-5 outlines the server performance so that the CUP Server cluster can be properly designed to meet the necessary requirements.

> **Note** You can find the latest platform information on the Cisco 7800 Series Media Convergence Servers (MCS) at http://tinyurl.com/8raxul.

CUCM Deployments

CUP Server can support integration into the four main CUCM deployment models:

- Single site
- Multisite WAN with centralized call processing

- Multisite WAN with distributed call processing

- Clustering over the WAN (CoW)

Table 2-5 *CUP Server Supported Platform and Users Maximums*

Server Platform*	CPU	Physical Memory	Users Supported
Cisco MCS 7816	One 3.2 GHz Celeron D	2 GB	500
Cisco MCS 7825	One 3.0 GHz Dual Core Xeon	2 GB	1000
Cisco MCS 7835	One 2.3 GHz Xeon	2 GB	2500
Cisco MCS 7845	Two 2.3 GHz Xeon	4 GB	5000

*Cisco recommends that all servers in a CUP Server cluster run on the same MCS platform.

Note For more detailed information on CUCM deployments, review the chapter titled "Unified Communications Deployment Models" in the *Cisco Unified Communications SRND Based on Cisco Unified Communications Manager 7.x*, available at http://tinyurl.com/ygsf9wt.

The CUCM deployment model will have an impact on what CUP Server deployment model will be most effective. Cisco recommends that all CUP Server subscriber servers be colocated within the CUP cluster. There are a couple of exceptions to this rule, and one that we will review later in the chapter addresses geographic separation for data center requirements in a multinode solution. The main rule that applies to the CUCM deployment is that only one CUCM cluster is supported for each CUP Server cluster. For the single site, multisite WAN with centralized call processing and CoW options, you would use the CUP Server single cluster deployment model. For the multisite WAN with distribute call processing option (assuming multiple Unified CM clusters), there would be one CUP Server cluster for every CUCM cluster; however, both options could include redundancy and high availability features with a multinode cluster design.

Note CUP Server can be integrated into only a single CUCM cluster. If the CUP Server/cluster needs to be integrated into another CUCM cluster, this requires a reinstall of the CUP Server/cluster.

CUP Server Single Cluster Deployment

The CUP single-cluster deployment defines a single CUP Server cluster connecting to a single CUCM cluster. This section refers to the CUP Server cluster as a single entity and its relationship with the CUCM cluster and does not cover details about redundancy and high availability. Those details are covered later in this chapter.

CUP Server requires several communication components with the Unified CM cluster for a successful integration. Figure 2-7 shows a visual representation of the communication requirements between the CUCM cluster and the CUP Server cluster.

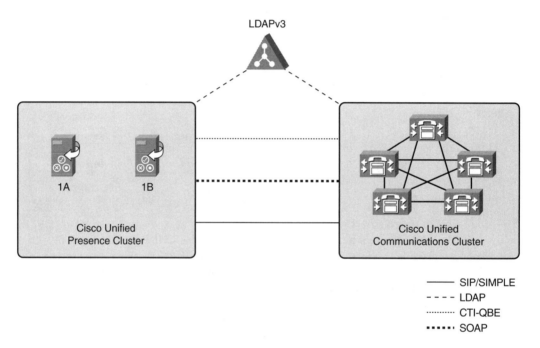

Figure 2-7 *CUP Server Cluster Interaction with LDAP and Unified CM Cluster*

When setting up a CUP Server, the server with CUCM 5.x and 6.x, the server must be added as an application server, and a SIP trunk must be configured within the CUCM cluster. Introduced in CUCM 7.0(3), this can be done automatically with the AXL/SOAP interface through the system topology page in the CUP Server administration. Highly available DNS that support DNS SRV is recommended when implementing an enterprise CUP Server solution. Chapter 4 provides step-by-step details of integrating a CUP Server into a CUCM cluster.

Computer Telephony Integration Quick Buffer Encoding (CTI-QBE) is between the CUCM cluster and the CUP Server cluster for CTI functionality at a user level. This enables the CUP Server to control the IP Phones and provides for functionality such as Cisco Unified Personal Communicator (CUPC) and Microsoft Office Communicator

(MOC) to control a desk phone via the software client. Chapter 5, "Cisco Unified Personal Communicator," covers this in detail using the CUPC software client.

LDAP is important to a seamless solution at the enterprise level. CUCM has the capability to synchronize with an LDAP solution, such as Microsoft Active Directory (AD), so that there is one uniform source of user management. Manual user management is available but must be done with CUCM; then CUP Server fully synchronizes with the CUCM cluster. When LDAP is used it provides for directory synchronization and authentication. There is no direct integration into LDAP and no schema changes; it is a one-way user synchronization and a pass-through authentication design with the CUCM cluster. The CUP Server does a full synchronization with the CUCM cluster for LDAP users and authenticates those users to the CUCM cluster.

AXL/SOAP is an interface on the CUP Server cluster that is leveraged to provide database synchronization services from the CUCM cluster. The Synch Agent is the service that runs on the CUP Server during the synchronization process. Refer to Tables 2-3 and 2-4 when determining the time requirements for database synchronization with one server or multiple servers in the CUP Server cluster. When performing the initial database synchronization, the Synch Agent does a balanced user distribution across multiple servers. To change this behavior, you need to modify the User Assignment setting in the Synch Agent Service Parameter.

Remember that a single cluster CUP Server deployment can support Presence service for CUCM deployed in a single cluster, multisite WAN with centralized call processing, and Clustering over the WAN (CoW). Federation with other CUCM clusters and a Microsoft Office Communications Server can be done on the same CUP Server cluster. This concept is discussed in a more detail later in this chapter along with the multinode high availability concept to address the CoW deployment model of Unified CM.

CUP Server Multicluster Deployment

Enterprises with multiple CUCM clusters will likely have the requirement to have Presence and IM functionality enterprisewide rather than contained within a single CUCM cluster. The multicluster CUP Server deployment provides this functionality for this exact reason. Figure 2-8 depicts a Cisco CUCM multisite WAN with distributed call processing deployment. This distributed call processing solution is built entirely upon CUCM clusters and not Unified CM Express or third-party call processing solutions. It is also important to note that this deployment addresses only multicluster design and is not addressing a federated design dealing with multiple domains. This solution must exist in the same domain.

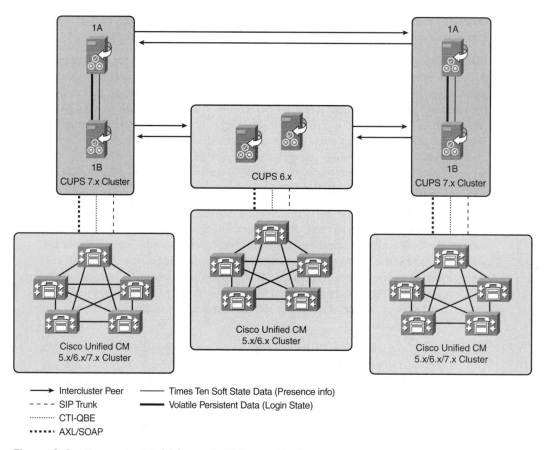

Figure 2-8   *Enterprise Multicluster CUP Server Deployment*

Each CUP Server cluster can be implemented as a standalone server, redundancy with a primary and backup server, or multinode with subclusters as previously outlined in this chapter.

Remember to outline the redundancy and high availability needs in the solution to make sure there are enough servers and the cluster design meets the necessary requirements.

Figure 2-8 shows each CUP Server 7.x cluster with a primary and backup server solution and integration into a CUP Server 6.x solution supporting a CUCM 5.x/6.x cluster. The intercluster peer connection between each CUP Server cluster has an AXL/SOAP and a SIP connection. This connection can be designated as an IP address of the Presence servers in another cluster or as recommended using DNS SRV. The AXL/SOAP interface is leveraged for synchronization of user information related to the home cluster. The SIP connection is used for subscription and notification traffic between clusters.

Federated Deployment

Federation as defined for the purposes of this book is discussed as interdomain federation only. This means that when federating with other Presence services, such as another CUP Server cluster or Microsoft Office Communications Server (OCS), it must exist in another domain and cannot be a member for the current CUP Server cluster domain. Figure 2-9 shows how a federated CUP Server cluster would logically look.

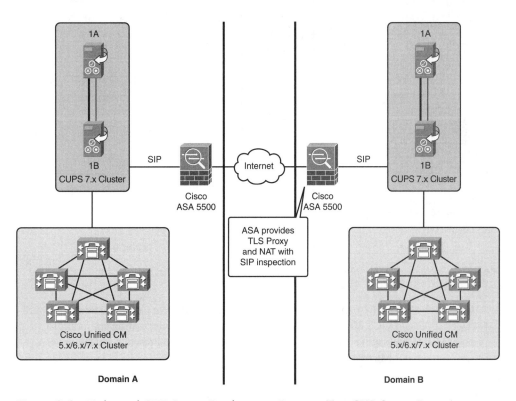

Figure 2-9   *Federated CUP Server Deployment Between Two CUP Server Domains*

Figure 2-9 outlines a Domain A and a Domain B both with CUCM and CUP Server clusters. The requirement is for Presence users to have Presence and IM functionality between each domain. The Cisco Adaptive Security Appliance (ASA) provides for Transport Layer Security (TLS) and NAT with SIP inspection services for secure communication between the CUP Server cluster in Domain A and the CUP Server cluster in Domain B. The intercluster peering between the two Presence domains propagates Presence and IM information between users in Domain A and Domain B. This intercluster peering allows for interdomain federation between CUP Server clusters and Microsoft OCS. Figure 2-10 shows the Microsoft OCS deployment model.

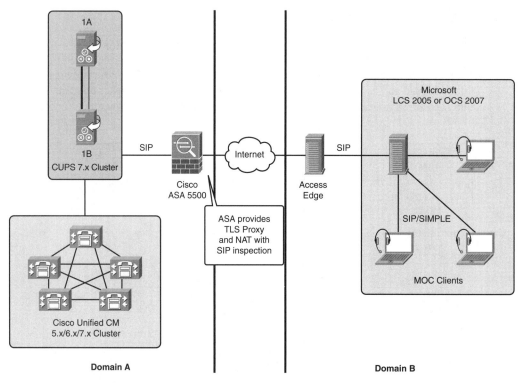

Figure 2-10 *Federated CUP Server Deployment with Microsoft OCS*

Federation with a Microsoft deployment can be done with Live Communications Server (LCS) 2005, and OCS 2007 and provides for basic Presence information and point-to-point instant messaging. Table 2-6 shows the mappings of the Presence states between CUP Server and Microsoft OCS.

Table 2-6 *Presence Mappings for CUP Server and OCS*

Cisco Status	Cisco Color	Status on OCS
Out of Office	RED	Away
Do not disturb	RED	Busy
Busy	RED	Busy
On the phone	YELLOW	Busy
In a meeting	YELLOW	Busy
Idle on all clients	YELLOW	Away
Available	GREEN	Available
Unavailable/offline	GREY	Offline

When federating a CUP Server cluster with a Microsoft OCS domain, the DNS SRV configuration is required because the Cisco Presence solution is considered a Public IM service on the OCS Access Edge servers. Redundancy in a federated solution can be attained by using load balancers or leveraging redundant ASA devices.

CUP Server Scalability and High Availability

This last section covers how to design a CUP Server solution that offers scalability and high availability. Previously in this chapter, there was clarification of redundancy and high availability. There will be deployment models that offer high availability with limited or no redundancy. The term *multinode* has been touched on earlier in this chapter, and the rest of this chapter focuses on multinode deployment models.

CUP Server Multinode Scalability

CUP multinode scalability is relevant to a single cluster implementation. The same parameters exist in a multicluster deployment.

The services delivered with a CUP Server solution (Presence, IM, directory services, CTI, and so on) and the platform used play a role in how many users can be deployed in a cluster. One of the user limitations is the number of contacts users can have in their client. The system maximum is currently at 200 contacts. There are other sizing limitations to adhere to when implementing a cluster maximum to meet the CUCM cluster maximum. A single CUCM cluster can support up to 30,000 users, and the following must be complied with when deploying a CUP Server cluster to meet that 30,000 maximum:

- CUP Server cluster can have a maximum of six nodes consisting of a maximum of three subclusters.

- 5000 users per node with a Unified IP Phone and a Presence client (10,000 endpoint maximum per node).

- Each user can have a maximum of 100 contacts, which only applies to the 30,000 cluster deployment.

The next section covers the details around user balancing and handling failures. Table 2-5 provided for platform performance maximums based on a 70 percent server CPU utilization. Those platform numbers are used in calculations moving forward to determine what is a redundant and nonredundant multinode solution.

Multinode Deployment Models

Multinode deployments contain multiple servers (nodes) in a cluster that increase scalability, high availability, or both. The four multinode deployments for CUP Server implementations follows:

- Balanced redundant high-availability deployment

- Balanced nonredundant high-availability deployment

■   Active/standby redundant high-availability deployment

■   Nonhigh-availability deployment

Balanced Redundant High-Availability Deployment

In this deployment model, the requirement is to provide a highly available CUP Server solution with full redundancy. The users must have full services during peak hours if a single node fails. Figure 2-11 shows a CUP Server solution that can handle 6000 users with the capability to grow to the deployment model maximum of 15,000 users.

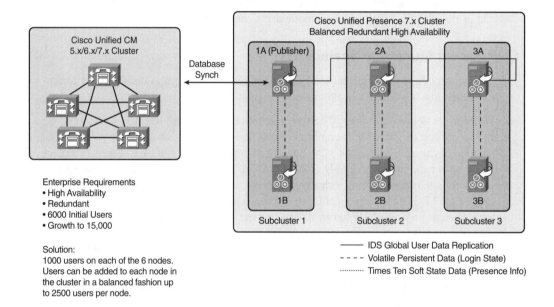

Figure 2-11 *Balanced Redundant High-Availability CUP Server Deployment*

The platform chosen for this solution is an MCS 7845 that supports up to 5000 users per node at 70 percent CPU utilization. The requirement is also to have high availability and full redundancy and provide support for the maximum number of users allowed by the deployment model, in this case 15,000.

Full redundancy now means that the chosen platform supports half of the supported amount of users because the platform needs to handle another server's load if that server fails. This means that to support 15,000 users, there needs to be six MCS 7845 servers in a three subcluster design. Six servers will be deployed with support for up to 2500 users on each server, and each subcluster will have a primary and backup server for full redundancy. The initial deployment will have only 6000 users, so to provide for a balanced cluster solutions (the default setting for the Synch Agent), there will be 1000 users configured across each of the six servers in the cluster. There can be up to 9000 more users added to the cluster; if a server fails at any time, the backup server can handle full services during peak hours.

This is the most resilient and high performance CUP Server cluster that can be implemented. This does not scale to meet the maximum number of users supported on a CUCM cluster.

Balanced Nonredundant High-Availability Deployment

How does an enterprise deploy a single CUP Server cluster to support a Unified CM cluster that has between 15,000 and 30,000 users? Nonredundant high-availability deployment helps address this situation and still offers some resiliency in the solution.

Figure 2-12 shows a CUP Server cluster that has 18,000 users. The customer still wants high availability and would like as much resiliency as possible with the capability to grow to 30,000 users.

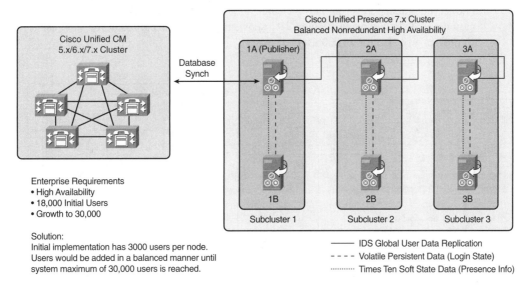

Figure 2-12 *Balanced Non-Redundant High-Availability CUP Server Deployment*

Three thousand users can be configured on each of the six nodes in the cluster. The platform used is still the MCS 7845 server; it can scale to 5000 users per server. The reason this is nonredundant is that with 3000 users assigned to each node, if one fails, 6000 users are on the backup server in the subcluster. This exceeds the 5000 user support on the MCS 7845, but it will be technically allowed in a failover situation. The idea here is that even though the number of users exceeds the platform supported amount, there are times in the day when the system might not be running at capacity. If all the users on the node use the system heavily (peak hours), potentially services can be impacted for some of those users, and that impact is not predictable. It is important with this deployment model that when a failure occurs there is active monitoring on the backup servers' CPU utilization to ensure the service interruption, if any, is not impacting end users widely.

Because this deployment model is used to scale beyond the redundant 15,000 users, it is highly recommended that active monitoring tools be in place for your voice network. This is a good idea in any voice over IP deployment but is especially recommended when deploying services such as a CUP Server in a nonredundant fashion. Cisco Unified Operations Manager and Cisco Unified Service Monitor are good places to start for actively managing and providing day-2 support services in a Unified Communications environment. You can find more information on those tools here (CCO account required): www.cisco.com/en/US/partner/products/ps5747/Products_Sub_Category_Home.html.

Active/Standby Redundant High-Availability Deployment

This deployment model provides the same level of redundancy and high availability as outlined in the "Balanced Redundant High-Availability Deployment" section in this chapter. The only difference is that users are not deployed in a balanced fashion, but rather all reside on the primary server in the subcluster, and the backup server is there as a standby option if a node failure occurs. Figure 2-13 shows this type of deployment for 5000 users with growth provided for 10,000 users.

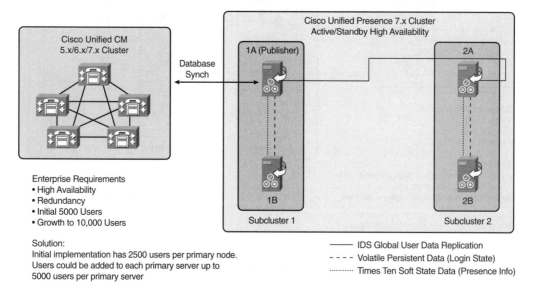

Figure 2-13 *Active/Standby Redundant High-Availability CUP Server Deployment*

Although there is little difference between the redundant deployment options provided for a multinode cluster in terms of feature and functionality, you need to understand the growth capacity required prior to implementation so that both deployment models can be considered closely prior to deploying.

Nonhigh-Availability Deployment

This deployment model offers the lowest capital cost to implement and can often be used for a starting point for a pilot or initial enterprise solution. In this deployment model, there is no redundancy or high availability in the cluster. If a node fails, all the users assigned to that node will experience an outage. Figure 2-14 shows a single cluster deployed with no high-availability options. The requirement is to support 1000 users with no redundancy in the cluster. The solution will be to assign all 1000 users to a single node in the CUP Server cluster. Technically, this is the primary server of subcluster 1.

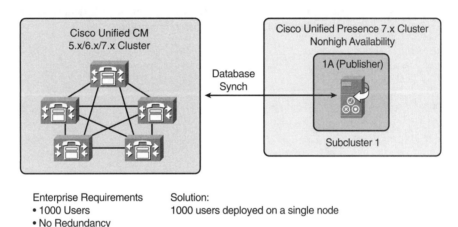

Figure 2-14 *Nonhigh-Availability CUP Server Deployment*

Although this might be a good solution for a pilot or an initial deployment, it is not recommended for a long-term strategy. The types of services that CUP Server offers to end users are increasingly seen as critical business applications. End users with the ability to leverage Presence at the desktop level, take advantage of IM for quick real-time communications, and integrate desktop applications to the desk phone, and so on are becoming less tolerant of service outages than ever before.

You need to implement a solution that can scale and offer high availability and redundancy. The great thing about this solution and all the other deployment models is that nodes and subclusters can be easily added to allow for a change in the deployment model to happen while deployed. In this scenario, it would be easy to add a second node as a backup server in the first subcluster, quickly offering redundancy and high availability to the 1000 users. Extending the solution for greater scalability is just a matter of adding additional nodes and subclusters to the solution.

Summary

This chapter covered several items of the Cisco Unified Presence (CUP) solution. There are several components involved when extending the Presence services offered by the Cisco Unified Communication platform to the desktop, other applications, and third-party communication platforms. The Cisco solution focuses on the needs that end users have in today's enterprise environment. There are several deployment models that support most business communication environments today, from the single-cluster nonredundant solution to the multicluster, large-scale, and multiple-vendor solution. CUP Server flexibility and services offered are robust. The chapters that follow provide details on how to configure the solution and how to leverage it in different markets.

Chapter 3

Installing Cisco Unified Presence Server 7

Since the advent of the appliance model, the installation process of Cisco Unified Communications components has been greatly simplified. All the appliance model components, including Cisco Unified Communications Manager (CUCM), Cisco Unity Connection and Cisco Unified Presence Server (CUPS), all now run the same underlying operating system. This is a custom operating system specifically crafted to support the Cisco appliance models. No third-party Linux (or Windows) operating systems or application can be used with CUPS. Also note that root access to the operating system is not available outside of Cisco TAC.

The installation processes have distinct similarities. They all begin with a rather 1980s looking text-based installation script and end in a command prompt. It is somewhat reminiscent of what might result if WordPerfect 5 and DbaseIII were blended.

Obviously, what goes on before, during, and after the installation script is quite different. But when you know the basic installation steps of one component, you know the others as well. As you might expect, this chapter covers the installation procedure for CUPS version 7.0.

Because CUPS is meant to interact with the CUCM cluster, you need to perform some configuration tasks on both. The CUCM-specific tasks are covered along with those tasks necessary to get CUPS installed and running. The CUCM-related tasks need to be done prior to the beginning of the actual CUPS installation. Stay tuned for further discussion.

Preinstallation Tasks

As with any preinstall checklist, this one includes a number of hardware-related items. Quite a few pieces of information need to be in hand prior to setting off on the adventure of the CUPS installation. Aside from the obvious IP addressing, gateway, Domain Name Service (DNS), and other relevant information, various usernames and passwords need to be created in accordance with the system.

Supported Server Platforms

Along with software information, significant hardware information is required. First and foremost is the server itself. That said, this presents an excellent opportunity to discuss the supported platforms list, which can be found here: www.cisco.com/en/US/docs/ voice_ip_comm/cups/7_0/english/compatibility/cupcompatibility.html.

The short version of the story is that the server platform must be a Cisco MCS server. Older platforms are supported with CUPS 6.0 and later, though there might be some necessary memory and hard drive upgrades needed to get the desired performance.

Also note that the web page is a CUCM-compatibility table. It shows which CallManager/Communications Manager versions are compatible with varied versions of the CUPS software. Of particular note is that CallManager 4.x is not Presence-capable; therefore, it is not supported with any version of CUPS.

As a matter of best practice, you can save time and effort by keeping the CUPS version as close as possible to the CUCM version number. To ease the potential for confusion, as of version 7, all Cisco Unified Communications (UC) products were advanced to 7, so some gaps exist in the numbering sequence for some products. For example, Cisco Unity jumped from version 5.x to 7.x; similarly, Unity Connection jumped from 2.x to 7.

CUCM and CUPS (along with most other Cisco UC components) are supported only on Cisco-provided platforms; that is, you must purchase the server from Cisco. You may not provide your own in most cases. If you purchase the identical servers directly from HP or IBM, they might be supported; however, if any differences exist, the install will likely fail. If you get an Unsupported Model error during the install, the best course of action is to open a case with Cisco TAC. You want to provide installation logs for the engineer. To get to them, press Alt-F2 on the server console during installation. The installation logs are in the /tmp directory on the server. Alternately, you can download a recovery CD from Cisco.com.

RAID and BIOS Settings

Although there should typically be no reason to alter the settings for RAID and BIOS, a quick rundown of the key settings is in order. The servers in question are either IBM- or HP-manufactured, so the amount of information required is mercifully limited. Should the hardware configuration process fail for any reason, the boot-time utilities on the servers can allow for manual configuration.

The BIOS configuration settings for HP servers include

- **OS Selection:** Linux

- **Boot Order:** CD/DVD, hard disk, floppy

- **Post F1 Prompt:** Delayed

- **Hyperthreading:** Enabled

The configuration for IBM servers is identical, but there is no need for OS Selection, so that should be considered not applicable for IBM. On the newer HP servers, the OS selection is unnecessary as well. Because it is not uncommon to see servers repurposed, however, not every install will include the latest, greatest servers.

The RAID configuration is somewhat simple as well. Both the IBM and HP versions of the MCS-7825 use the same settings. SATA RAID is enabled and the RAID type is 1(1+0) and one logical drive.

For the MCS-7835 and MCS-7845, again, both IBM and HP servers use the same settings. The MCS-7835 uses one logical drive, whereas the MCS-7845 uses two logical drives. Both utilize RAID Type 1(1+0).

Supported Browsers

At the current time, only Internet Explorer 6.0 or higher is officially supported for CUPS administration. This is not to say that Firefox, Safari, and others will not work properly for the job, just that they might be quirky, and you cannot open a TAC case for them because they haven't been tested and certified.

Preparing for the Installation

Among the things that should be placed high on the to-do list in preparing for the installation of the Presence Server are a few that are obvious and a few that are simply not. Among the obvious items are the crucial details such as IP address, default gateway, DNS Servers, NTP Servers and other network-related information. Also of particular interest is verification of network accessibility for the Presence Server because it will need to make contact with the Communications Manager Publisher.

If relying on DNS entries for IP address resolution, ensure ahead of time that the names of both the Communications Manager and the Presence Server can be resolved. Although not entirely necessary, there will be some sanity gained by resolving the addresses of both servers utilizing both the Fully Qualified Domain Name (FQDN) and the short name (or hostname).

The Administrative XML Layer (AXL) Application Programming Interface (API) provides a mechanism for inserting, retrieving, updating, and removing data from the database by using an eXtensible Markup Language (XML) Simple Object Access Protocol (SOAP) interface. This enables a programmer to access Cisco UC data by using XML and receive the data in XML form, instead of using a binary library or DLL.

The AXL API methods, known as requests, use a combination of HTTP and SOAP. SOAP is an XML remote procedure call (RPC) protocol. Users perform requests by sending XML data to the Cisco UC server. The server then returns the AXL response, which is also a SOAP message.

It is critical that the Cisco Web AXL Service be activated and running on the Communications Manager Publisher, which is discussed in the next section.

CUCM Installation Tasks

By now, you are likely ready to get this installation moving. Most likely, you have already placed the DVD into the drive and powered up the server. You're asking, "Okay, what's next?" Well, next is a small bit of configuration on the Communications Manager. Some tasks need to be performed in expectation of the Presence Server making contact and synchronizing with the CUCM publisher. These major tasks include the following:

- Adding an Application Server

- Adding an AXL group and user

- CUCM/CUPS synchronization

- Adding a Presence gateway

During the CUCM installation, you entered a security password. This is the same password that was necessary when adding subscribers to the cluster. That password will be needed quite soon, so now would be a good time to track it down if it's an unknown element because it will certainly come into play soon.

Adding an Application Server

The first step in preparing for the Presence Server installation is to tell the Communications Manager that it will be making contact. This is done by adding it as an Application Server. Open the ccmadmin page and log in. It is accessible via https://publisher-ip-address/ccmadmin. When logged in, click **System > Application Server**. Most likely, there will be few, if any, items listed here. If you click **Find** with a blank search, it returns all records. Honestly, none of that is of concern because you need to add a new server. That said, click **Add New**.

At this point, you will be presented with a drop-down box to specify the type of Application Server. Figure 3-1 shows the options available.

From the figure, it is clear that the choice should be Cisco Unified Presence Server. Select it, and then click the **Next** button.

The final step in this task is to enter the name of the Presence Server. Note that this is not the FQDN. DNS names are irrelevant to this step. Figure 3-2 shows this configuration page.

As evident in the figure, this entry is solely the hostname that will be assigned to the Presence Server during its installation. Optionally, the URL and User URL can be entered here, though they are not necessary. After the name is entered, click **Save**.

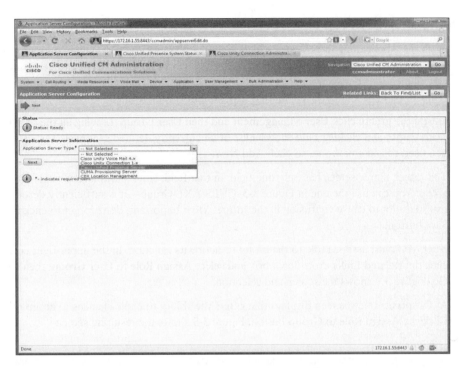

Figure 3-1   *Adding the Presence Server as an Application Server*

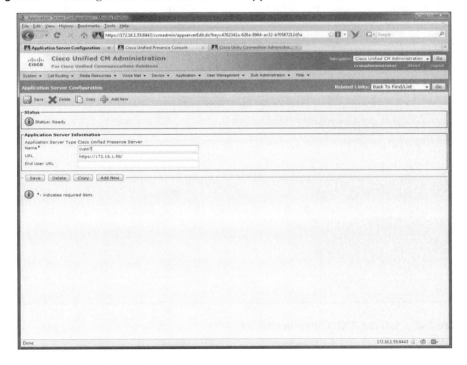

Figure 3-2   *Naming the Presence Server*

Adding an AXL Group and User

With the Application Server entry added, the final phase of the CUCM preconfiguration can be handled. This involves adding a group and user for the AXL service to utilize in communications between the Presence Server and CUCM. This portion of the configuration will be done via the Cisco Unified CM Administration (ccmadmin for short) page.

To add the group, click **User Management** and then **User Group**. Leaving all the search fields empty and clicking **Find** shows a list of all currently defined groups. In this case, you need to add a new one, so click **Add New**.

This rather simple screen has only one field. In that field, enter a meaningful name for this group. You can use the one in Figure 3-3, CUPS-AXL-Group—it is sufficiently descriptive so as not to cause confusion in the future. Most important, don't forget to click the **Save** button.

Next, you must assign a role to the group to define its function. In the upper-right corner, click the **Related Links** drop-down box and select **Assign Role to User Group**; then click **Go**. Figure 3-4 shows the screen and selection.

At this point, a new screen displays that offers the ability to make chances to group roles. Click the **Assign Role to Group** button. Figure 3-5 shows the resulting screen.

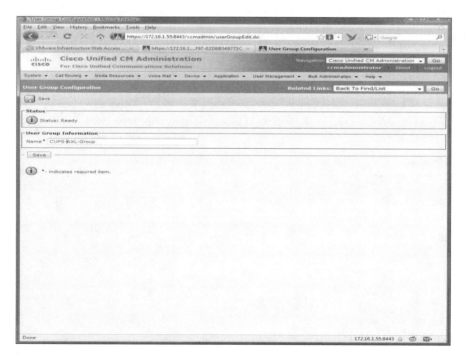

Figure 3-3   *Add the AXL Group in CUCM*

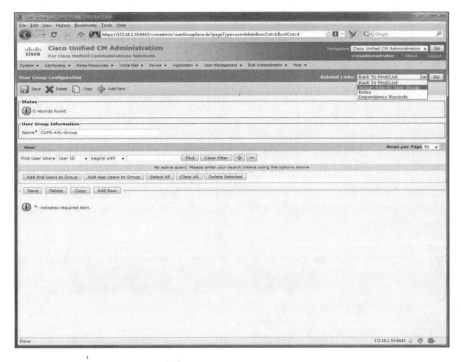

Figure 3-4   *Configuring the AXL Group*

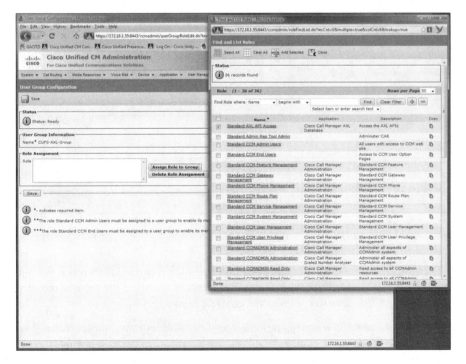

Figure 3-5   *Assigning the AXL API Access Role*

Check the box next to **Standard AXL API Access** followed by the **Add Selected** button at the top of the page. This returns you to the User Group Configuration page. Simply click **Save**.

The next task is to create an Application User (not an End User) that will be added to the AXL Group. To do this, click **User Management > Application User**.

Enter the User ID in the first field. Like the group name previously, this name should be something adequately descriptive and meaningful to be evident to future administrators who work with the system. Enter a password and confirm it. It defaults to the Standard Presence Group, so there's no need to change that field.

Scroll all the way down to the bottom of the page. The Permissions Information section is your destination. Click the **Add to User Group** button. Figure 3-6 shows the User and User Group pages.

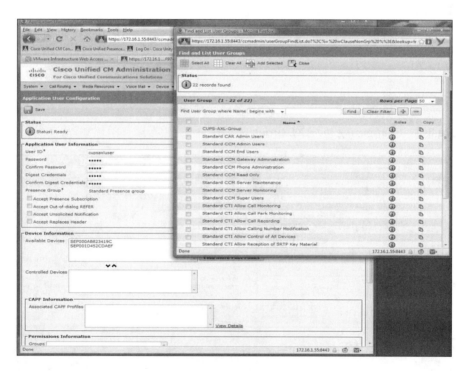

Figure 3-6   *Adding a User to the AXL Group*

Select the group you created in the prior step, and then click **Add Selected** at the top of the page. The User Group selection page disappears and you see the group name in the Groups box. Click **Save** to complete the configuration step.

At this point, the CUCM configuration is complete. The necessary pieces that will facilitate the integration between it and the Presence Server are in place. It is now time to move on to the actual installation of the CUPS software on the server platforms.

Installing the CUPS Software

As mentioned at the beginning of the chapter, all the Cisco UC appliance-based products use essentially the same underlying operating system. The media shipped to you by the fulfillment team at Cisco includes all the necessary files, drivers, images, and so on needed to complete the installation.

During the installation process, you will create an administrative ID to log in to the Cisco Unified Operating System Administration interface (also called the Platform Administration), the Disaster Recovery System Administration interface, and the command-line interface (CLI). The ID used for these will not be the same ID used to access the CUPS Administration page. This is identical in practice as the use of Administrative IDs on the Communications Manager.

Power on the Presence Server and insert the media into the DVD drive. The server boots from the CD image and launches the installer. It configures the necessary RAID settings and other hardware drivers as the installation progresses.

After the server's power on self-test (POST), a screen displays asking if you want to do a media check, as shown in Figure 3-7.

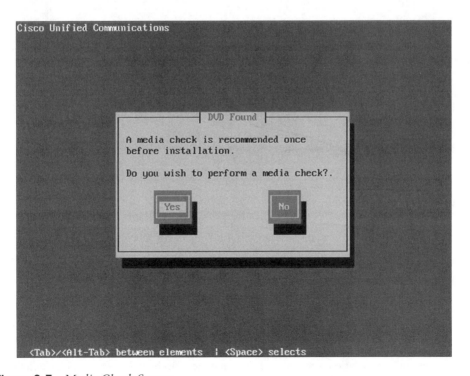

Figure 3-7   *Media Check Screen*

If this is the first time the media has been used, it is worth the effort to allow the media check to progress. If it is known good media, this step can be skipped because it is somewhat time-consuming. If the affirmative selection is made, the media check begins and a screen displays with a progress bar. Should the negative selection be made, a confirmation screen displays showing what is currently installed on the server's disk drives and what is about to be installed. Figure 3-8 shows the screen as presented on a new installation.

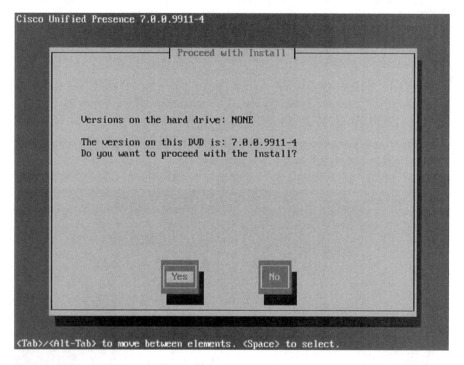

Figure 3-8   *Proceed with Install Screen*

Choosing **No** aborts the install. Because it is assumed that this is not the desired action at this point, choosing **Yes** might be the better way to go.

With the confirmation out of the way, you are presented a bit of information explaining that a wizard is launching that can set up the initial configuration of the platform. It explains how to navigate the following pages using the Tab and Alt-Tab keystrokes to go forward and back respectively. Figure 3-9 shows the Platform Installation Wizard screen.

Although three options, Proceed/Skip/Cancel, are presented, only one is actually an option if the installation is to succeed. Pressing the spacebar while Proceed is highlighted launches the wizard and progresses to the next screen. If you're feeling somewhat adventurous and daring, click the **Skip** button to see what lies down the road less traveled. Only wimps use the wizard, right?

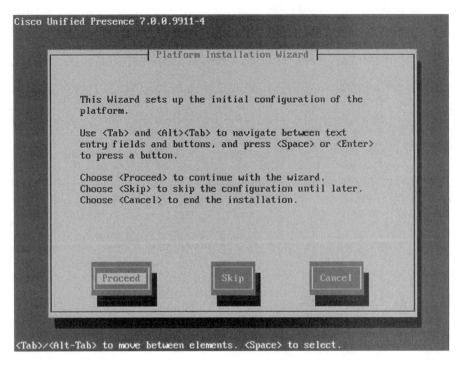

Figure 3-9 *Platform Installation Wizard*

Assuming the sane choice was made and **Proceed** was clicked, you are offered the chance to include a Service Release (SR) or an Engineering Special (ES) as part of the upgrade. Figure 3-10 shows the Apply Additional Release screen.

Appropriately, the No button is highlighted by default, so go ahead and click it. If that is an SR/ES you want, clicking the **Yes** button provides the opportunity to indicate the desired image file.

The next screen is informational in nature. It discusses the fact that the software version from the DVD will be installed and will not use any imported data. Figure 3-11 shows the Basic Install screen.

Selecting **Continue** takes you to the next step.

Up next is the Timezone Configuration screen. Using the arrow keys, scroll up or down the list to find the time zone in which the server exists. Select it and press **Tab** to drop down to the OK button. Figure 3-12 shows the Timezone Configuration screen. Click **OK** to progress on to the next step.

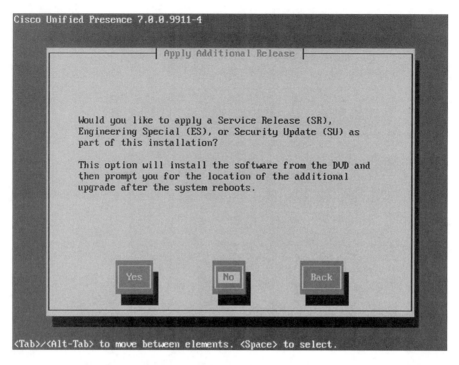

Figure 3-10   *Apply Additional Release Screen*

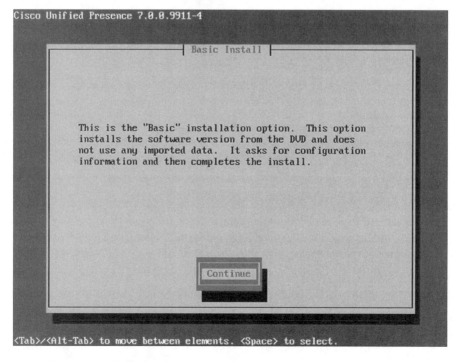

Figure 3-11   *Basic Install Screen*

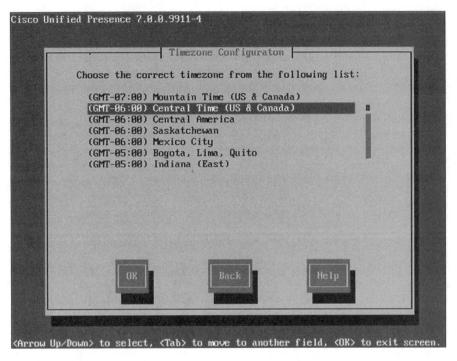

Figure 3-12 *Timezone Configuration Screen*

The basic configuration of the networking components is composed of the next few screens. The first piece of information concerns the duplex and link speed of the server's network connection. Figure 3-13 shows the Auto Negotiation Configuration screen.

If you want the link auto negotiated, select **Yes** to move on. Otherwise, selecting **No** provides the opportunity to manually set the duplex and link speed for the server. If presented with the option to alter the Maximum Transmittable Unit (MTU), you will typically refuse to do so. It is recommended that you avoid altering the MTU unless specifically required by specific circumstances. This setting must match the configuration of the Communications Manager or the install will fail. If auto negotiation is used, it is important that the settings be checked on the appliance and switch after the installation is complete to ensure that the desired settings are negotiated (for example, 100/full).

Moving on to the next screen brings you to the Dynamic Host Configuration Protocol (DHCP) Configuration screen. Though it might be difficult to think of a case in which to use DHCP on a server, you can quickly notice that **Yes** is highlighted automatically. Figure 3-14 shows the DHCP Configuration screen.

Select **No** to move on to the next step in the network configuration.

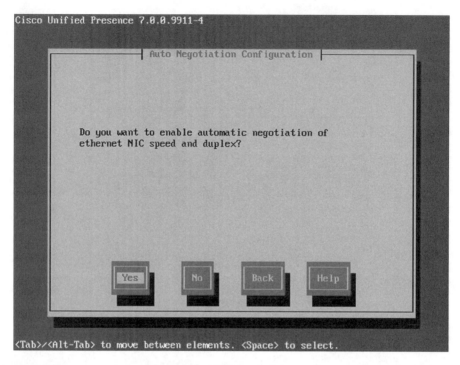

Figure 3-13 *Auto Negotiation Configuration Screen*

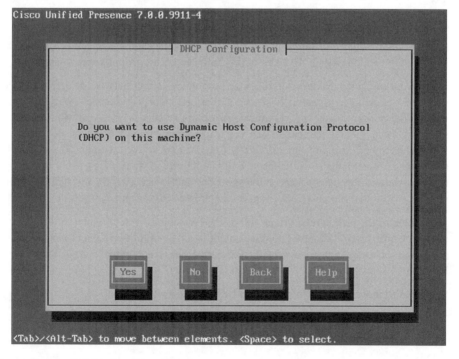

Figure 3-14 *DHCP Configuration Screen*

Having successfully disabled DHCP, the next screen provides the opportunity to set the Host Name, IP Address, IP Mask, and Gateway Address. Figure 3-15 shows the Static Network Configuration Screen.

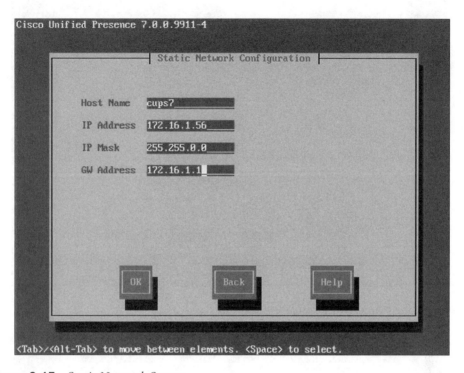

Figure 3-15 *Static Network Screen*

The Host Name must be filled in with the identical entry that was made in the CUCM earlier when you added the Application Server name. Again, this is not the FQDN, just the Host Name. Set the IP Address and Subnet Mask as appropriate. Don't forget the Gateway Address if you want any traffic to leave the local subnet. With all that information entered and verified, **Tab** your way down to the **OK** button and select it to move on.

The next question presented is one regarding DNS. Do you want to use it? Typically, in Cisco UC deployments, DNS is to be relied upon as little as possible. Wherever possible, use IP addresses rather than hostnames. Doing so removes a layer of dependency on supplemental services. Figure 3-16 shows the DNS Client Configuration screen.

If you want to specify DNS servers, click **Yes**; otherwise, click **No** to progress. Clicking **Yes** takes you to a screen where multiple DNS server addresses can be entered. This concludes the network configuration portion of the installation.

The next screen is the Administrator Login Configuration screen. At the beginning of this section, Administrator IDs were discussed briefly. This is the place where that ID is defined. Figure 3-17 shows the Administrator Login Configuration Screen.

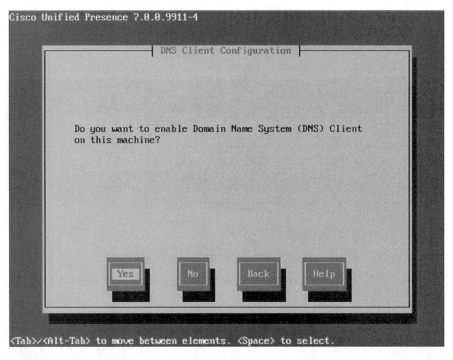

Figure 3-16   *DNS Client Configuration Screen*

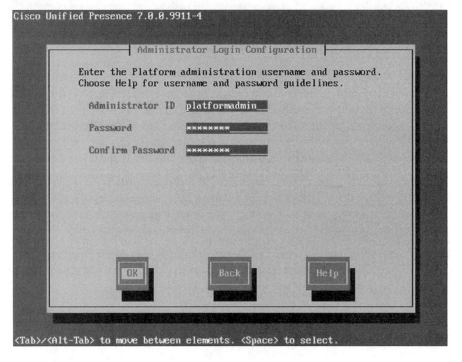

Figure 3-17   *Administrator Login Configuration Screen*

Enter the ID you want to use for the Cisco Unified OS Administration page, Disaster Recover page, and CLI. The Administrator login must start with an alphabetical character, be at least six characters in length, and contain alphanumeric characters, hyphens, and underscores.

With the administrative username and password set, the next screen presented is the Certificate Information screen. This is where the server's security certificate will be configured. Figure 3-18 shows the Certificate Information screen.

Enter the appropriate information for Organization, Unit, Location, State, and Country. Select **OK** when finished to progress to the next screen.

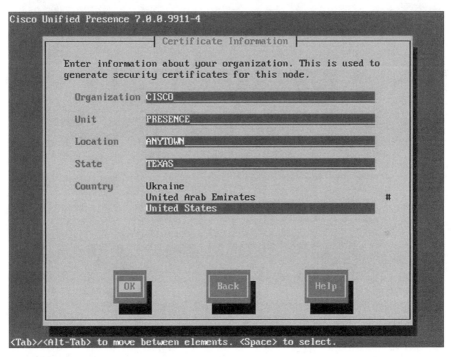

Figure 3-18 *Certificate Information Screen*

The next screen presents you with a crucial step that asks whether this is the first node in the cluster. CUPS works on a similar premise as CUCM. It has a publisher/subscriber architecture. If this is the CUPS Publisher node, answer **Yes**. If it is a subsequent node, answer **No** and provide the relevant publisher information as the installation requests it. Figure 3-19 shows the First Node Configuration screen.

The next decision placed before you, the installer, is whether to make use of the Network Time Protocol (NTP). It is strongly recommended that you *do* use NTP on all Cisco UC components to keep the clocks in synch. For those of you who actually read the entire screen, take particular note of the final paragraph. It states that the CUCM Publisher will be set as the *only* NTP server when available. So even if you do set an external source, it will be overridden when the CUCM is available. This ensures a consistent time source throughout.

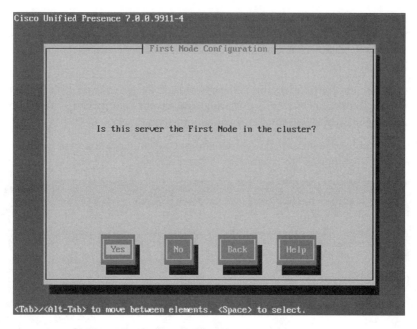

Figure 3-19   *First Node Configuration Screen*

Figure 3-20 shows the Network Time Protocol Client Configuration screen.

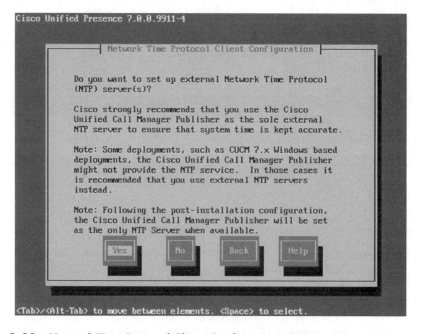

Figure 3-20   *Network Time Protocol Client Configuration Screen*

Selecting **Yes** on this screen progresses to a new screen with multiple fields for entering the IP addresses of NTP Server entry, as illustrated in Figure 3-21.

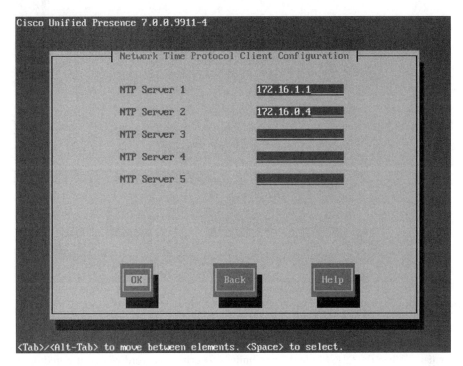

Figure 3-21 *Network Time Protocol Client Configuration Screen: Entering NTP Server IP Addresses*

When you finish entering the NTP Server IP addresses, select **OK** to progress to the Hardware Clock Configuration screen where the time and date settings can be manually configured. Figure 3-22 shows the Hardware Clock Configuration screen.

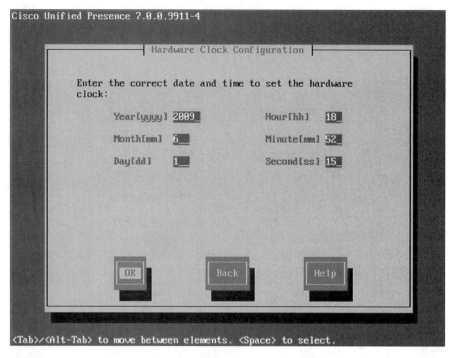

Figure 3-22   *Hardware Clock Configuration Screen*

Now that the bulk of the initial Configuration Wizard is complete, only a few parameters remain. When the CUCM cluster was built, a security password was configured on the Publisher. Each Subscriber configuration included this password to authenticate to the Publisher and join the cluster. This same password concept is utilized in the Presence cluster. If this is the first node, the password can be set. If it is a subsequent node, the password must match what was set on the first node when it was built. Figure 3-23 shows the Security Password Configuration screen.

During the post-install phase of the configuration, you have an opportunity to set this password to match that of the CUCM Publisher.

With the security password set, the option to configure Simple Mail Transfer Protocol (SMTP) settings for the server is offered. Figure 3-24 shows the SMTP Host Configuration screen.

If **Yes** is selected here, options will be presented to specify SMTP account settings for the Presence Server. This account will be used to send alerts, alarms, and other messages.

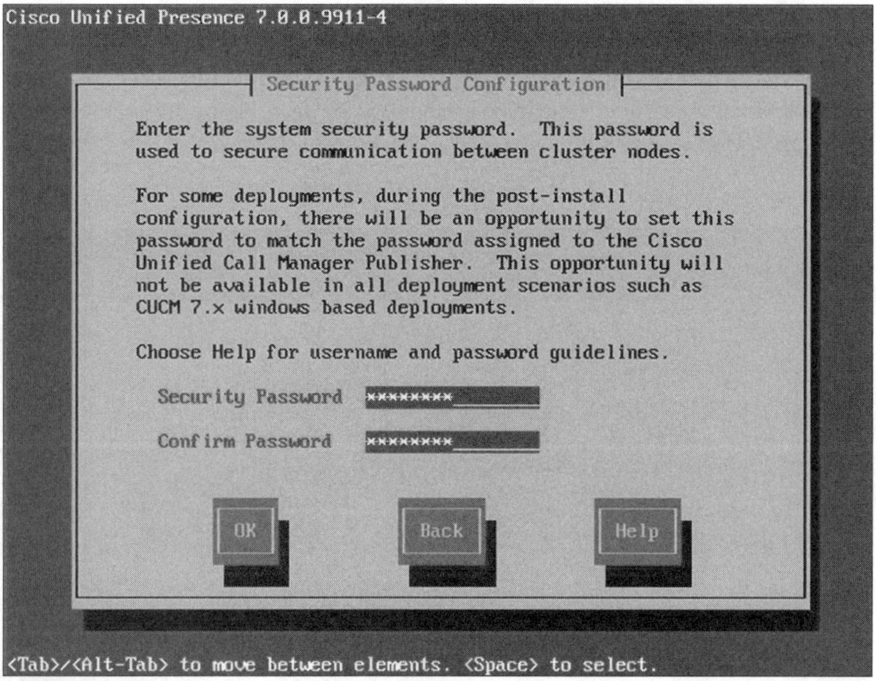

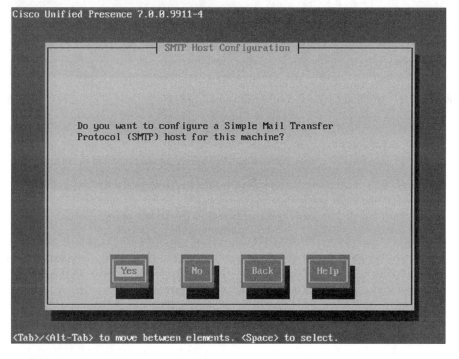

Figure 3-23 *Security Password Configuration Screen*

Figure 3-24 *SMTP Host Configuration Screen*

With the Administrator ID and password set along with the security password, only one password remains, which is the application user password. The application user is the administrative user credentials to log you in to the Cisco Unified Presence Administration and Cisco Unified Serviceability web pages. Figure 3-25 shows the Application User Configuration screen.

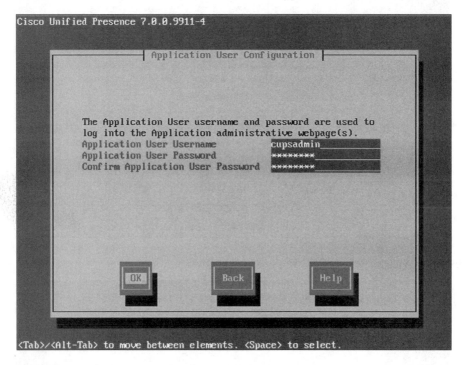

Figure 3-25 *Application User Configuration Screen*

Please don't confuse this username and password with the platform administration username and password. They are separate entities. Keep these passwords in a safe place.

All the network-related information is set, usernames and passwords configured, and NTP, SMTP, and other acronyms all acknowledged. The initial Configuration Wizard is nearly done. Figure 3-26 shows the Platform Configuration Confirmation screen.

The primary message of this screen is that you're done, for the most part. It provides you one last chance to go back and make changes. After you click **OK** on this page, the configuration is set. No further changes are possible. Figure 3-27 shows your reward for a well-configured server, the Platform Installation screen.

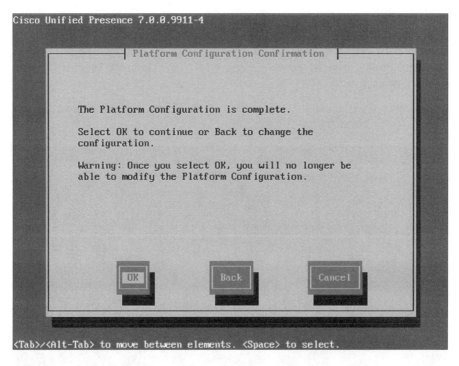

Figure 3-26 *Platform Configuration Confirmation Screen*

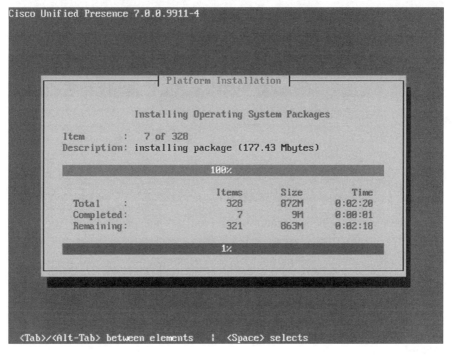

Figure 3-27 *Platform Installation Screen*

From here, it's time for a coffee break, Red Bull break, or whatever the chosen drink of the hour might be. This portion of the installation takes a while. The installation script is using all the information provided thus far to build the server image. When the entire process is finally complete, the end result is simply a login prompt. Figure 3-28 shows the completed server install.

At this point, the configuration continues in the web-based Administration tool. The really fun parts are all behind you now.

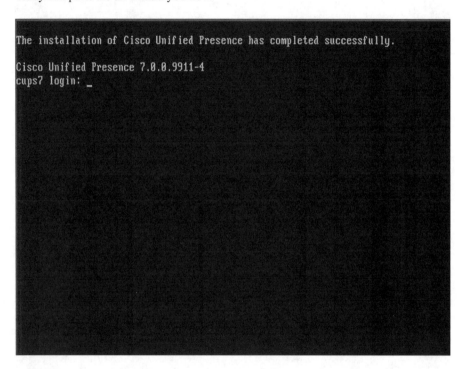

Figure 3-28   *Platform Login Screen*

Post-Install Configuration

The first time you log in to the Cisco Unified Presence Administration page, the Post-Install Wizard runs. This wizard runs only once and cannot be rerun, so be ready when you launch it. The tool can be accessed at **https://*CUPSIPAddress*/ccmadmin**. You can access the server directly by IP address. Links to the Administration and User Options pages are accessible there.

The Post-Installation Wizard runs only on the CUPS Publisher, and then, only once. On subsequent nodes, it does not run. This is where the AXL link between the CUCM and Presence server is configured.

The launching of the Post-Installation Wizard is a confirmation of sorts that the initial installation was a success. Figure 3-29 shows the opening page of the Post-Installation Wizard.

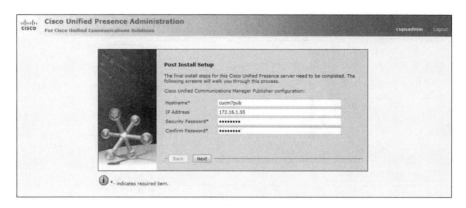

Figure 3-29 *Post-Installation Wizard, Page 1*

The first page requests information regarding the CUCM Publisher. In the Hostname field, input only the Publisher's hostname, not its FQDN. Enter its IP Address and then the security password configured during the initial installation wizard phase of the CUPS installation. Click **Next.**

The second page of the Post-Installation Wizard requests AXL user information. Figure 3-30 shows the second page of the Post-Installation Wizard.

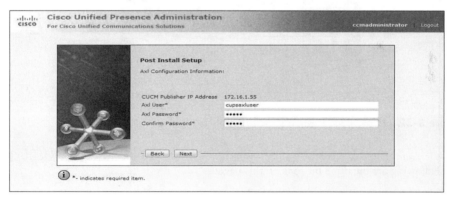

Figure 3-30 *Post-Installation Wizard, Page 2*

At the beginning of the installation (and this chapter) an AXL user was created specifically for this role. Enter that username and password here and click **Next.**

The third page of the Post-Installation Wizard is simply a confirmation page. Figure 3-31 shows the third page of the Post-Installation Wizard.

Verify the CUCM Publisher hostname, IP address, and the username of the AXL user; then click **Confirm.**

Figure 3-31   *Post-Installation Wizard, Page 3*

The fourth and final page denotes that the installation is complete. Figure 3-32 shows the fourth and final page of the Post-Installation Wizard.

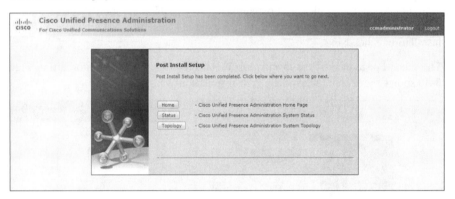

Figure 3-32   *Post-Installation Wizard, Page 4*

Following are the three buttons on this page:

■ **Home:** Loads the Cisco Unified Presence Administration page

■ **Status:** Loads the Cisco Unified Presence Administration System Status page

■ **Topology:** Loads the Cisco Unified Presence Administration System Topology page

Click the button corresponding to the page you'd like to load.

Licensing

To activate the CUPS services, the license files must be uploaded. The license files were discussed earlier in the "Preinstallation Tasks" section. If you have not yet obtained the license files, stop now and do so.

When obtained, the license file should be uploaded to the Presence Server via the CUPS Admin page. Log in to the CUPS Admin interface and click **System > Licensing > License File Upload**. Figure 3-33 shows the License upload screen.

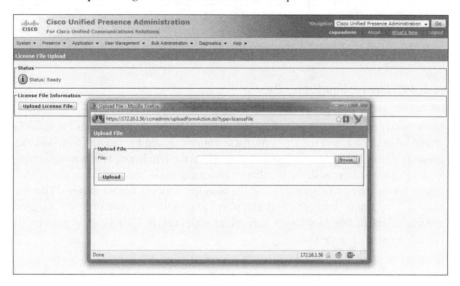

Figure 3-33 *License Upload Page*

The license files should have been e-mailed to the address in your Cisco Connection Online (CCO) profile. Open the message and save the license file to your local hard drive. Do not alter the file because it is digitally signed, and you will invalidate it. Also, Mac users, take notice. Your e-mail client might rewrite the file and invalidate it without your knowledge. If need be, retrieve the file via web-based e-mail client.

Start by clicking the **Upload License File** button. Browse to the location where you saved the file to your hard drive and select it. Click **Open** and then **Upload**. The window closes and the screen refreshes to show you that the license file has indeed been received.

To verify the licensing, click **System > Licensing > License Unit Report**. Figure 3-34 shows the License Unit Report page.

Two tables appear on this screen. The first is for Proxy Server licensing. CUPS can perform the role of SIP Proxy Server for Unified Contact Center Enterprise deployments.

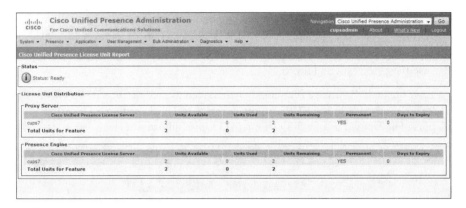

Figure 3-34   *License Unit Report Page*

The second table is the Presence Engine licensing. The hostname of your Presence Server should be in the list, and the Units Available column should be updated to reflect the contents of the license file you uploaded. It shows the number of CUPS node licenses available, the number used, the number of remaining node licenses, the status of the license (Permanent or Temporary), and the time left until the license expires. This is applicable only to temporary licenses. If you plan a multinode Presence deployment, go ahead and upload the license files for the subscriber nodes via the CUPS Admin page on the Publisher Presence node now.

In Figure 3-34, note that the Units Used is 0. This is because none of the CUPS Services have yet been activated. When the services are activated, the numbers will increment/decrement properly.

Service Activation

The Installation Wizards are complete and the installation steps closely followed. There is another task to be accomplished. None of the services are started by default, so you need to activate processes such as the Presence Engine, AXL Web Service, and others.

Launch the Serviceability page. To do so, select Cisco Unified Serviceability from the Navigation drop-down box and click **Go.** When on the Serviceability page, log in if need be. **Click Tools > Service Activation**. Figure 3-35 shows the Service Activation page.

Select the server you've just configured. For the easy way out, check the box labeled **Check all Services** and click **Save** at the top of the page. After a brief period of time, the page refreshes, and all services show as Activated. The Presence Server is now ready to do its job.

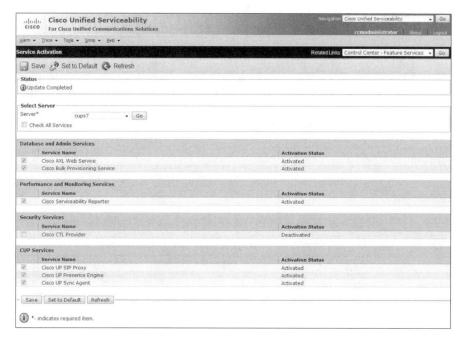

Figure 3-35 *CUPS Serviceability Page*

Rerun the License Unit Report, and you will see that the numbers have appropriately changed. Figure 3-36 shows the License Unit Report after service activation.

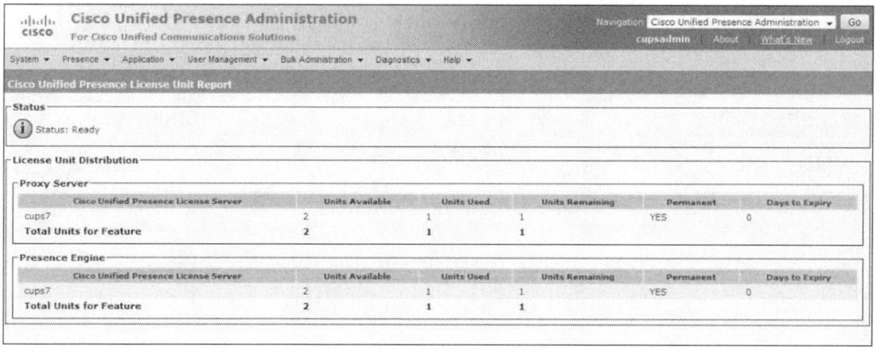

Figure 3-36 *License Unit Report Page After Service Activation*

CUCM/CUPS Synchronization

After the installation is complete and the necessary services started, wait a few minutes and check the System Status page. The Presence Server will make contact with the CUCM and synchronize databases with it. On the Serviceability page, you might have noticed the Cisco UP Sync Agent. This is the service that will make contact with the CUCM. It uses AXL to pull in relevant information from the CUCM. As you might guess, it does use the AXL user created as part of this installation.

Depending on the size of the database (number of phones, other endpoints, gateways, and so on), the sync might take a while. To see the status of the sync process, click **Diagnostics > System Status** from the CUPS Admin page. Figure 3-37 shows the System Status page.

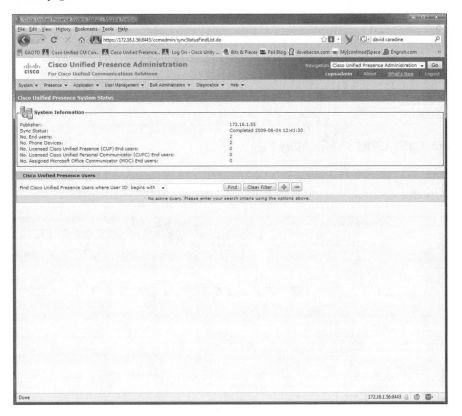

Figure 3-37   *System Status Page*

In the figure, the Sync Status can be seen with a time/date stamp. The number of end users and phones is shown. Additionally, the number of licensed Presence users, Cisco Unified Personal Communicator (CUPC) users, and the number of Microsoft Office Communicator (MOC) client users is shown. Currently, those numbers are set to 0. This indicates that the databases might have synchronized properly, but the users have not been Presence-enabled on the Communications Manager.

To enable them for the features available, launch the ccmadmin page and click **System > Licensing > Capabilities Assignment**. Figure 3-38 shows the Find and List Capabilities Assignments Page.

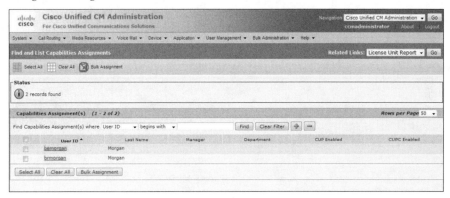

Figure 3-38 *Find and List Capabilities Assignments Page*

A list of users will be presented, along with columns indicating their license status. Specifically of interest are the two columns on the right side of the page: CUP Enabled and CUPC Enabled. CUP Enabled means that Presence services are permitted for this user. CUPC Enabled means that the user can use the CUPC client on their workstation.

Capabilities can be assigned individually or in bulk. Select all the users for which you want Presence enabled and click **Bulk Assignment**. A screen displays that has two check boxes on it; one is for Presence and the other for CUPC. Check both of them; then click **Save**. After saving the changes, the Find and List Capabilities Assignment page refreshes and shows the check marks by those users enabled for both services. Figure 3-39 shows the Find and List Capabilities Assignment page after enabling the features for users.

Return to the Presence Server admin page and click **Diagnostics > System Status** again. Now you should see that the users are enabled for Presence and CUPC. Figure 3-40 shows the System Status page after the features for the users.

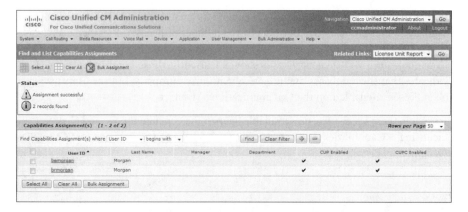

Figure 3-39 *Find and List Capabilities Assignment Page After Bulk Assignment*

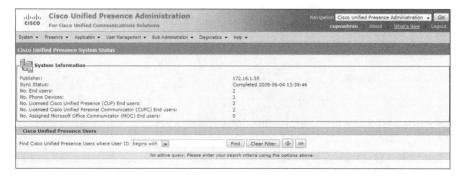

Figure 3-40 *Cisco Unified Presence System Status Page Updated*

Adding a Presence Gateway

The Presence Gateway is an entity connected to the Presence Server via a Session Initiation Protocol (SIP) trunk. In this case, the entity will be the Communications Manager. This will be used to pass Presence indication (on-hook, off-hook, and so on) between the CUCM and the Presence Server. To add a Presence Gateway, log in to the CUPS Admin page and click **Presence > Gateways > Add New**. Figure 3-41 shows the Presence Gateway Configuration screen.

The Presence Gateway Type field has two options: CUCM and Outlook. Creating an Outlook gateway is beyond the scope of this book, so select the CUCM option. The Description field is just that. Enter a meaningful description for this gateway. The Presence Gateway field can hold the IP address of the CUCM Publisher.

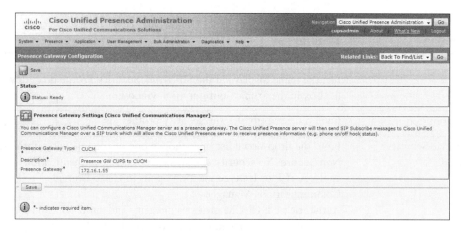

Figure 3-41 *Presence Gateway Configuration Screen*

Creating a SIP Trunk on the CUCM

For the Presence Gateway entry to function, a SIP Trunk must be configured on the CUCM. The first step completing that task is to configure a SIP Security Profile for Presence. This is done on the Communications Manager. Click **System > Security Profile > SIP Trunk Security Profile**. Ensure that the search field is blank, and click **Find**. Select the **Non Secure SIP Trunk Profile** to get to its configuration page.

Verify that the following settings are in the configuration:

- **Device Security Mode:** Non Secure

- **Incoming Transport Type:** TCP+UDP

- **Outgoing Transport Type:** TCP

- **Incoming Port:** 5060

- **Enable Application Level Authorization:** uncheck

- **Accept Presence Subscription:** check

- **Accept Out-of-Dialog REFER:** check

- **Accept Unsolicited Notification:** check

- **Accept Replaces Header:** check

- **Transmit Security Status:** uncheck

Complete the configuration by clicking **Save**. The next task is to add a SIP Trunk to the CUCM configuration that points back to the Presence Server. Table 3-1 provides some additional detail about the fields on this screen.

Table 3-1   *SIP Trunk Security Profile Field Descriptions*

Setting	Description
Name	Enter a name for the security profile. When you save the new profile, the name displays in the SIP Trunk Security Profile drop-down list box in the Trunk Configuration window.
Description	Enter a description for the security profile.
Device Security Mode	From the drop-down list box, choose one of the following options: **Non Secure:** No security features except image authentication apply. A TCP or UDP connection opens to Cisco Unified Communications Manager. **Authenticated:** CUCM provides integrity and authentication for the trunk. A TLS connection that uses NULL/SHA opens. **Encrypted:** CUCM provides integrity, authentication, and signaling encryption for the trunk. A TLS connection that uses AES128/SHA opens for signaling.
Incoming Transport Type	When Device Security Mode is Non Secure, TCP+UDP specifies the transport type. When Device Security Mode is Authenticated or Encrypted, TLS specifies the transport type. Note: The Transport Layer Security (TLS) protocol secures the connection between CUCM and the trunk.
Outgoing Transport Type	From the drop-down list box, choose the outgoing transport mode. When Device Security Mode is Non Secure, choose TCP or UDP. When Device Security Mode is Authenticated or Encrypted, TLS specifies the transport type. **Note:** TLS ensures signaling integrity, device authentication, and signaling encryption for SIP trunks. **Tip:** You must use UDP as the outgoing transport type when connecting SIP trunks between CUCM systems and IOS gateways that do not support TCP connection reuse.
Nonce Validity Time	Enter the number of minutes (in seconds) that the nonce value is valid. The default value equals 600 (10 minutes). When the time expires, CUCM generates a new value. Note: A nonce value, a random number that supports digest authentication, calculates the MD5 hash of the digest authentication password.

Setting	Description
X.509 Subject Name	This field applies if you configured TLS for the incoming and outgoing transport type. For device authentication, enter the subject name of the X.509 certificate for the SIP trunk device. If you have a CUCM cluster or if you use SRV lookup for the TLS peer, a single trunk might resolve to multiple hosts, which results in multiple X.509 subject names for the trunk. If multiple X.509 subject names exist, enter one of the following characters to separate the names: space, comma, semicolon, or a colon. You can enter up to 4096 characters in this field. **Tip:** The subject name corresponds to the source connection TLS certificate. Ensure that subject names are unique for each subject name and port. You cannot assign the same subject name and incoming port combination to different SIP trunks. Example: SIP TLS trunk1 on port 5061 has X.509 Subject Names my_cm1, my_cm2. SIP TLS trunk2 on port 5071 has X.509 Subject Names my_cm2, my_cm3. SIP TLS trunk3 on port 5061 can have X.509 Subject Name my_ccm4 but cannot have X.509 Subject Name my_cm1.
Incoming Port	Choose the incoming port. Enter a value that is a unique port number from 1024–65,535. The default port value for incoming TCP and UDP SIP messages specifies 5060. The default SIP secured port for incoming TLS messages specifies 5061. The value that you enter applies to all SIP trunks that use the profile. **Tip:** All SIP trunks that use TLS can share the same incoming port; all SIP trunks that use TCP + UDP can share the same incoming port. You cannot mix SIP TLS transport trunks with SIP non-TLS transport trunk types on the same port. **Tip:** If the incoming packet rate on a SIP trunk UDP port from a single IP address exceeds the configured SIP Trunk UDP Port Throttle Threshold during normal traffic, reconfigure the threshold. When a SIP trunk and SIP station share the same incoming UDP port, CUCM throttles packets based on the higher of the two service parameter values. You must restart the Cisco CallManager service for changes to this parameter to take effect.

continues

Table 3-1   *SIP Trunk Security Profile Field Descriptions   (continued)*

Setting	Description
Enable Application Level Authorization	Application-level authorization applies to applications that connect through the SIP trunk. If you check this check box, you must also check the Enable Digest Authentication check box and configure digest authentication for the trunk. CUCM authenticates a SIP application user before checking the allowed application methods. When application level authorization is enabled, trunk-level authorization occurs first, and application-level authorization then occurs, which means that CUCM checks the methods authorized for the trunk (in this security profile) before the methods authorized for the SIP application user in the Application User Configuration window. **Tip:** Consider using application-level authorization if you do not trust the identity of the application or if the application is not trusted on a particular trunk; that is, application requests might come from a different trunk than you expect.
Accept Presence Subscription	If you want CUCM to accept presence subscription requests that come via the SIP trunk, check this check box. If you checked the Enable Application Level Authorization check box, go to the Application User Configuration window and check the Accept Presence Subscription check box for any application users that are authorized for this feature. When application-level authorization is enabled, if you check the Accept Presence Subscription check box for the application user but not for the trunk, a 403 error message gets sent to the SIP user agent connected to the trunk.
Accept Out-of-Dialog Refer	If you want CUCM to accept incoming non-INVITE, Out-of-Dialog REFER requests that come via the SIP trunk, check this check box. If you checked the Enable Application Level Authorization check box, go to the Application User Configuration window and check the Accept Out-of-Dialog Refer check box for any application users that are authorized for this method.
Accept Unsolicited Notification	If you want CUCM to accept incoming non-INVITE, unsolicited notification messages that come via the SIP trunk, check this check box. If you checked the Enable Application Level Authorization check box, go to the Application User Configuration window and check the Accept Unsolicited Notification check box for any application users that are authorized for this method.

Setting	Description
Accept Replaces Header	If you want CUCM to accept new SIP dialogs, which have replaced existing SIP dialogs, check this check box. If you checked the Enable Application Level Authorization check box, go to the Application User Configuration window and check the Accept Header Replacement check box for any application users that are authorized for this method.
Transmit Security Status	If you want CUCM to transmit the security icon status of a call from the associated SIP trunk to the SIP peer, check this check box.

Log in to the CUCM Admin page and click **Device > Trunk > Add New**. The Trunk Type and Device Protocol will both be SIP. Select **SIP Trunk** for the Trunk Type and the Device Protocol automatically populates. Click **Next**.

Figure 3-42 shows the SIP Trunk Configuration page as it needs to be when the configuration is complete.

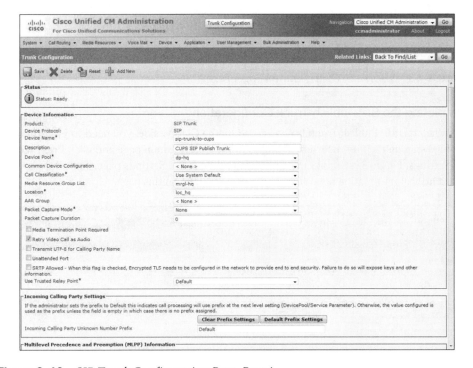

Figure 3-42   *SIP Trunk Configuration Page, Part 1*

Figure 3-43 shows the relevant SIP Trunk settings from the bottom of the SIP Trunk page.

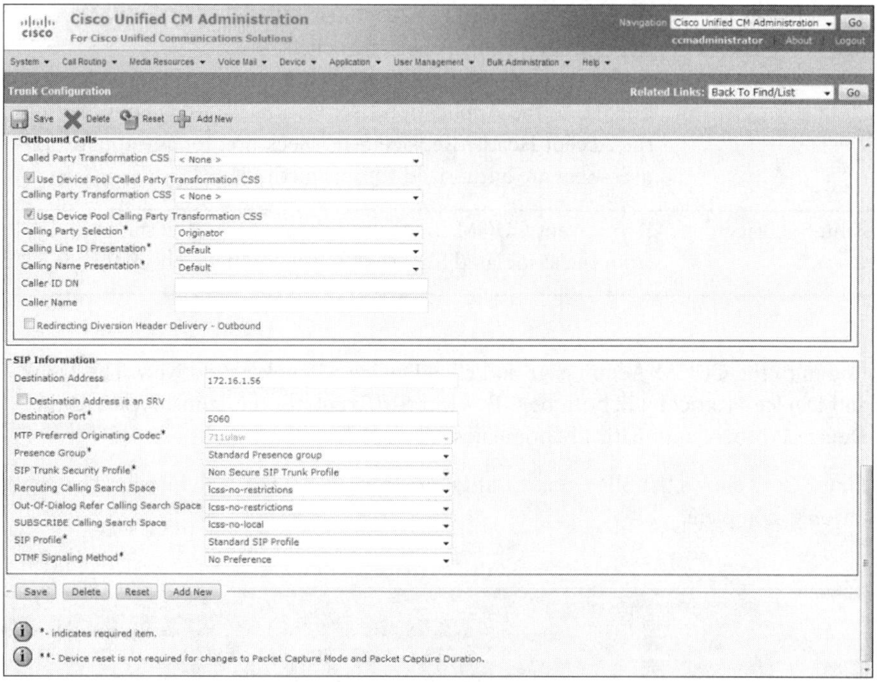

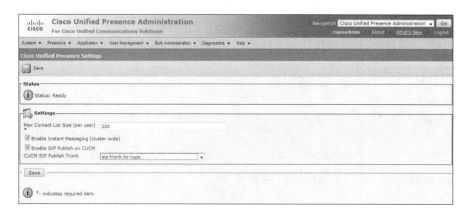

Figure 3-43   *SIP Trunk Configuration Page, Part 2*

Completing the SIP Publish Trunk Configuration

When the SIP Publish Trunk is configured on the CUCM side, you need to perform one final step on the Presence Server. Log in to the CUPS Admin page and click **Presence > Settings.** Figure 3-44 shows the Cisco Unified Presence Settings page. Table 3-2 provides additional information regarding the fields referenced on this page.

Figure 3-44   *Cisco Unified Presence Settings Page*

Table 3-2 *Cisco Unified Presence Settings Page Field Description*

Field	Description
Max Contact List Size (per user)	Enter the maximum size for a contact list in the range of 0–200. Default setting: 200 contacts **Note:** This setting controls the maximum number of contacts per user for both CUPC and IP Phone Messenger (IPPM).
Enable Instant Messaging (check box)	Check this check box to enable Instant Messaging on this Cisco Unified Presence cluster. This setting affects the Cisco IPPM service, the SIP Proxy, and CUCP. Default setting: Enabled
Enable SIP Publish on CUCM (check box)	Check this check box to enable PUBLISH to the associated CUCM. This setting affects the IPPM service, the SIP Proxy, and CUPC. Default setting: Disabled **Note:** This field displays only when you connect to CUCM Release 6.0 or higher.
CUCM SIP Publish Trunk	From the drop-down list, choose the appropriate SIP PUBLISH trunk to allow Cisco Unified Presence to monitor phone status from CUCM. **Note:** You must check the Enable Publish to CUCM check box to enable this parameter. **Note:** This parameter changes the SIP Publish Trunk on CUCM. In addition, if you change the SIP Publish Trunk parameter on CUCM, this also changes this setting because they are connected. Default setting: Current CUCM SIP Publish Trunk, as read from AXL. **Note:** This field displays only when you connect to CUCM Release 6.0 or higher.

This page has only one configuration item. The CUCM SIP Publish field needs to be populated with the name of the trunk just built in the CUCM. Click the drop-down box and select the **SIP Publish Trunk**, and then click **Save**.

Other Important Settings for Presence Server Configuration

Some tasks involved in the configuration of the Presence server simply don't categorize well but are necessary nonetheless. This section covers those so-called miscellaneous configuration items. In particular, this portion of the discussion covers the Proxy Domain, IPPM, and CTI Gateway configuration.

Proxy Domain

The proxy domain is utilized in routing requests among various entities. For example, if a SIP request came in to sip:brmorgan@cisco.com, the proxy would service the request because it belongs to the proxy domain. A request coming in for brmorgan@mysipuri.com would not be serviced by this server.

The Proxy Domain field in the service parameters needs to be set. The Proxy Domain is typically the default domain of the Enterprise Proxy server. In other words, set this field to the domain name of your company, department, or other entity. For purposes of this example, it has been set to cisco.com. To access it, launch the CUPS Admin page and click **System > Service Parameters**. Select the **CUPS Server**, and then select the **Cisco UP Proxy Service** from the second drop-down list. This takes you to the SIP Proxy Service Parameters page. The Proxy Domain is the first field. Set it to your company's top-level domain name, for example cisco.com, and click **Save**. Figure 3-45 shows the SIP Proxy Service Parameters page with the Proxy Domain filled in.

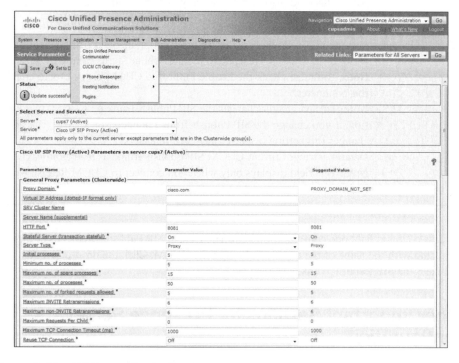

Figure 3-45   *SIP Proxy Service Parameters*

The Virtual IP Address field is an address by which this server (or cluster, if using a clustered Presence Server model) is known by external systems. This enables load balancing and redundancy. This address is used in addition to the actual IP address of the servers in the Presence cluster. If there is only one Presence Server, it will be the actual IP address of the Presence Server itself.

The SRV Cluster Name field enables the user of a DNS SRV that overrides the default value in the Proxy Domain field. For this to function properly, the Address Resolution Type (the last field in the General Proxy Parameters section on this page) needs to be set to SRV. It defaults to IP, though it can be alternatively set to utilize an A-Record. That's a bit out of scope but worth mentioning. The port of the SRV should be set to 5060. This SRV record might not be used by the CUCM SIP Trunk for the same cluster because the SRV Record used by the SIP Trunk should define port 5070.

The Server Name is simply a hostname for this particular server. It might be an IP address as well. It is used by clients in Request-URIs that are different from those that the server would typically use. This is typically useful in a clustered or server-farm implementation where a single hostname for the farm/cluster is published.

As evident in the figure, each of these service parameters is an HTML link. Clicking each can provide more information on each parameter. That said, no further discussion will be covered here. For the most part, aside from those parameters discussed here, there should be little need to adjust the remaining fields on this page.

IP Phone Messenger

The IP Phone Messenger (IPPM) provides an IM client on a Cisco IP Phone with availability-enabled contact lists. This feature provides users with a quick way to check availability of co-workers through the sending and receiving of short text messages typed out on the phone's keypad. The IPPM includes a number of standard phrases utilized in day-to-day text conversation. This can give users the ability to select common phrases or sentences without having to type them out. Message recipients can type out a reply on the keypad or simply press the **Dial** softkey on their phones to call a message sender directly.

The IPPM is an integral part of the overall Presence experience. The configuration is relatively simple and straightforward. It begins with the creation of an Application User. To do this, launch the CUCM Admin page and log in. Click **User Management > Application User > Add New**. Figure 3-46 shows the Application User Configuration page.

The first field is User ID. Choose an ID that is descriptive and meaningful, such as ippm-user or phonemessenger. The system uses a default name of PhoneMessenger in the Presence Server config, so it might be best to match that. If not, be sure to change it in the Presence IP PhoneMessenger Settings. You'll need to go there to alter the password regardless of which username is used. Any of them will do the job quite well. Enter a password and confirm it.

Select the devices to be controlled by this use. That is, choose the devices that you want to be IPPM-capable. Select all the wanted phones, and click the down arrow to move them into the Controlled Devices box. This provides IPPM the access it needs to the phones.

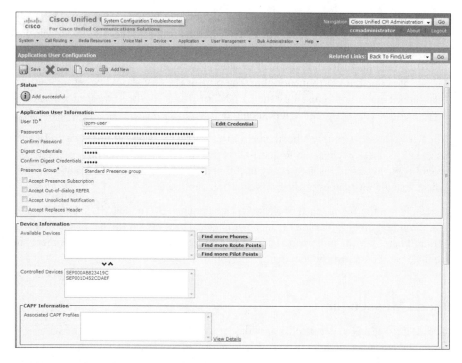

Figure 3-46 *Application User Configuration Page*

With the user added and phones under control, the next step is to subscribe the phones to the IPPM service. To do this, of course, the IPPM service must be created. Click **Device > Device Settings > Phone Services > Add New.** The settings will be as follows:

■ **Service Name:** IPPM

■ **ASCII Service Name:** IP PhoneMessenger

■ **Service Description:** IP PhoneMessenger

■ **Service URL:** http://<cupserverIP>:8081/ippm/default?name=#DEVICENAME#

■ **Service Category:** XML Service

■ **Service Type:** Standard IP Phone Service

■ **Service Vendor:** <blank>

■ **Service Version:** <blank>

■ **Enable:** check

■ **Enterprise Subscription:** uncheck

Figure 3-47 shows the IP Phone Services Configuration page.

When the settings are properly entered, click **Save** and move on to the next task.

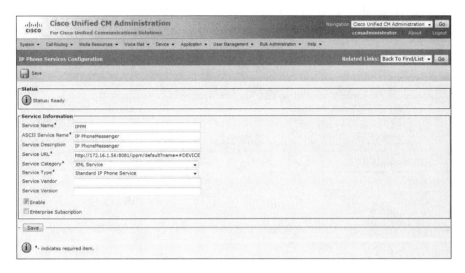

Figure 3-47 *IP Phone Services Configuration Page*

To wrap up the IPPM configuration, subscribe the phones to the new service just created. To do this, click **Device > Phone > Find**. Choose a phone from the list to be subscribed to the service. Note that the phone being subscribed must have been in the list of controlled devices added to the IPPM user created previously.

Select a phone by clicking on its Device Name. Click the drop-down box labeled Related Links and select the **Subscribe/Unsubscribe Services** option and click **Go**. The service subscription page pops up. Select the IPPM Service from the drop-down box and click **Next**. The screen refreshes and provides a Subscribe button for you to click. When the Subscribe button is clicked, this part of the task is complete. Close the window. Repeat the process on all desired phones. You can also use the Bulk Administration Tool (BAT) to accomplish the phone subscriptions rather than reconfiguring every phone manually. Figure 3-48 shows the IP Phone Subscribe/Unsubscribe page.

It is necessary to configure the Presence Server side of the IPPM application. To do this, log in to the CUPS Admin page and click **Application > IP PhoneMessenger > Settings**. On this page, you need to modify the username (if you used something other than PhoneMessenger) and password. Figure 3-49 shows the IP Phone Messenger Settings page.

After you make the necessary changes, click **Save**.

CTI Gateway

The Computer Telephony Interface (CTI) handles the communications required for the Presence Server to control phones on the CUCM. This is one of the more crucial pieces of the entire puzzle because it relates to the user experience. That said, there is a requirement for CTI services to be active on both the CUCM and the Presence Server.

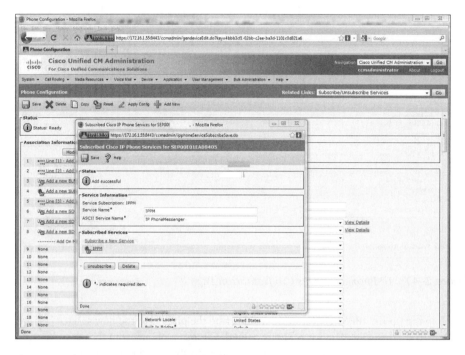

Figure 3-48   *IP Phone Subscribe/Unsubscribe Page*

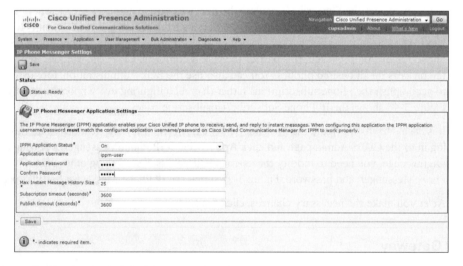

Figure 3-49   *IP Phone Messenger Settings Page*

Presence users must be associated with a CTI-enabled group and the primary extension of their phones. The phones must be enabled for CTI use as well. All this communication is facilitated by the CTI Gateway. The CTI Gateway must be enabled on the Presence Server. Database sync between the CUCM and the Presence Server has already created the CTI configuration for the CUPC client. The CTI conversation occurs between the CUCM and CUPC directly, not through the Presence Server.

Like other processes in this task list, the CTI Gateway configuration requires the creation of an Application User. In this case, we'll use the name CtiGw. Log in to the CUCM Admin page and click **User Management > Application User > Add New.** In the User ID field, enter a name of your choice followed by the password, and then confirm the password. Click **Save.** Figure 3-50 shows the Application User Configuration page.

Now it is time to add the newly created user to the CTI Enabled Group. Click **User Management > User Group > Find.** Select the Standard CTI Enabled group. Once again, click **Find.** Click **Add App Users to Group** and check the box next to the newly created CtiGw user. Click **Add Selected** to close the window.

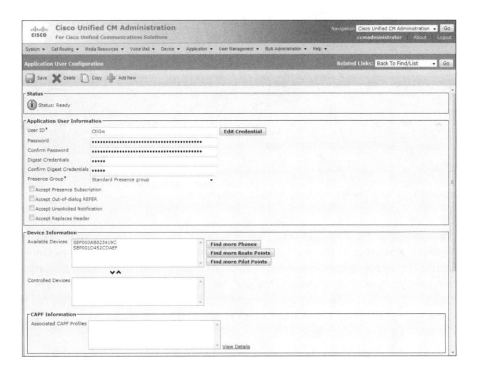

Figure 3-50 *Application User Configuration Page*

The next step involves adding another role to the CtiGw user. Click **User Management > User Group > Find**. From the list, click **Standard CTI Allow Control of All Devices**. Add the CtiGw user to this group by clicking **Add App Users to Group**. Check the box next to the CtiGw user and click **Add Selected** to close the window. Figure 3-51 shows the CTI User Group Configuration page for this step.

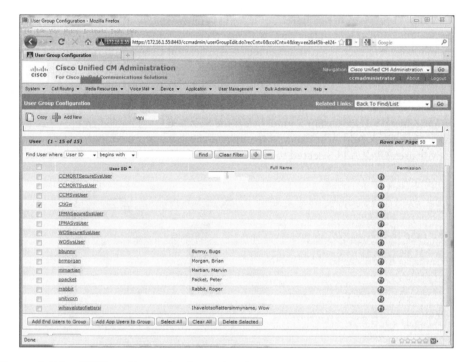

Figure 3-51   *CTI User Group Configuration Page*

Finally, log in to the Presence Server Admin page and click **Application > CUCM CTI Gateway > Settings**. In the first field, Application Status, change the setting to **On**. Enter your CTI Gateway username into the Application Username blank followed by the password and password confirmation in the next two fields, respectively. Drop down to the Cisco Unified Communications Manager Address fields and enter the addresses of the Publisher and all subscribers. Click **Save** to complete the task. Figure 3-52 shows the CTI Gateway Application Settings.

With the CTI Gateway settings complete, log in to the CUPS Serviceability page and restart the SIP UP Proxy Service. On the Serviceability page, click **Tools > Control Center Feature Services**. This brings up a list of services and their respective statuses. Click the radio button next to the Cisco UP SIP Proxy entry, and click the **Restart** button at the top of the page. Figure 3-53 shows the Feature Service Control Center page.

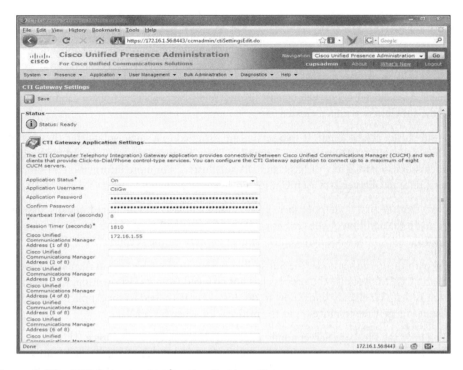

Figure 3-52   *CTI Gateway Application Settings Page*

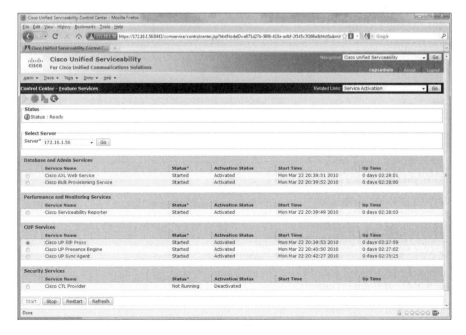

Figure 3-53   *CTI Gateway Application Settings Page*

Adding Additional Nodes to the CUPS Cluster

CUP consists of up to six servers. One is the Publisher node whereas the remaining five servers will be Subscriber nodes. Within a cluster, individual servers can be grouped to form a subcluster. A subcluster can include only two servers at most. In a basic deployment, a subcluster might well consist of only one server. That said, there can be only three subclusters within a cluster.

A subcluster acts as a unit. If two servers are assigned to a single subcluster, they act as a High Availability (HA) pair providing redundancy for Presence features and functionality. A cluster can have a mix of basic and HA subclusters. For more information on subclusters, refer to Chapter 2, "Cisco Unified Presence Overview."

Now that the first node/publisher server is built and largely configured, the discussion turns to the addition of subscriber nodes to the cluster. Many of the details are already configured, so the work here centers almost entirely on the secondary Presence server.

As with the Publisher node, the Subscriber node must be added as an Application Server to the CUCM. Because the process has not changed from its last mention, the assumption is that you already know how to do this. After it's added to the Application Server list, it will be time to move on to the primary Presence Server.

Log in to the Presence Server admin page and click **System > Topology**. This screen has a number of options that allow for user and node manipulation. In the right window pane, there is an option to **Add New Node**. Click it and provide the hostname of the new subscriber node. Add a description that is meaningful. Figure 3-54 shows the Topology page.

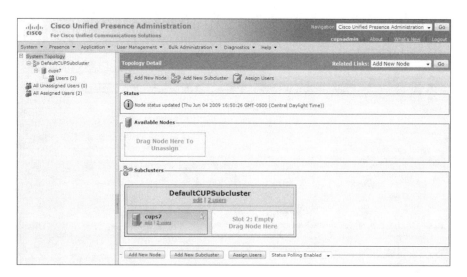

Figure 3-54   *Topology Page*

When the hostname (not FQDN or IP address) and description are entered, click **Save**.

The page refreshes and a new entry exists on the page with a nice red X, denoting that it cannot be reached. We know that is because it has not yet been installed, but the server sees only that it can't reach its companion. Figure 3-55 shows the Topology Detail page.

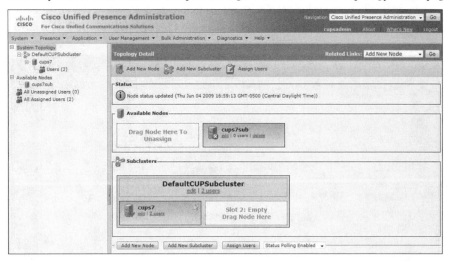

Figure 3-55 *Topology Detail Page*

At this point, the initial install of the second server can begin. It starts off much like that of the first; however, when you get to the point where it asks if this is the first node, you select **No**. It then tells you that you must add the new node to the first node prior to starting. Luckily, that was just done. Figure 3-56 shows the First Node Configuration page.

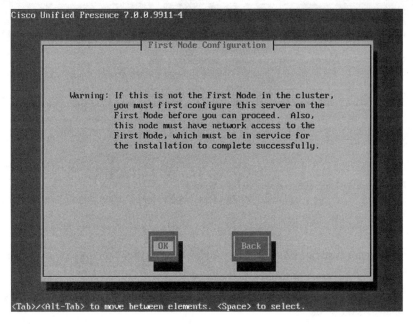

Figure 3-56 *First Node Configuration Page*

If that has not yet been done, stop and do so now; otherwise, select **Continue** to move on to the next screen where contact is to be made with the First Node. Enter the hostname of the CUPS Publisher, its IP address, and the security password along with a confirmation of the password. Click **OK** to move on. Figure 3-57 shows the First Node Access Configuration page.

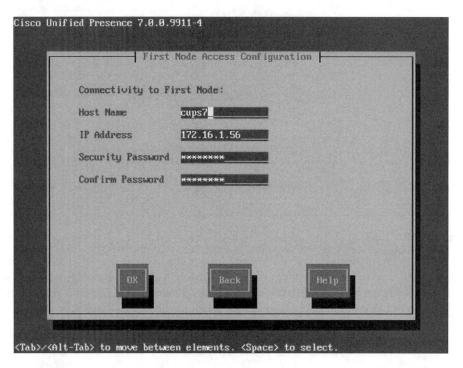

Figure 3-57   *First Node Access Configuration Page*

The last step in this phase is to decide whether to make use of an SMTP server. Configure this option exactly as you did on the first node's installation. When you click **OK** on this page, the installation begins copying files to the server. Just as with the first node, it's time for a break.

When the install is complete and the subscriber console shows the command prompt, log in to the CUPS Admin page and click **System > Topology**. Drag the newly added subscriber node from the Available Nodes section into the existing cluster. Navigate to the Serviceability page. You need to restart the services on both servers for the configuration to complete.

When all services show as Activated, return to the **System > Topology** screen to verify cluster health. Figure 3-58 shows the Topology Detail screen as it should show at this point.

As shown in the figure, the Subclusters section should show both Presence Servers with green checks on them.

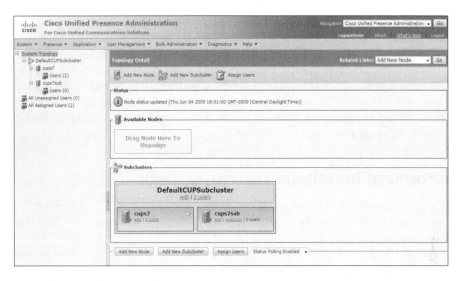

Figure 3-58   *Topology Detail Page*

At this point, you need to add a SIP Trunk to the CUCM pointing at the Presence Subscriber. This allows for redundancy. Match the settings on the SIP Trunk previously configured to complete the Subscriber configuration.

CUPS Redundancy Configuration

CUPS redundancy functions in much the same manner as that of CUCM. Users are assigned primary and backup facilities in both cases. In the case of CUPS, adding a second node is easy enough. Following this chapter, you might have just done so. So the question remains, how do I set up the redundancy so that it is most effectively deployed? What is to be avoided is to have one node under heavy load while the other sits in an almost entirely idle state.

Obviously, the server platform dictates how many CUPS users can be supported per server. Multiple CUPS clusters can be grouped together to reach the full capacity of a single CUCM cluster. Table 3-3 shows the number of users supported by each server platform. The numbers are the same for both HP and IBM server platforms.

Table 3-3   *CUPS Platform User Support*

Platform	Users Supported
MCS-7816	500
MCS-7825	1000
MCS-7835	2500
MCS-7845	5000

In the **System > Topology** screen of the CUPS Admin interface, users can be assigned individually, or in bulk, to subclusters. Within a subcluster, they can be assigned to individual servers. In a basic deployment, there will only be one server in the subcluster. So, all users in the subcluster will be assigned to that server. In an HA subcluster, the users can be split half and half across the servers to spread the load rather than having one server doing all the work. In a failover scenario, this lessens the impact because all users are not failing at once to the second server. At any given time, only half of the users in the subcluster are impacted by the loss of a single server.

Unattended Installation

Using the Cisco Unified Communications Answer File Generator, a file can be created for unattended installation of the Presence Server. This is a web application that supports the simultaneous creation and saving of answer files for the publisher node and all subscriber nodes. It also provides validation of syntax for data entries. Finally, it does include online help resources if there are any questions as to its use. The tool is available at www.cisco.com/web/cuc_afg/index.html.

The answer files are to be copied to a USB key or floppy disk that will be used with the DVD installation media. The USB key must be formatted using the FAT32 file system, not NTFS.

Note that the Answer File Generator does not support upgrades. It is for use only with new installations. Additionally, it supports Internet Explorer 6.0 and higher and Mozilla 1.5 and higher.

To use the tool, point your browser to the aforementioned URL and fill out the web form. It requests the same information covered in this chapter (that is, information required for the install). When completed, click the **Generate Answer Files** button at the bottom of the page. Example 3-1 shows the output from an answer file that would match the configuration of the CUPS servers installed for this chapter. The highlighted lines point out some of the more relevant features.

Example 3-1 *Primary Node Answer File Output*

```
<?xml version="1.0"?>
<PlatformData>
  <Version>7.0(1)</Version>
  <ProductDeployment>
    <ParamNameText>Deployment</ParamNameText>
    <ParamDefaultValue>CallManager</ParamDefaultValue>
    <ParamValue>cups</ParamValue>
  </ProductDeployment>
  <PlatformConfigurationDone>
    <ParamNameText>Status of platform configuration</ParamNameText>
    <ParamDefaultValue>no</ParamDefaultValue>
    <ParamValue>no</ParamValue>
```

```
</PlatformConfigurationDone>
<PreLoadedSoftware>
   <ParamNameText>Create a pre loaded software node</ParamNameText>
   <ParamDefaultValue>no</ParamDefaultValue>
   <ParamValue>yes</ParamValue>
</PreLoadedSoftware>
<InstallType>
   <ParamNameText>Install or upgrade type</ParamNameText>
   <ParamDefaultValue>basic</ParamDefaultValue>
   <ParamValue>Basic Install</ParamValue>
</InstallType>
<LocalHostNICAuto>
   <ParamNameText>Auto Configure speed and duplex</ParamNameText>
   <ParamDefaultValue>yes</ParamDefaultValue>
   <ParamValue>yes</ParamValue>
</LocalHostNICAuto>
<LocalHostName>
   <ParamNameText>Host Name for this machine</ParamNameText>
   <ParamDefaultValue>localhost</ParamDefaultValue>
   <ParamValue>cups7</ParamValue>
</LocalHostName>
<LocalHostDHCP>
   <ParamNameText>Is DHCP enabled for this machine</ParamNameText>
   <ParamDefaultValue>no</ParamDefaultValue>
   <ParamValue>no</ParamValue>
</LocalHostDHCP>
<LocalHostIP0>
   <ParamNameText>Host IP0 addr for this node</ParamNameText>
   <ParamDefaultValue>127.0.0.1</ParamDefaultValue>
   <ParamValue>172.16.1.56</ParamValue>
</LocalHostIP0>
<LocalHostMask0>
   <ParamNameText>Host IP0 mask for this node</ParamNameText>
   <ParamDefaultValue>255.255.255.0</ParamDefaultValue>
   <ParamValue>255.255.0.0</ParamValue>
</LocalHostMask0>
<LocalHostGW0>
   <ParamNameText>Gateway for this node</ParamNameText>
   <ParamDefaultValue>127.0.0.1</ParamDefaultValue>
   <ParamValue>172.16.1.1</ParamValue>
</LocalHostGW0>
<LocalHostDnsPrimary>
   <ParamNameText>Primary DNS server IP address</ParamNameText>
   <ParamDefaultValue>0.0.0.0</ParamDefaultValue>
```

```
      <ParamValue>4.2.2.1</ParamValue>
   </LocalHostDnsPrimary>
   <LocalHostDnsSecondary>
      <ParamNameText>Secondary DNS server IP address</ParamNameText>
      <ParamDefaultValue>0.0.0.0</ParamDefaultValue>
      <ParamValue>172.16.1.201</ParamValue>
   </LocalHostDnsSecondary>
   <LocalHostDomain>
      <ParamNameText>Domain name for this machine</ParamNameText>
      <ParamDefaultValue>cisco.com</ParamDefaultValue>
      <ParamValue>cisco.com</ParamValue>
   </LocalHostDomain>
   <LocalHostTimezone>
      <ParamNameText>Timezone for this node</ParamNameText>
      <ParamDefaultValue>America/Los_Angeles</ParamDefaultValue>
      <ParamValue>America/Chicago</ParamValue>
   </LocalHostTimezone>
   <LocalHostContinent>
      <ParamNameText>Continent for this node</ParamNameText>
      <ParamDefaultValue>America</ParamDefaultValue>
      <ParamValue>America</ParamValue>
   </LocalHostContinent>
   <LocalHostCity>
      <ParamNameText>City for this node</ParamNameText>
      <ParamDefaultValue>Los_Angeles</ParamDefaultValue>
      <ParamValue>Chicago</ParamValue>
   </LocalHostCity>
   <LocalHostAdminName>
      <ParamNameText>Administrator name for this node</ParamNameText>
      <ParamDefaultValue>administrator</ParamDefaultValue>
      <ParamValue>platformadmin</ParamValue>
   </LocalHostAdminName>
   <LocalHostAdminPwCrypt>
      <ParamNameText>Admin PW for this node</ParamNameText>
      <ParamDefaultValue>password</ParamDefaultValue>
<ParamValue>A928BD9C5090F599831812812AB2825C831812812AB2825C831812812AB2825C</Param
   Value>
   </LocalHostAdminPwCrypt>
   <CertX509>
      <Org>
         <ParamNameText>Certification Signing Request Organization</ParamNameText>
         <ParamDefaultValue>none</ParamDefaultValue>
         <ParamValue>CISCO</ParamValue>
      </Org>
```

```
  <Unit>
    <ParamNameText>Certification Signing Request Unit</ParamNameText>
    <ParamDefaultValue>none</ParamDefaultValue>
    <ParamValue>WWS</ParamValue>
  </Unit>
  <Location>
    <ParamNameText>Certification Signing Request Location</ParamNameText>
    <ParamDefaultValue>none</ParamDefaultValue>
    <ParamValue>IRVING</ParamValue>
  </Location>
  <State>
    <ParamNameText>Certification Signing Request State</ParamNameText>
    <ParamDefaultValue>none</ParamDefaultValue>
    <ParamValue>TEXAS</ParamValue>
  </State>
  <Country>
    <ParamNameText>Certification Signing Request Country</ParamNameText>
    <ParamDefaultValue>none</ParamDefaultValue>
    <ParamValue>US</ParamValue>
  </Country>
</CertX509>
<LocaleId>
  <ParamNameText>Microsoft assigned locale identifier value</ParamNameText>
  <ParamDefaultValue>00000409</ParamDefaultValue>
  <ParamValue/>
</LocaleId>
<CCMVersion>
  <ParamNameText>CM version on the server backed up</ParamNameText>
  <ParamDefaultValue>CCM ver 5.0</ParamDefaultValue>
  <ParamValue/>
</CCMVersion>
<CcmFirstNode>
  <ParamNameText>First CCM node in the cluster</ParamNameText>
  <ParamDefaultValue>yes</ParamDefaultValue>
  <ParamValue>yes</ParamValue>
</CcmFirstNode>
<SftpPwCrypt>
  <ParamNameText>Security PW for this node</ParamNameText>
  <ParamDefaultValue>password</ParamDefaultValue>

  <ParamValue>A928BD9C5090F599831812812AB2825C831812812AB2825C831812812AB2825C
  </ParamValue>
</SftpPwCrypt>
<IPSecFirstNode>
  <ParamNameText>First IPSec node in the cluster</ParamNameText>
```

```
        <ParamDefaultValue>yes</ParamDefaultValue>
        <ParamValue>yes</ParamValue>
    </IPSecFirstNode>
    <IPSecEnabled>
        <ParamNameText>IPSec Configuration for this node</ParamNameText>
        <ParamDefaultValue>no</ParamDefaultValue>
        <ParamValue>no</ParamValue>
    </IPSecEnabled>
    <IPSecSecurityPwCrypt>
        <ParamNameText>Security PW for this node</ParamNameText>
        <ParamDefaultValue>password</ParamDefaultValue>

        <ParamValue>A928BD9C5090F599831812812AB2825C831812812AB2825C831812812AB2825C
        </ParamValue>
    </IPSecSecurityPwCrypt>
    <NtpServer>
        <ParamNameText>Address Range for NTP server</ParamNameText>
        <ParamDefaultValue>none</ParamDefaultValue>
        <ParamValue>172.16.0.4</ParamValue>
    </NtpServer>
    <SMTPHostName>
        <ParamNameText>SMTP location for this node</ParamNameText>
        <ParamDefaultValue>smtp.host</ParamDefaultValue>
        <ParamValue>172.16.1.201</ParamValue>
    </SMTPHostName>
    <ApplUserUsername>
        <ParamNameText>Application User Username</ParamNameText>
        <ParamDefaultValue>CCMAdministrator</ParamDefaultValue>
        <ParamValue>cupsadmin</ParamValue>
    </ApplUserUsername>
    <ApplUserPwCrypt>
        <ParamNameText>Application User Password</ParamNameText>
        <ParamDefaultValue>password</ParamDefaultValue>

        <ParamValue>A928BD9C5090F599831812812AB2825C831812812AB2825C831812812AB2825C
        </ParamValue>
    </ApplUserPwCrypt>
</PlatformData>
```

A similar file was generated for the subscriber node. However, there seems to be little reason to include it here along with that of the primary node. The Answer File Generator works for the following installations:

■   Cisco Unified Communications Manager

■   Cisco Unified Communications Manager, Business Edition

- Cisco Unified Presence Server

- Cisco Unified Expert Advisor

- Cisco Unity Connection

Copy the output to a text file and place the file on the FAT32 formatted USB Key. Insert it upon beginning the installation. When the installation script begins, it provides an option to proceed with the basic Installation Wizard or skip it. To use the answer file, you must skip the basic Installation Wizard. For reference, refer to Figure 3-9.

After you select the **Skip** option, insert the USB key, if not already inserted. The next screen asks for it. Click **Continue** when the key or floppy disk containing the answer file is inserted. If a window pops up stating that new hardware has been found, press any key; then select **Install** on the next screen. The system reads the file and commences with the Platform Installation Wizard. Simply select **Proceed** to move on. On the Apply Additional Release screen, skip the procedure describing how to apply a release; then select **No** to install the software on the DVD without upgrading.

Do not remove the USB key or floppy disk containing the answer files. The wizard reads it during the course of the installation, so it must remain in place.

Troubleshooting the Installation

Like any installation, a number of things can be missed, mistyped, or simply just don't work. The goal of this section is to discuss some of the most common issues and their resolutions.

Recap of Dependencies

Communications between the Presence Servers and the CUCM Cluster depend on AXL, SIP, and CTI components. During the installation, you configured all these various components on both CUPS and CUCM. Figure 3-59 shows the interconnections between the CUCM cluster, CUPS, endpoints, and LDAP Directory Server.

Table 3-4 shows the configuration dependencies between CUCM and CUPS. The first step in troubleshooting the installation will be to verify that all these dependencies are properly configured and in place.

The tasks to be performed and information to be remembered is daunting. That said, it is important that you keep detailed notes of each step in the installation wherein input is required. There seems to be no shortage of opportunities to mistype usernames, passwords, or IP addresses.

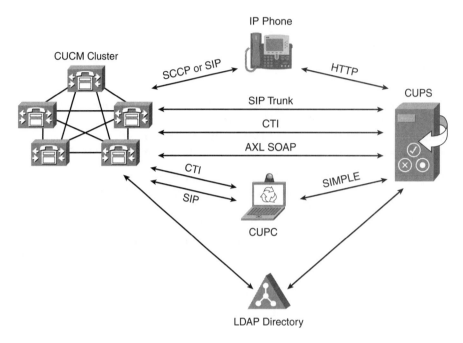

Figure 3-59   *CUPS/CUCM Connectivity*

Table 3-4   *CUCM-CUPS Dependencies*

CUCM Task	CUPS Task
Add Application Server	
Add AXL Group Add Standard AXL API Access to group Roles Add AXL user Assign user to group	Enter AXL User Credentials in Initial Install Wizard the first time CUPS Admin page is accessed.
Capabilities Assignment to enable CUP and CUPC for Users	Users will not show in CUPS until CUCM Capabilities Assignment is done.
Assign End Users to Standard CTI Enabled Group	
Create SIP Trunk to CUPS (if multinode, need a SIP trunk to each node)	Select SIP Trunk in SIP Publish Trunk Settings. Enter CUCM Publisher Address as Presence GW in Presence Gateway Settings.
Create IPPM User	Enter IPPM User credentials in IP PhoneMessenger Settings.

CUCM Task	CUPS Task
Create IPPM Phone Service Subscribe phones to the service	
Create CtiGW user Assign to Standard CTI Enabled group	Enter CTI User Credentials and all CUCM Addresses in CTI Gateway Settings.
	Set Proxy Domain in SIP Proxy Service Parameters.
	Load License files for CUPS Nodes and Users.
	Start Services in Service Activation Page.
Associate End Users with their Phones in Device Association section of End User Configuration Select Primary User Device in Mobility Information section of End User Configuration	
Configure Owner User ID at Phone Device Level Associate End Users at Phone Line (DN) Level	

Tools

For purposes of troubleshooting the installation process and the general health of the server thereafter, the CUPS Admin interface includes an extremely helpful tool called the System Troubleshooter. This tool queries the various dependencies, parts, and processes within the server and returns a status for each component. Figure 3-60 shows the System Troubleshooter page.

There is a legend at the top of the page explaining the various symbols, but they're self-explanatory. The difference between a green check and a red X are quite well known. As an example of how to make use of the System Troubleshooter, let's walk through a problem.

Notice that there are problems in the configuration. It seems that the AXL Sync Agent is not happy. When a problem is presented, a solution is offered in the right column along with a **fix** link to the page where the changes need to be made. Figure 3-61 shows the CUCM Publisher Page accessed by clicking the **fix** link.

Evidently, it thinks I entered the Publisher's name incorrectly as **cucm7pub**. Looking back at my documentation from the install of both the Presence Server and the Communications Manager, I see that it is correct in that assertion. The name as entered during the install is **cm7pub**. Changing the name and saving the change can provide the fix wanted by the System Troubleshooter page. Returning to it shows that one issue is corrected and the next one awaits. Figure 3-62 now shows a green check by the Sync Agent entries.

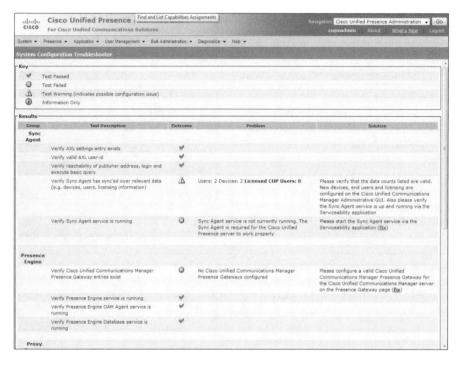

Figure 3-60   *System Troubleshooter Page*

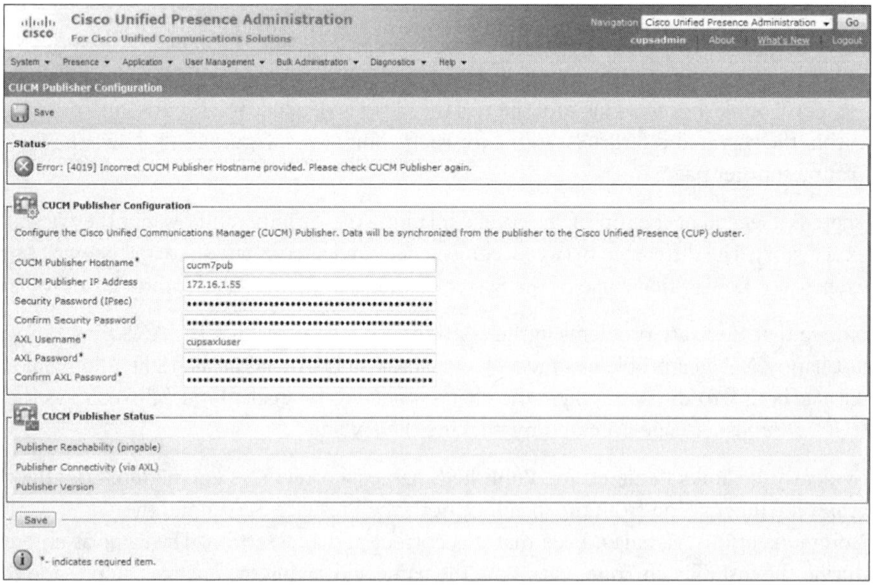

Figure 3-61   *CCM Publisher Page*

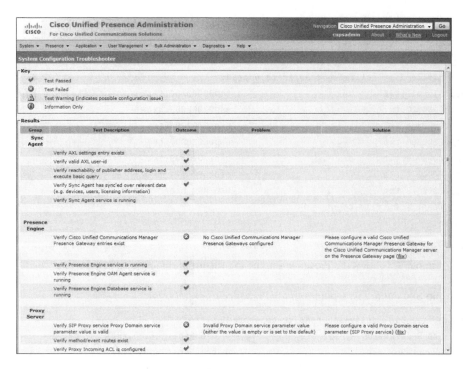

Figure 3-62 *System Configuration Troubleshooter Page*

Note   When the CUCM version is upgraded, the Sync Agent Service stops on the Presence server. It needs to be restarted on all servers in the cluster to begin functioning again. Use the System Troubleshooter to verify that all functions work properly.

If the information offered in the System Troubleshooter is inadequate to find the problem, CUPS does keep a collection of log files, which might be requested by a Cisco TAC engineer should you open a case. The most relevant logs and their locations are the Sync Agent, SIP Proxy, and Presence Engine. Example 3-2 shows the Sync Agent log file list and location.

Example 3-2 *File List Command for Sync Agent Logs*

```
admin:file list activelog epas/trace/epassa/log4j
syncAgent.bin                          syncAgent00001.log
syncAgent00002.log                     syncAgent00003.log
syncAgent00004.log                     syncAgent00005.log
syncAgent00006.log                     syncAgent00007.log
syncagentStatus.log
dir count = 0, file count = 9
admin:
```

Example 3-3 shows the SIP Proxy log file list and location.

Example 3-3 *File List Command for SIP Proxy Logs*

```
admin:file list activelog epas/trace/esp/sdi
esp-sipdctl.txt                    esp00000001.txt
esp00000002.txt                    esp00000003.txt
esp00000004.txt                    esp00000005.txt
esp00000006.txt                    esp00000007.txt
esp00000008.txt                    esp00000009.txt
esp00000010.txt                    esp00000011.txt
esp00000012.txt                    esp~num.bin
dir count = 0, file count = 14
admin:
```

Example 3-4 shows the Presence Engine log file list and location.

Example 3-4 *File List Command for Presence Engine Logs*

```
admin:file list activelog epas/trace/epe/sdi
epe-dropReplication.script.txt       epe-dropReplication.txt
epe-executeSql.txt                   epe-pres-postinstall.txt
epe-repAgent.txt                     epe-setupReplication.script.txt
epe-setupReplication.txt             epe-startup.txt
epe00000001.txt                      epe00000002.txt
epe00000003.txt                      epe~num.bin
dir count = 0, file count = 12
admin:
```

It might well be that the command line is not for the faint of heart. If you are an administrator who prefers a graphical interface for troubleshooting and information gathering, Cisco has included the Real Time Monitoring Tool (RTMT) for CUPS. It can be installed from the **Application > Plugins** page. Figure 3-63 shows the RTMT trace file collection dialog page.

When RTMT is launched, click **Trace & Log Central** in the far left pane; then double-click **Collect Files** in the middle pane. The Collect Files dialog box pops up. Check the files you want to collect, and click **Next** at the bottom. Another page of files ready for collection is presented, but the files of interest for this discussion are all on the first page. Click **Next**. Figure 3-64 shows the final page in the Collect Files dialog.

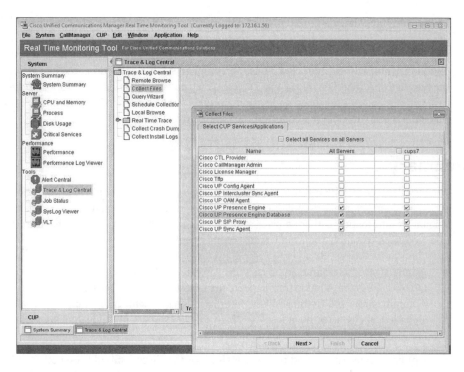

Figure 3-63 *Trace File Collection Dialog*

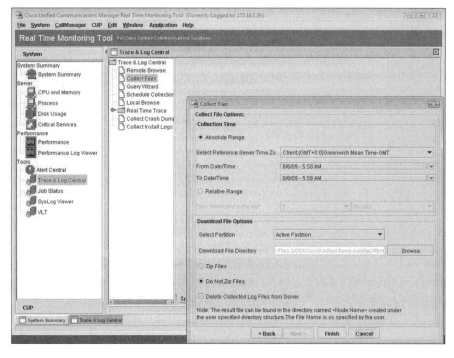

Figure 3-64 *Trace File Collection Dialog (Continued)*

It requests a time/date range and presents download options that enable you to specify the location of the files and whether to zip them. Of course, the more precise the time/date range, the easier it might be to pinpoint the specific event in question. When all options are properly entered, click **Finish** to complete the file collection. You can view the files in a specified Download File Directory. If you are collecting them for upload to a case with Cisco TAC, go ahead and have it zip them so that you need to deal only with a single file when attaching the collected files to the case.

Summary

The installation of CUPS is not overly difficult in the grand scheme of things. It is, however, a bit complex in places and does require some advance forethought and no small amount of information gathering prior to beginning the installation. During the installation, you need to supply the following usernames and/or passwords:

■ **Administrator username and password:** Used in the Cisco Unified Communications Operating System Administration page, the Disaster Recovery System Administration, and Command Line Interface. The username must start with an alphabetical character, be at least six characters in length, and can include hyphens, underscores, and alphanumeric characters.

■ **Application username and password:** Used for the Cisco Unified Presence Administration GUI.

■ **Security password:** Used to enable the first node to contact the CUCM Publisher Node. The security password must match the security password of the CUCM Publisher.

During the installation, you need to configure elements on both the CUCM and the Presence Server. Installation Wizards walk you through most of the essential configuration tasks associated with the CUPS Software install and subsequent configuration. There are numerous dependencies on both sides of the communications. For a list of dependencies on both the CUCM and CUPS servers, refer to Table 4-2.

At any point during the installation, the System Troubleshooter can be referenced as a general health check and next-steps tool. The System Troubleshooter indicates where errors exist in the configuration and offer suggestions and links to the page where those configuration errors can be fixed.

If problems persist, the RTMT can be a powerful troubleshooting tool. RTMT is a graphical interface that pulls real-time information from the servers in the CUPS cluster. If a TAC Case has been opened at any time, the RTMT can be used to gather trace files and zip them for download to your local machine so that they can be attached, uploaded, and attached to the TAC Case for review by the engineer.

Chapter 4

Cisco Unified Presence Integration with Cisco Unified Communications Manager

This chapter discusses the configuration of Cisco Unified Communications Manager (CUCM) with the Cisco Unified Presence Server (CUPS). This doesn't cover the Desktop Client integration, but instead focuses on the dependencies and configuration of the background administrative architecture.

The topics discussed in this chapter are as follows:

- LDAP integration
- CUCM configuration with CUPS
- LDAP profile creation
- Adding users and phone associations
- Configuring Cisco Unified Personal Communicator (CUPC) on CUP

LDAP Integration

Utilizing a Lightweight Directory Access Protocol (LDAP) directory in the integration of CUCM with CUPS is done to satisfy a few different requirements. The following are the four requirements that are a concern for every installation:

- Provisioning
- Authentication
- Directory Access
- Configuring LDAP

Provisioning

The ability to provision users automatically from the LDAP directory into the CUCM database gives the Presence server the capability to leverage the contact information fields that give administrators an easier means of user management. CUCM synchronizes with the LDAP directory content to avoid having to add, remove, or modify user information manually each time a change occurs in the LDAP directory. This also reduces the amount of network traffic and potential contention of resources that are now free for other tasks.

Authentication

Authenticating users using the LDAP directory credentials offers a means of security and user ease by using a single username and password to unlock the privileges and capabilities that have been administratively assigned.

CUP server synchronizes all the user information from CUCM to provide authentication for users of the CUPC client and CUP user interface.

Directory Access

With a properly configured and enabled LDAP directory, CUCP client users have the ability to search the user directory and add contacts from the LDAP directory. This gives the user access to directory photos, desk phone numbers, mobile phone numbers, e-mail addresses, and Instant Message (IM) addresses.

The LDAP integration can have dependencies based on customer requirements and environment that can largely vary between different implementations. The following list describes some potential LDAP integration scenarios ranked from recommended, functional, and not recommended respectively:

- **Recommended:** CUCM and CUCP are both integrated with the same LDAP directory.

- **Functional:** CUPC is integrated with an LDAP directory, but CUCM is not. This configuration is considered functional because it will work with desired results; however, the caveat with this type of integration is the administration costs go up because the user configuration will be manual for all users on CUCM at initial installation. This manual administration will also be required each time a change is made on the LDAP directory.

- **Not Recommended:** CUCM is integrated with an LDAP directory, but CUCP is not. This integration is not recommended because of the performance issues that can be experienced and the negative impact on CUCP functionality.

Note   The user ID in CUCM must match the LDAP user ID for each user.

Configuring LDAP

Cisco LDAP synchronization uses the Cisco Directory Synchronization tool on CUCM to synchronize information from a SunOne/Netscape, OpenLDAP, Microsoft Active Directory (AD) or Microsoft Active Directory Application Mode (ADAM) LDAP directory. The synchronization of LDAP can be configured for manual or automatically at prescribed intervals.

The first step in enabling Directory Synchronization is starting the DirSync Service on the CUCM Publisher. To do this, open a browser and navigate to the CUCM Serviceability Page. Click **Tools > Service Activation**. Scroll all the way to the bottom of the page and check the Cisco DirSync box; then click the **Save** button. The service starts. Figure 4-1 shows the Service Activation page.

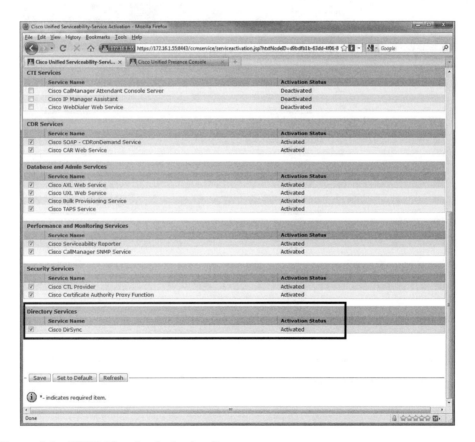

Figure 4-1   *CUCM Service Activation Page*

When the DirSync service is enabled, users are automatically provisioned from the corporate directory. Due to the noninvasive manner that CUCM uses to synchronize with the LDAP server, using the LDAP server's interface to manage adding, deleting, or changing the user contact information simplifies administration.

The DirSync service needs to be activated before configuring the LDAP synchronization; otherwise, the service will fail the synchronization until it is enabled on CUCM. LDAP synchronization does not apply to application users on CUCM.

Configuring LDAP Synchronization

Step 1.   Select **Cisco Unified CM Administration > System > LDAP > LDAP System**, as shown in Figure 4-2.

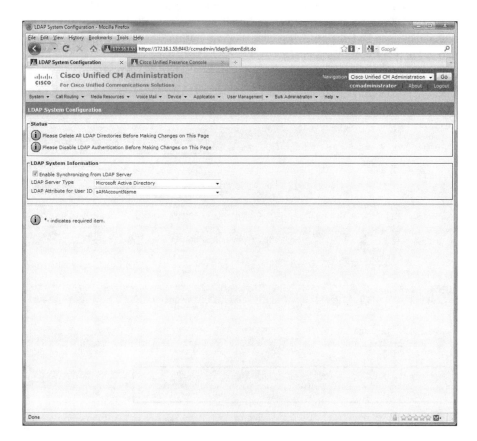

Figure 4-2   *CUCM LDAP System Page*

Step 2.   Configure the LDAP server type and attribute.

Step 3.   Enable synchronization of data from the LDAP server.

Step 4.   Select **Cisco Unified CM Administration > System > LDAP > LDAP Directory**, as shown in Figure 4-3.

Step 5.   Configure the following items:

- LDAP directory account settings

- User attributes to be synchronized

- Synchronization schedule

- LDAP server hostname or IP address, and port number

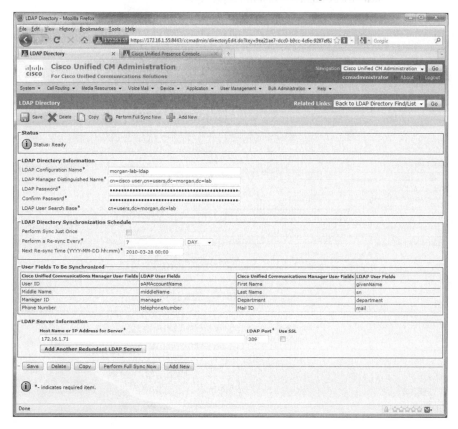

Figure 4-3 *CUCM LDAP Directory Page*

Step 6.   Check **Use SSL** to use Secure Socket Layer to communicate with the LDAP
directory, if SSL is desired.

To have a secure connection between the CUCM and the LDAP server, Secure Socket
Layer (SSL) needs to be established for the LDAP server on CUCM. The SSL certificate
should be configured as a trust certificate on CUCM.

After the LDAP SSL certificate is in place, a restart of the following services on the
CUCM Serviceability Page will be required:

- Directory service

- Tomcat service

Configuring LDAP Authentication

The LDAP authentication feature enables CUCM to authenticate user passwords against the LDAP directory.

Passwords of application users are authenticated against the CUCM internal database:

Step 1.　Select **Cisco Unified CM Administration > System > LDAP > LDAP Authentication**, as shown in Figure 4-4.

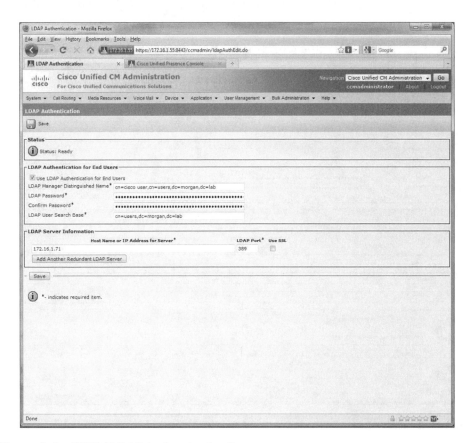

Figure 4-4　*CUCM LDAP Authentication Page*

Step 2.　Enable LDAP authentication for users.

Step 3.　Configure the LDAP authentication settings.

Step 4.　Configure the LDAP server hostname or IP address, and port number.

Configuring a Secure Connection Between Cisco Unified Presence and the LDAP Directory

These steps are applicable only if you're configuring a secure connection between CUPS and the LDAP directory.

These steps need to be replicated to all CUPS in the cluster.

Step 1.   Select **Cisco Unified Operating System Administration > Security > Certificate Management,** as shown in Figure 4-5.

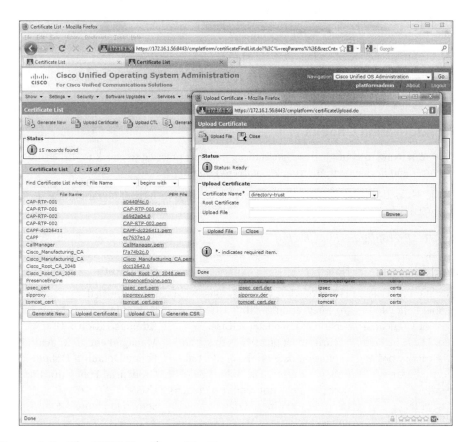

Figure 4-5   *The CUPS Certificate List Page*

Step 2.   Select **Upload Certificate.**

Step 3.   Select **directory-trust** from the Certificate Name menu.

Step 4.   Browse and select the LDAP server certificate from the local computer.

Step 5.   Select **Upload File.**

Step 6.   Restart the Tomcat service from the Serviceability Page on the CUPS.

Cisco Unified Communications Manager Configuration with Cisco Unified Presence Server

This section focuses on the configuration steps for CUCM integration with CUPS Configuration procedures.

Putting this in sequential order, the topics being discussed are

1. Preconfiguration checks

2. Configuring CTI gateway settings

3. Configuring Presence service parameter

4. Configuring the SIP trunk on CUCM

5. Profile creation

6. Adding users and making device associations

Preconfiguration Checks

Before starting to configure the integration, it is best practice to check to make sure that the user and device configuration is completed on CUCM.

Table 4-1 outlines the steps to check before continuing with the integration of CUCM and CUPS.

Table 4-1 *Preconfiguration Checks*

Task	Notes	Menu Path
Modify the End User Credential Policy for the type of Credential desired. These include End User Password Application user Password End User PIN.	This procedure is only applicable if the integration is with CUCM version 6.0 or a later release. Security best practice is to set an expiration date on the credential policy for users. The only type of user that does not require a credential policy expiration date is an application user. When configured to use an LDAP server for user authentication, the credential policy for End User Password is not used.	**Cisco Unified Communications Manager Administration > User Management > Credential Policy Default > Default Credential Policy** (for End Users) Shown in Figure 4-6
Configure the phone devices, and associate a Directory Number with each device.	Check Allow Control of Device from CTI to enable the phone to interoperate with the CUCP client.	**Cisco Unified Communications Manager Administration > Device > Phone > Find > Select Phone** to be CTI Enabled Shown in Figure 4-7

Task	Notes	Menu Path
Configure the users, and associate a device with each user.	Deploying CUPC, make sure that the user ID value is unique for each user. The softphone device name is derived by a conversion of the user ID. When two users share the same softphone device name, CUPC cannot derive the softphone device name causing improper functionality.	**Cisco Unified Communications Manager Administration > User Management > End User** Shown in Figure 4-8
Associate a user with a line appearance.	This procedure is only applicable to CUCM version 6.0 or a later release.	**Cisco Unified Communications Manager Administration > Device > Phone** Shown in Figure 4-9
Add users to CTI-enabled user group.	This procedure is needed when planning to deploy CUPC. This configuration enables the feature of controlling the desk phone.	**Cisco Unified Communications Manager Administration > User Management > User Group** Shown in Figure 4-10

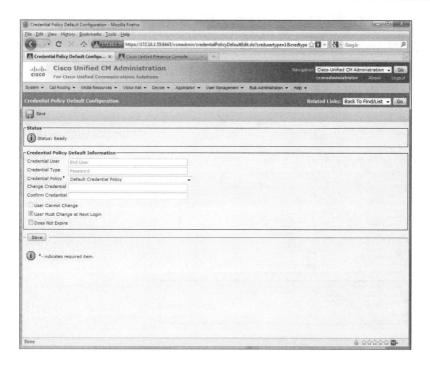

Figure 4-6 *Credential Policy Default Page*

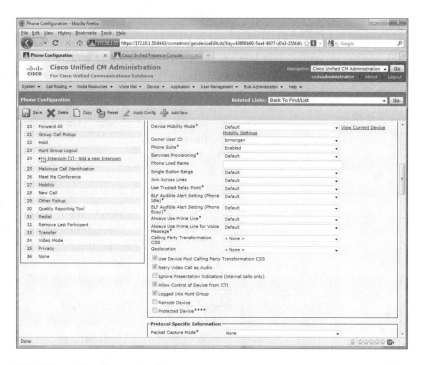

Figure 4-7   *Phone Configuration Page*

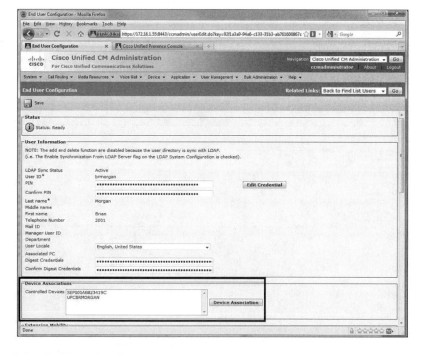

Figure 4-8   *End User Configuration Page*

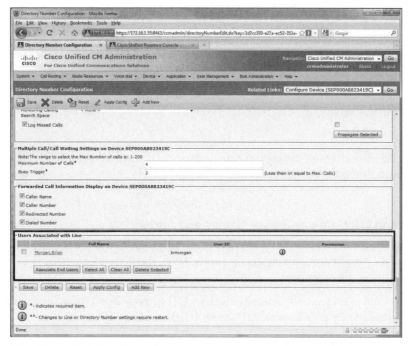

Figure 4-9 *Phone DN Configuration Page*

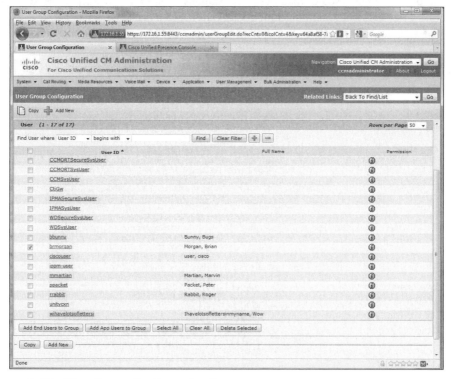

Figure 4-10 *User Group Configuration Page*

Configuring CTI Gateway Settings

The CTI gateway provides desk phone control when users are configured for phone-association mode. Proper installation calls upon information to specify CTI gateway server names, addresses, ports, and protocols on CUPS.

Configured correctly, the CTI gateway enables users logging in to CUPC to reach the CTI gateway server.

Note   The procedures in this topic are applicable only if you're configuring CUPC for desk phone control.

Configuring CTI Gateway Server Names and Addresses

If the IP address was previously configured through the **Cisco Unified Communications Manager Administration > System > Server** menu, the steps documented in the list that follows won't be necessary.

Cisco Unified Presence dynamically creates a CTI gateway host profile for that address and automatically populates the CTI gateway fields on the CUP server.

Before starting, be sure to get the hostnames or IP addresses of the CTI gateway:

Step 1.   Select **Cisco Unified Presence Administration > Application > Cisco Unified Personal Communicator > CTI Gateway Server**, as shown in Figure 4-11.

Step 2.   Select **Add New**.

Step 3.   Enter information into the fields.

Table 4-2 illustrates the field name and the settings for each.

Step 4.   Select **Save**.

Tip   The CTI gateway information can be seen in the Server Health window in CUPC.

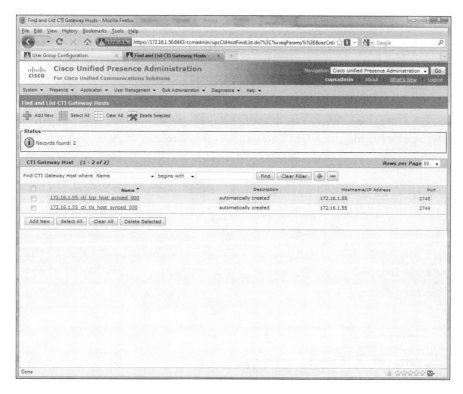

Figure 4-11   *The CUPS CTI Gateway Configuration Page*

Table 4-2   *Field Names and Settings for CTI Gateway*

Field	Setting for CTI Gateway
Name	Enter the server name.
Description	Enter a server description. This is to distinguish it uniquely so that it will be easier to locate.
Hostname or IP Address	Enter an IP address or the Fully Qualified Domain Name of CUCM that runs the CTI service.
Port	Enter 2748.
Protocol Type	Select TCP.

Creating CTI Gateway Profiles

CTI gateway profiles are created in CUP Administration. This is also where to assign primary and backup servers for redundancy.

Configuration should begin with creating the CTI gateway profile. This needs to happen before adding CUPC users to the application profile.

Specify CTI gateway server names and addresses in **Application > Cisco Unified Personal Communicator > CTI Gateway Server** before selecting what server will act as primary or backup, as shown in Figure 4-12.

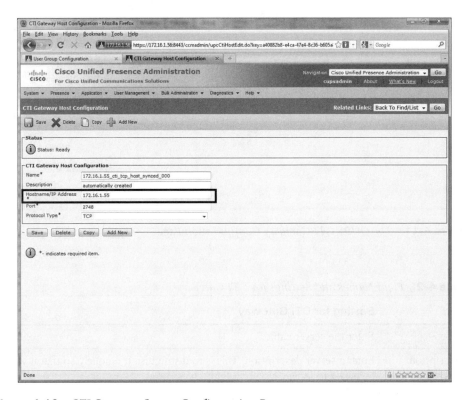

Figure 4-12 *CTI Gateway Server Configuration Page*

CUP dynamically creates a CTI gateway profile based on the *hostname* of CUCM. Before using this profile, verify that CUP and CUPC clients can ping CUCM by its DNS name.

If the server is unreachable, check for the DNS entry and if not present, add the *IP address* of the CUCM in CUPA. If it is present by DNS name, it might be worth changing the DNS name to the IP address of the server for troubleshooting purposes. This is done by going to **Application > Cisco Unified Personal Communicator > CTI Gateway Server**.

The field and settings are in Table 4-3. The steps for CUPS are as follows:

Step 1. Select **Application > Cisco Unified Personal Communicator > CTI Gateway Profile**, as shown in Figure 4-13.

Step 2. Select **Add New**.

Step 3. Enter information into the fields as outlined in Table 4-3.

Step 4. Select **Add Users to Profile**.

Step 5. Use the Find and List Users window to find and select users.

Step 6. Select **Add Selected** to add users to the profile.

Step 7. Select **Save** in the main CTI Gateway Profile window.

Table 4-3 *Field Names and Settings for CTI Gateway*

Field	Setting
Name	Enter the profile name.
Description	(Optional) Enter a profile description.
Primary CTI Gateway Server and Backup CTI Gateway Server	Select a primary server and backup servers.
Make this the Default CTI Gateway Profile for the System	Check so that any new users that are added to the system are automatically placed into this default profile. Users who are already synchronized to CUP from CUCM are not added to the default profile. However, when the default profile is created, any users synchronized after those are added to the default profile.

Configuring Firewalls to Pass CUPC Traffic

With security a major concern and how information traverses the network internally or externally, firewalls and other security measures are present, and applications need to work with a firewall to maintain as much security as possible. The traffic moves through a firewall based on service identification numbers known as ports. Certain ports must be open for CUPC to work like any other application. Network administrators typically open a minimal number of network ports, allowing the traffic for approved applications to enter and leave the network while blocking other network traffic.

Identify whether there is a firewall (hardware or software) in the network between CUP and CUPC.

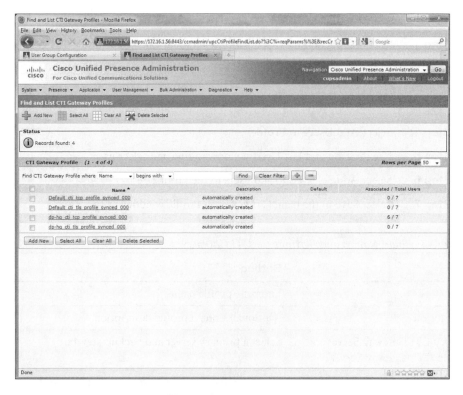

Figure 4-13 *CTI Gateway Profile Configuration Page*

Configure the firewall to pass CUPC traffic or an inconsistent user experience will occur. Some of the symptoms are missing, incorrect, or intermittent display of availability status.

Like other applications of this nature, CUPC expects inbound and outbound traffic to occur on particular ports through particular protocols.

The operating system is what chooses a port for the origination of traffic, except for the Real-Time Transport Protocol. CUPC selects a port on which to send and receive Real-Time Transport Protocol traffic. The application uses port 16384 as the base port for the initial stream and uses higher port numbers for additional streams.

For details, see Table 4-4 and Table 4-5.

Configuring Presence Service Parameter

The Inter-Presence Group Subscription parameter enables users in one Presence Group to subscribe to the availability information for users in a different Presence Group.

The Inter-Presence Group Subscription parameter can be enabled only when the subscription permission for the default Standard Presence Group, or any new Presence Groups, is set to Use System Default.

Table 4-4 *Network Ports for Inbound Traffic*

Protocol	Ports	Description
RTP	16384 to 32767	Receives RTP media streams for audio and video
SIP	50000 to 50063	Permits TCP or UDP traffic directed at the client computer; provides SIP presence information
TFTP	69, then Ephemeral UDP	Permits UDP traffic from the IP Phone endpoint to the Server resource for phone configuration files

Table 4-5 *Network Ports for Outbound Traffic*

Protocol	Ports	Description
HTTP	80	Connects to Cisco Unified MeetingPlace Express or Cisco Unified MeetingPlace servers
HTTP/HTTPS	80	Connects to Cisco WebEx servers
HTTP/HTTPS	80/443	Connects to Cisco Unity via Simple Object Access Protocol service to decrypt the session keys for secure voicemails
IMAP (SSL, TCP, TLS)	143, 993, and 7993	Connects with the Cisco Unity Connection mail-store for voicemail retrieval
IMAP (SSL, TCP, TLS)	143, 993	Connects with the Cisco Unity mail-store (with Microsoft Exchange) for voicemail retrieval
RTP	16384 to 32767	Sends Real-Time Transport Protocol media streams for audio and video. UDP
SIP	5060	Registers the softphone with CUCM and used for call signaling. TCP and UDP Registers with the Cisco Unified Presence SIP proxy for SIMPLE presence, publishes and subscribes to CUP
SOAP over HTTPS	443	Downloads configuration data from the CUPS, manages contact lists and privacy, searches for user IDs, sets persistent presence states, and so on Connects with Cisco Unified MeetingPlace Express servers Connects to Cisco Unity for secure message services
TCP	389 2748	Connects to the LDAP server for the CUPC contact searches Connects to the CTI gateway, which is the CTIManager component of CUCM
TFTP	69, then Ephemeral UDP	Permits UDP traffic from the IP Phone endpoint to the Server resource for phone configuration files

To configure Presence Groups, perform the following tasks:

Step 1. Select **Cisco Unified Communications Manager Administration > System > Presence Group**.

Step 2. Click **Add New** or reconfigure the existing Presence Group. In Figure 4-14, a new Presence Group called pg_hq was created. Choose the relationship with other configured Presence Groups. You can Allow or Disallow Subscription or simply use the system default setting.

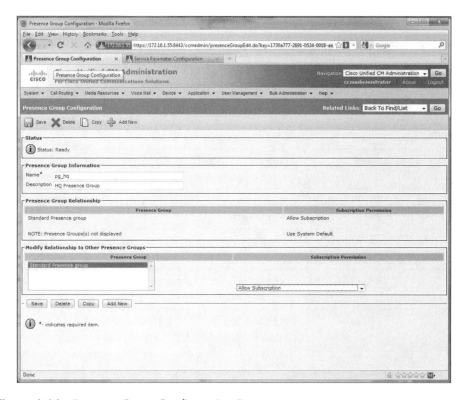

Figure 4-14 *Presence Group Configuration Page*

Step 3. Select **Cisco Unified Communications Manager Administration > System > Service Parameters**.

Step 4. Select **Cisco Unified Communications Manager** server from the Server menu. and select the Cisco CallManager Service from the Service drop-down box.

Step 5. Scroll down to the **Clusterwide Parameters (System - Presence)** section and change the field entry for **Default Inter-Presence Group** to **Allow Subscription**, as shown in Figure 4-15.

Step 6. Select Save.

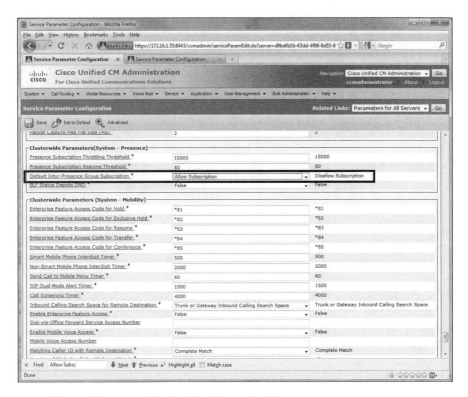

Figure 4-15 *CallManager Service Configuration Page*

Configure the SIP Trunk on CUCM

Although this was covered in Chapter 3, "Installing Cisco Unified Presence Server 7," it is important to go over the settings when configuring the SIP trunk. An option in adding a SIP trunk is to create a DNS SRV record. This allows for Presence information to be shared among all Presence servers used for the exchange of Presence information. The DNS SRV record needs to be created for each of the Cisco Unified Presence Publisher and Subscriber servers in the cluster. An additional DNS SRV record entry is required on the CUPS for each of the CUCM subscriber servers.

Before adding the SIP trunk, it is necessary to create the Security Profile for the SIP trunk.

The steps for creating the Security Profile for the SIP trunk are as follows:

Step 1.   Select **Cisco Unified Communications Manager Administration > System > Security Profile > SIP Trunk Security Profile**.

Step 2.   Select **Find**.

Step 3.   Select **Non Secure SIP Trunk Profile**, as shown in Figure 4-16.

Step 4.   Verify that the setting for Device Security Mode is **Non Secure**.

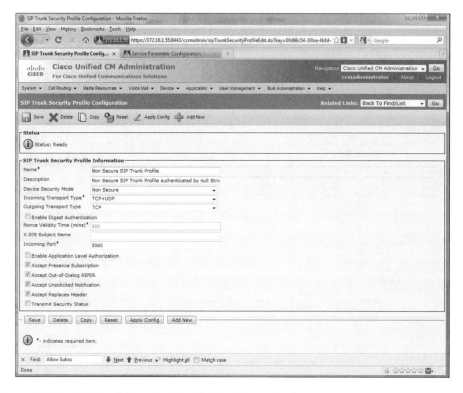

Figure 4-16   *SIP Trunk Security Profile Configuration Page*

Step 5.   Verify that the setting for Incoming Transport Type is **TCP+UDP**.

Step 6.   Verify that the setting for Outgoing Transport Type is **TCP**.

Step 7.   Check to enable these items:

■   Accept Presence Subscription.

■   Accept Out-of-Dialog REFER.

■   Accept Unsolicited Notification.

■   Accept Replaces Header.

Step 8.   Select **Save**.

When the SIP trunk Security Profile is in place, the SIP trunk can be created. To create the new SIP trunk reference, follow these steps:

Step 1.   Select **Cisco Unified Communications Manager Administration > Device > Trunk**.

Step 2.   Select **Add New**.

Step 3.   Select **SIP Trunk** from the Trunk Type menu.

Step 4.   Select **SIP** from the Device Protocol menu.

Step 5.   Select **Next**.

Step 6.   Enter **CUPS-SIP-Trunk** for the Device Name, as shown in Figure 4-17.

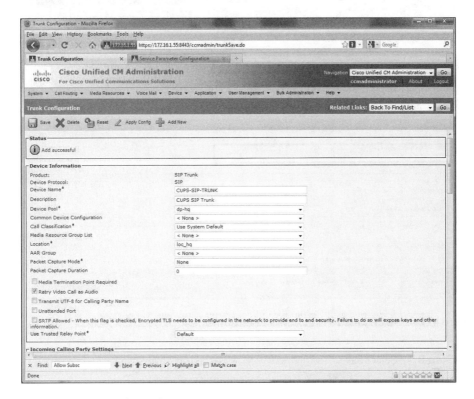

Figure 4-17   *SIP Trunk Configuration Page*

Step 7.   Select a device pool from the Device Pool menu.

Step 8.   In the SIP Information section at the bottom of the window, configure the following values, as shown in Figure 4-18:

- In the Destination Address field, enter IP address, or the Fully Qualified Domain Name, or the DNS SRV record for the CUPS.

- Check that the Destination Address is an SRV if a DNS SRV record was configured for the Destination Address value.

- Enter **5060** for the Destination Port for CUPS 7.x. For CUPS 6.x, use 5070.

- Select **Non Secure SIP Trunk Profile** from the SIP Trunk Security Profile menu.

- Select **Standard SIP Profile** from the SIP Profile menu.

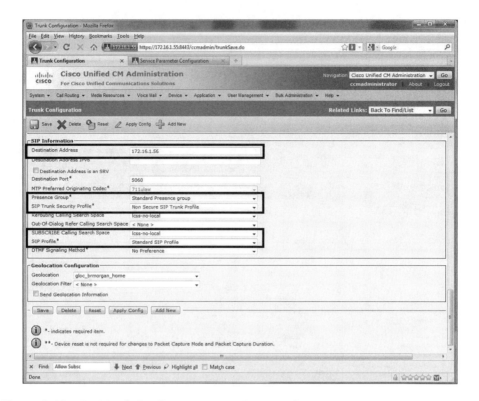

Figure 4-18   *SIP Trunk Configuration Page Continued*

Step 9.   Select **Save**.

LDAP Profile Creation

These topics have a direct effect on the CUPC capabilities, so close attention should be paid as not to negatively affect the user experience.

The sections that follow describe how to configure the LDAP settings on CUP to enable CUPC users to search and add contacts from the LDAP directory.

Creating LDAP Profiles and Adding Users to the Profile

CUPC connects to an LDAP server on a per-search basis.

Redundancy can be built into the LDAP servers by identifying the LDAP servers as a Primary or Secondary.

The CUPC automatically reaches out to the Primary LDAP server. If the Primary is out of service, the Secondary LDAP server will be referenced. Intelligence has been programmed into the client to periodically try to reconnect with the Primary. This reduces the time spent having to administer to the client for an issue with LDAP connection.

A prerequisite before adding users is to create an LDAP Profile. To create the profile, follow these steps:

Step 1.   Select **Cisco Unified Presence Administration > Application > Cisco Unified Personal Communicator > LDAP Profile**. This is illustrated in Figure 4-19.

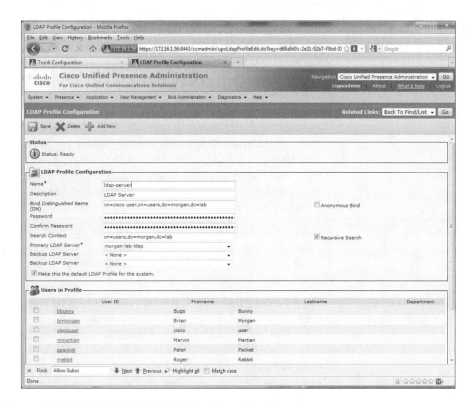

Figure 4-19   *CUPS LDAP Profile Configuration Page*

Step 2.   Select **Add New**.

Step 3.   Enter information into the fields outlined in Table 4-6.

Step 4.   Select **Save**.

Adding Users and Making Device Associations

The process of adding users was already discussed earlier as a part of the precheck process for configuring CUCM with a CUPS. Users need additional configuration to complete the user experience, which is what this section covers.

Table 4-6   *Field Name and Settings for LDAP Profiles*

Field	Setting
Name	Enter the profile name limited to 128 characters.
Description	Enter a description limited to 128 characters.
Bind Distinguished Name	Enter the administrator-level account information limited to 128 characters.
Anonymous Bind	Uncheck this option to use the user credentials to sign in to this LDAP server. For nonanonymous bind operations, CUPC receives one set of credentials. These credentials must be valid on the backup LDAP servers, if they are configured. If selecting Anonymous Bind, users can sign in anonymously to the LDAP server with read-only access. Anonymous access might be possible on the directory server, but it is not recommended. Instead, create a user with read-only privileges on the same container where the users to be searched are located. Specify the directory number and password in CUP for CUPC to use.
Password	Enter the LDAP bind password limited to 128 characters. This is the password for the administrator-level account used in the Bind Distinguished Name string that enables users to access this LDAP server.
Confirm Password	Enter the same password as the one entered in the Password field. After configuring CUP for authenticated bind with the LDAP server, configure the LDAP server for anonymous permissions and anonymous login so that all directory information (name, number, mail, fax, home number, and so forth) is passed to the CUPC client.
Search Context	Enter the location where all LDAP users are configured. This location is a container or directory. The name is limited to 256 characters. Only a single OU/LDAP search context is supported. When integrating with Microsoft AD: OU must contain users, for example: ou=users,dc=cisco,dc=com Another Example: cn=users,DC=EFT-LA,DC=cisco, DC=com The search base should include all users of CUPC.

Field	Setting
Recursive Search	Check to perform a recursive search of the directory starting at the search base.
Primary LDAP Server and Backup LDAP Server	Select the primary LDAP server and optional backup servers.
Make this the Default LDAP Profile for the System	Check so that any new users who are added to the system are automatically placed into this default profile. Users who are already synchronized with CUP from CUCM are not added to the default profile. However, when the default profile is created, any users synchronized after that is added to the default profile.
Add Users to Profile	Select the button to open the Find and List Users window. Select **Find** to populate the search results fields, or search for a specific user, and then select **Find**. Select users, and add them to this profile by selecting **Add Selected**.

Adding a Softphone Device for Each User

Enabling the CUPC softphone features requires a new softphone device for each user to be created. These steps are outlined in the following list.

Note Note the auto-registration features in CUCM are not supported with CUPC.

Step 1. Select **Cisco Unified Communications Manager Administration > Device > Phone.**

Step 2. Select **Add New.**

Step 3. Select **Cisco Unified Personal Communicator** from the Phone Type menu.

Step 4. Select **Next.**

Step 5. Configure the following information, as shown in Figure 4-20:

- Specify the softphone device name in the Device Name field. The device name must begin with UPC followed by up to the first 12 characters of the user ID. Shorter names are permissible, of course.

- Enter a descriptive name for the phone in the Description field. For example, enter *<username>*-softphone.

- Configure the Device Pool, Phone Button Template, Calling Search Space, Media Resource Group List, MoH Sources, User, and Network Locales as appropriate for the environment. All fields marked with a * beside them are mandatory.

- Select the user ID from Owner User ID drop-down box, as shown in Figure 4-21.

- Select the device name of the Cisco Unified IP Phone to associate with CUPC from Primary Phone.

- Uncheck Allow Control of Device from CTI to disable the capability of CTI to control and monitor this device.

- Enter information in the Protocol Specific Information section, as outlined in Table 4-7.

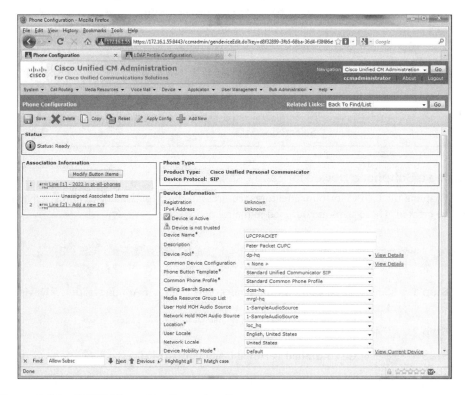

Figure 4-20   *CUPC Phone Configuration Page*

Step 6.   Select **Save**.

Step 7.   Select the **Add a New DN link** in the Association Information pane that displays on the left side of the window.

Step 8.   Configure the following information:

- Enter the directory number and route partition for the CUPC.

- Enter the caller ID in Display (Internal Caller ID), in the Line 1 on Device Device-Name section.

■ In the Multiple Call/Call Waiting section, specify the maximum number of calls that can be presented to CUPC in the Maximum Number of Calls field.

■ In the Multiple Call/Call Waiting section, specify the trigger after which an incoming call receives a busy signal in the Busy Trigger field.

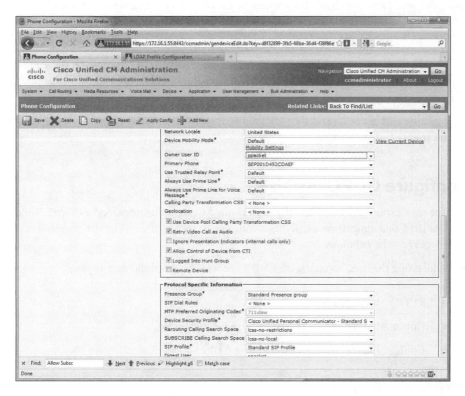

Figure 4-21 *CUPC Phone Configuration Page Continued*

Table 4-7 *Field Name and Settings for Softphone Device Profiles*

Field	Setting
Presence Group	Select **Standard Presence Group.**
Device Security Profile	Select **Cisco Unified Personal Communicator - Standard SIP Non-Secure Profile.**
SIP Profile	Select **Standard SIP Profile** to specify the default SIP profile. SIP profiles provide specific SIP information for the phone such as registration and keep-alive timers, media ports, and Do Not Disturb control.
Digest User	Select the user ID. This is the same user ID as the one selected for Owner User ID.

Step 9.   Select **Save**.

> **Note**   The Busy Trigger and Number of Calls settings work with each other. The maximum number of calls and busy trigger are set to a specific numerical value in the number of calls that are available to be taken or made. When that value is reached, the next incoming caller will follow the Busy Trigger action. This action could forward to voicemail, another extension, or play back a busy tone.

The directory numbers and route partitions configured for CUPC must be the same values used by the Cisco Unified IP Phone for this user to take advantage of a Shared Line.

The Shared Line benefits of the association between the user and a line are demonstrated by single number reach and showing the Presence availability based on the device on which the user is currently active.

Configure CUPC on CUP

The user experience is the key driver in Unified Communications, and as Web 2.0 and Unified Communications capabilities continue to merge or develop, the enablement process can be nebulous.

Addressing the need to configure CUPC is covered in the following topics:

- TFTP server connection
- Configuring the Proxy Listener and TFTP addresses
- Configuring the Service Parameter for CUPC

TFTP Server Connection

CUPC connects to the primary Trivial File Transfer Protocol (TFTP) server derived from the Presence server at startup. When the connection is established, CUPC downloads the UPC*<username>*.cnf.xml configuration file from CUCM for each user.

The configuration file contains the list of CUCM primary and failover server addresses and the transport protocol for CUPC to use in softphone mode to connect to CUCM. The TFTP service is on by default with the installation of the first node or Publisher in a CUCM environment. For more information on how to configure a TFTP server, follow these links:

CUCM 7.X SRND:
http://www.cisco.com/en/US/partner/docs/voice_ip_comm/cucm/srnd/7x/callpros.
html#wp1043790

CUCM Administration Guide:
http://www.cisco.com/en/US/docs/voice_ip_comm/cucm/admin/7_1_2/ccmcfg/bccm-712-cm.html

After CUPC downloads the configuration file, that information is made available to CUPC and then disconnects from the TFTP server.

Each time a connection attempt is tried from CUPC to the TFTP server, the Primary TFTP server is contacted first, and if a connection cannot be made, an attempt to connect to the secondary TFTP server is made. If all TFTP server connections fail, CUPC tries to load the last valid local copy of the configuration file.

If both the connection to the TFTP server and the local configuration file fails, the CUPC switches to Disabled mode.

Some configuration expectations should be set with the CUPC or CUPC client that are noteworthy. With CUPC, Auto Registration, Auto Updates or Upgrades are not supported; however, this doesn't stop the functionality of the client, but rather is more of an administration task that should be planned for.

Configuring the Proxy Listener and TFTP Addresses

When configuring the Proxy Listener, it is highly recommended that CUPC use TCP to communicate with the proxy server.

Using UDP to communicate with the proxy server leaves the user in a state that does show the Presence state for the contacts being searched against with large contact lists.

Following are the steps to configure a Proxy Listener server and setting the TFTP addresses:

Step 1.   Select **Cisco Unified Presence Administration > Application > Cisco Unified Personal Communicator > Settings**, as shown in Figure 4-22.

Step 2.   Select the **Proxy Listener Default Cisco SIP Proxy TCP Listener**.

Step 3.   Assign the primary and backup TFTP server addresses. Valid entries are an IP address or a Fully Qualified Domain Name.

Step 4.   Select **Save**.

Configuring the Service Parameter for CUPC

The Service Parameter for CUPC allows for the availability messages that occur between the CUPC client and CUPS.

Perform the following steps to ensure this is configured:

Step 1.   Select **Cisco Unified Presence Administration > System > Service Parameters**.

Step 2.   Select a CUPS from the Server menu.

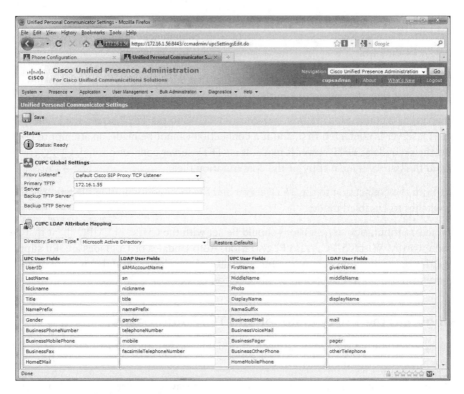

Figure 4-22   *Unified Personal Communicator Settings Page*

Step 3.   Select **Cisco UP SIP Proxy** as the service on the Service Parameter Configuration window.

Step 4.   Scroll down to the SIP Parameters section of the page. Set **Use Transport in Record-Route Header** to **On**, as shown in Figure 4-23.

This forces the Proxy to use the transport parameter in the record-route header.

Step 5.   Select Save.

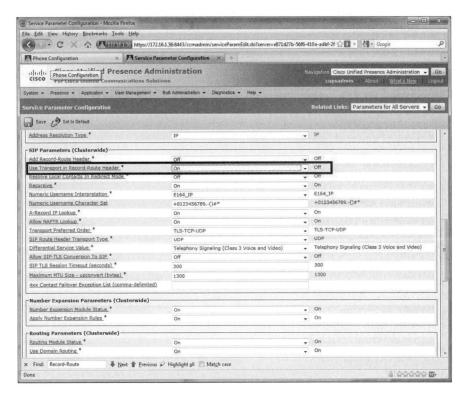

Figure 4-23 *SIP Proxy Service Parameter Configuration Page*

Summary

This chapter covered the integration with LDAP, Presence Server, and Client configuration. These steps help serve as reference material while deploying a Cisco Presence solution. When implementing applications or Unified Communications, it is always best that a certified partner or integrator be contracted to help configure and deploy.

Chapter 5

Cisco Unified Personal Communicator

Cisco Unified Personal Communicator (CUPC) is the client application that integrates into the Cisco Unified Presence Server (CUPS). This client runs on a Windows or Macintosh desktop environment and provides for several integrated communications features such as desk phone control, Instant Messaging (IM), Presence, softphone, communication escalation, and so on. This chapter covers the client installation, configuration, basic and advanced features, and client-side troubleshooting.

Figure 5-1 illustrates the communications in a basic CUP deployment with an IP phone and CUPC client.

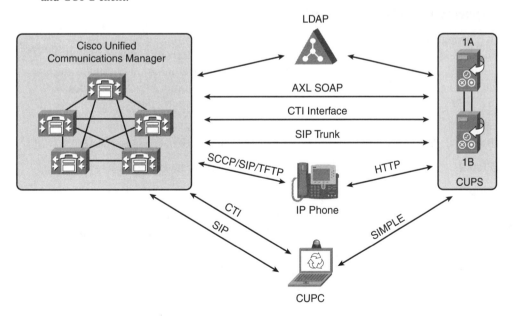

Figure 5-1 *Communications of a Basic CUP Deployment*

Note   CUPS enables Presence information to be populated by many types of presentities; however, CUPC is the only software client supported directly by CUPS.

CUPC Configuration

The configuration of a user leveraging CUPC has several basic steps that need to be completed:

Step 1.   Configure user in CUCM.

Step 2.   Configure desk phone device in CUCM (optional).

Step 3.   Configure the CUPC device in CUCM.

Step 4.   Configure CUPS advanced end-user features:

- Voicemail

- Conferencing

- Lightweight Directory Access Protocol (LDAP)

Step 5.   Install CUPC software on the client machine.

The following sections describe these configuration steps in greater detail.

Configuring CUPC User in CUCM

It is strongly recommended having LDAP synchronization configured in any CUCM installation. This brief section covers the steps required to configure a user in CUCM *without* LDAP integration. This is because when LDAP synchronization is enabled, the ability to add/delete users in the CUCM user interface is removed. All users are added or removed via the LDAP management interface. Figure 5-2 illustrates the concepts for the following steps:

Step 1.   In CUCM Administration, select **User Management > End User > Add New**.

Step 2.   Fill in at least the required user information (User ID and Last Name).

Step 3.   Device Associations can be left at the default.

Step 4.   If this user will use extension mobility services, configure the required settings. Make sure to select the correct Presence group because this impacts what Presence visibility this user has.

Step 5.   Leave directory number associates at the default setting unless you already have a desk phone and directory number configured for this user.

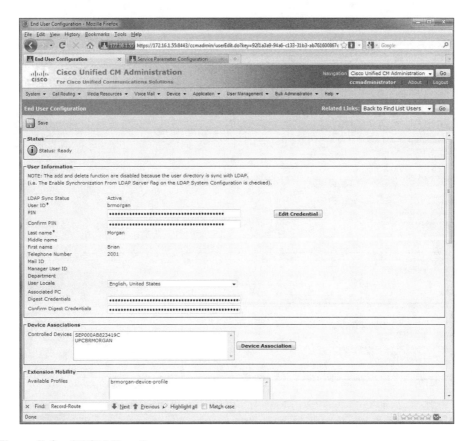

Figure 5-2   *CUCM User Page*

Step 6.   The mobility section enables the user to configure single number reach access and mobile voice access (directory assistant IVR). Configure this section according to the end user's needs.

Step 7.   Ensure that the user roles include **Standard CTI Enabled** and **Standard CTI Allow Control of All Devices**, as shown in Figure 5-3.

Step 8.   Select the **Save** button.

Step 9.   In CUCM Administration, select **System > Licensing > Capabilities Assignments**.

Step 10.   Select the users recently added that will have Presence and CUPC capabilities.

Step 11.   Click both check boxes to enable CUP and CUPC features for the users.

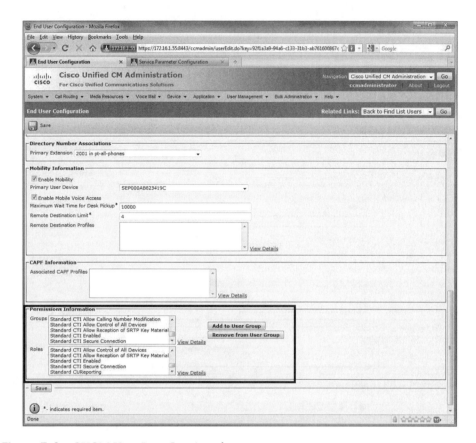

Figure 5-3   *CUCM User Page Continued*

Tip   The user might not show up for several minutes on the CUP server. If it is taking too long, go to **Cisco Unified Serviceability > Tools > Control Center-Feature Services**, select the CUP server (publisher if in a cluster), and then start or restart Cisco UP Sync Agent.

When the user has been added to CUCM, it will be synchronized over to the CUP server. There is no need to add the user separately to the CUP server. LDAP synchronization is strongly recommended so most of these steps would not be necessary, and the rest can be done when doing the phone device provisioning in CUCM. For more information on CUCM synchronization with LDAP, refer to the "LDAP System Configuration" section in the *Cisco Unified Communications Manager Administration Guide* at http://tinyurl.com/yaoy42m.

Configuring IP Phone in CUCM

A common deployment model is for a single user to have both a desk phone and have CUPC act as a softphone during communications that take place away from the desk. CUPC offers a softphone capability that enables it to act as a phone device on a computer without the requirement of a desk phone, making the desk phone an optional device in a deployment. The use of a desk phone is optional and not required when deploying and configuring CUPC. This section covers the basic steps necessary in setting up an IP Phone to be used with CUPC. Figure 5-4 shows the addition of a physical desk phone.

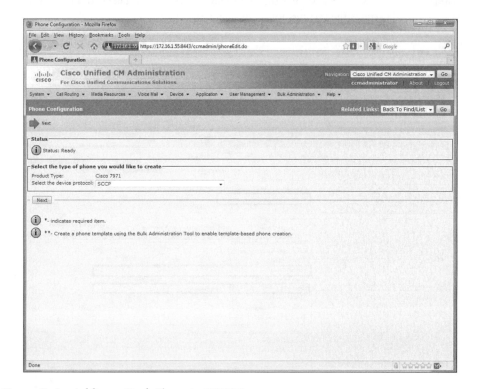

Figure 5-4   *Adding a Desk Phone in CUCM*

Step 1.   In CUCM Administration, select **Device > Phone**.

Step 2.   Click the **Add New** button.

Step 3.   Select the device for the desk phone; then click the **Next** button. *Do not* select Cisco Unified Personal Communicator.

Step 4.   Select the protocol for the phone to use.

Step 5.   Make sure the Presence Group and SUBSCRIBE Calling Search Space are defined according to your Presence policy.

Note   Presence authorization works with Presence Groups to allow or block Presence requests between groups. This enables greater granularity in offering Presence services to groups or departments.

The SUBSCRIBE calling search space determines how CUCM routes Presence requests that come from the phone. This setting enables you to apply a calling search space separate from the call-processing search space for Presence (SUBSCRIBE) requests for the phone.

Step 6.   Make sure that Allow Control of Device from CTI is checked. Figure 5-5 illustrates the settings for Steps 5 and 6.

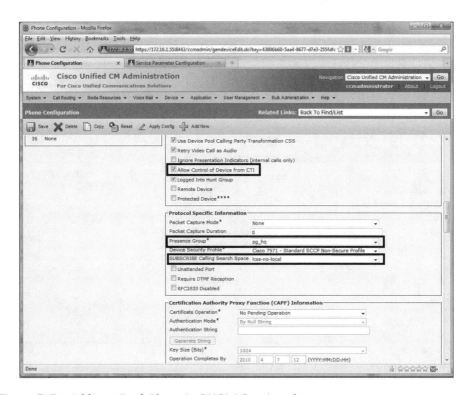

Figure 5-5   *Adding a Desk Phone in CUCM Continued*

Step 7.   Configure all the remaining required settings for the phone and end-user requirements.

Step 8.   Associate the user to the phone, as shown in Figure 5-6.

The phone now registers to CUCM with the proper settings and user association. Adding the phone allows users to have the option to control their phone through a computer telephony interface (CTI) with the CUPC client. This allows for the added software features offered by the CUPC client and still has a desk phone for a more reliable voice experience.

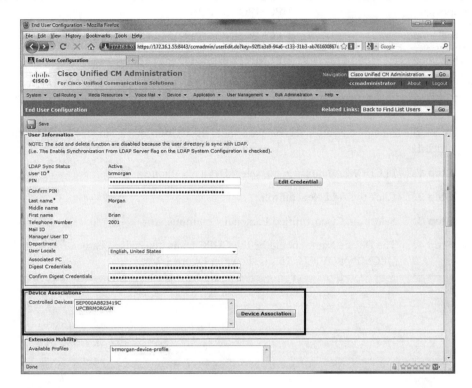

Figure 5-6   *Associating Phones with Users*

Configuring a CUPC Device in CUCM

The next step is to set up a CUPC device in CUCM associated to the appropriate user and potentially connected to a desk phone. The first step in planning for the CUPC device configuration is to understand the naming convention required in CUCM. These requirements follow:

- Derives from the username

- Starts with *UPC*

- Contains only uppercase letters or numerals

- Contains no more than 12 additional characters after *UPC*

Table 5-1 provides some examples that outline these requirements.

Table 5-1   *Username Examples for CUPC in CUCM*

CUCM Username	Associated Softphone Device Name
mpopovich	UPCMPOPOVICH
michael_popovich	UPCMICHAELPOPOV
michaelpopovich	UPCMICHAELPOPOV
mike.popovich	UPCMIKEPOPOVICH

When the naming convention has been decided, the CUPC device can now be added to CUCM:

Step 1.   In CUCM Administration, select **Device > Phone**.

Step 2.   Click the **Add New** button.

Step 3.   Select the **Cisco Unified Personal Communicator**.

Step 4.   The Device Name should be the CUPC name determined earlier, for example, UPCMPOPOVICH. This is shown in Figure 5-7.

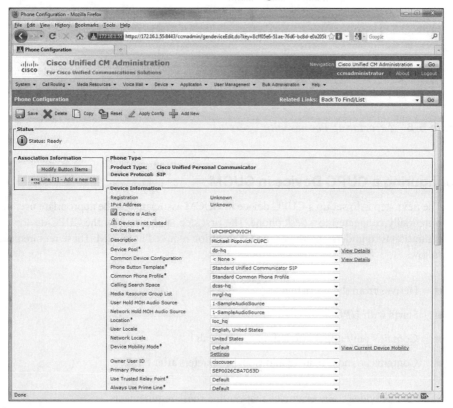

Figure 5-7   *Adding a CUPC Endpoint in CUCM Continued*

Step 5.   Uncheck the box for Allow Control of Device from CTI.

Step 6.   Specify the correct Presence Group and SUBSCRIBE Calling Search Space.

Step 7.   Set the Owner User ID field to the appropriate user.

Step 8.   Configure the rest of the settings according to system/user policy.

Step 9.   Click the **Save** button.

Step 10.   Click the **Line[1] > Add a new DN link**.

Step 11.   Assign the directory number to the line. If a phone device is already configured, use the same DN as the phone. If this is a CUPC-only user, enter a new DN, as shown in Figure 5-8.

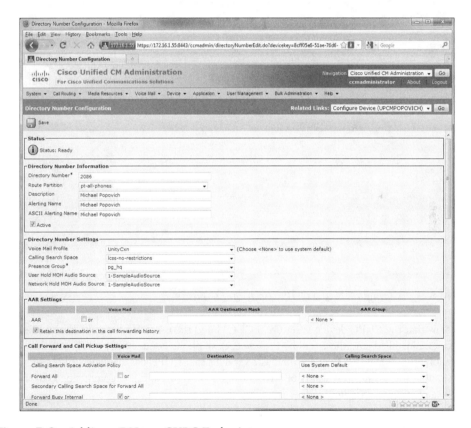

Figure 5-8   *Adding a DN to a CUPC Endpoint*

Step 12.   Uncheck the box for Allow Control of Device from CTI.

Step 13.   Configure the rest of the settings according to system policy.

Step 14.   Click Save.

When saved, a new screen comes up that shows what devices are associated to the DN. This field should at least have the CUCP device associated with it. If it is a shared DN with a phone device, two devices should be listed: the CUPC and the phone device. This is shown in Figure 5-9.

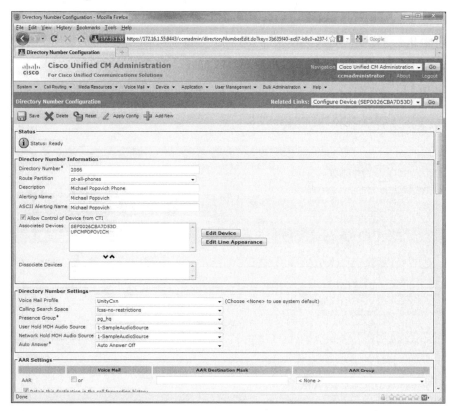

Figure 5-9   *Adding a DN to a CUPC Endpoint Continued*

Now that the CUPC device is set up in CUCM and the users are configured, the client can be installed, and there will be Presence, desk phone connectivity (CTI), and softphone functionality. These are the basic services that CUPC has available, and in the next section, the advanced features of CUPC will be configured. It is recommended to have these features configured before installing the client.

Configuring Advanced Features for CUPC

The advanced features available to the CUPC client consist of Unity voicemail, MeetingPlace conferencing, video, and LDAP integration. The following sections describe the configuration of these advanced features in greater detail.

Voicemail Configuration for CUPC

CUPC has the capability to access Unity voicemail directly through the client interface. This is useful to the end user by providing a visual interface to the Unity voicemail system, enabling the user to prioritize voicemails by name, timestamp, duration, and so on without having to listen to the messages first.

Two primary prerequisites must be completed before integrating CUPS to Unity:

■ Implement a supported version of Unity or Unity Connection, which are the only two supported messaging platforms for CUPS integration.

■ Complete the integration of CUCM and Unity/Unity Connection, and make sure all voice ports are working properly.

The sections that follow discuss how to satisfy these prerequisites in more detail.

Cisco Unity Connection

The following steps describe the Cisco Unity Connection (CUC) provisioning steps for CUPC users. Use Figure 5-10 with the following steps.

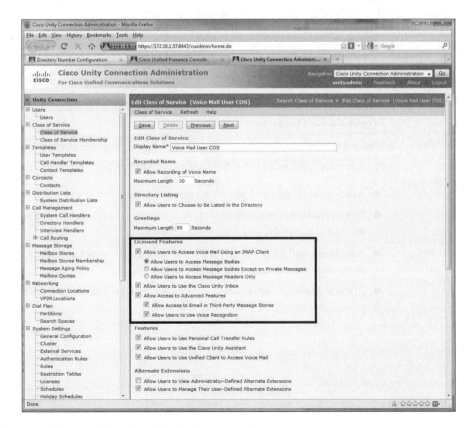

Figure 5-10 *Enabling IMAP in Unity Connection*

Step 1.   Configure a class of service in CUC with IMAP enabled:

a. Select **Class of Service** in the left navigation pane.

b. Select or add the desired class of service in the list.

c. Check the **Allow Users to Use Unified Client to Access Voice Mail** box. This allows access to port 7993 and TLS for the CUPC client support.

d For IMAP client support as well, check the **Allow Users to Access VoiceMail Using an IMAP Client** box and select the **Allow Users to Access Message Bodies** button.

e Click **Save.**

Step 2.   Create a CUC user account and voicemail box for each CUPC user.

Step 3.   Make sure the web application password is set for the user.

Note   Secure messaging is optional, and a set of features offered in Unity Connection enables several security features that provide control for access and distribution to messages. Several caveats need to be understood before enabling these features. You can find detailed information on these caveats at http://tinyurl.com/y9uuu2q.

Use Figure 5-11 with the following steps to enable secure messaging:

Step 1.   Enable secure messaging:

a. Select **Class of Service** using the navigation panel; then click the Class of Service the CUPC users are a part of.

b. Under the Message Options section of the Class of Service; select the type of secure messaging next to the **Require Secure Messaging** option:

- **Always:** Messages will always be marked secure.

- **Never:** Messages will never be marked secure. (Users can still mark messages as private, and they will be secure.)

- **Ask:** Users will be prompted from the Special Delivery Options menu to select if the message is marked secure or not.

- **Private:** Messages are marked secure only when the user makes them a private message. This is the system default.

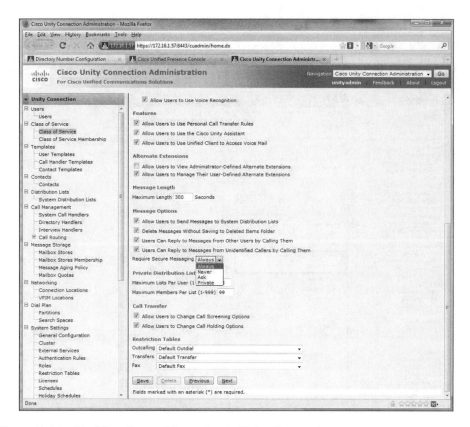

Figure 5-11 *Enabling Secure Messaging in Unity Connection*

Step 2. Configure unidentified caller message security settings, as shown in Figure 5-12:

a. Select **Users** in the navigation panel.

b. Select the desired user.

c. Select **Edit > Message Settings**.

d. Check **Mark Secure** in the Unidentified Callers Message Security section.

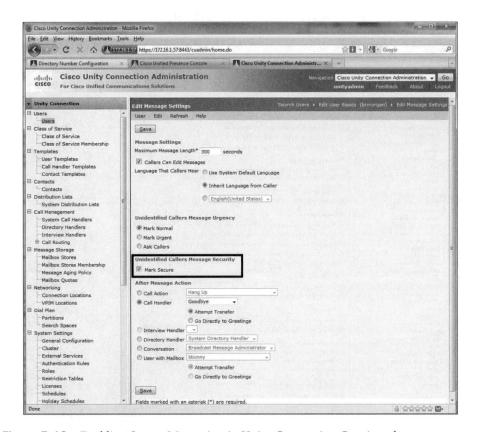

Figure 5-12   *Enabling Secure Messaging in Unity Connection Continued*

Cisco Unity

The next steps cover the configuration requirements for Unity as the message platform for the CUPC user:

Step 1.   Configure the Microsoft Exchange server to use IMAP by enabling the IMAP Connector. Refer to Chapter 9, "Troubleshooting Cisco Unified Presence," for step-by-step guidance.

Step 2.   Configure the port and encryption type. Ensure that SSL is the only encryption type being used and not TCP. This setting is manually done in Exchange 2003 but on Exchange 2007, SSL is the default.

Step 3.   Configure the user in Unity.

Step 4.   Create the exchange mailbox for the users. This step might not be necessary, depending on whether the user was added in Unity or AD first. If users were imported from AD into Unity, the mailbox should already be there as a result of the import process. For purposes of brevity, it is assumed that this is the case.

The following steps are necessary only if secure messaging is implemented with Cisco Unity:

Step 1.   Enable secure messaging through the Cisco Unity System Admin Page, as shown in Figure 5-13:

a. Select **Subscribers > Subscribers > Features.**

b. Select the desired option in the **Message Security When Sending a Message** list.

c. Select **Save.**

Step 2.   Configure unidentified caller message security settings, as shown in Figure 5-14.:

a. Select **System > Configuration > Message Security Settings.**

b. Select an option from the list on how messages should be secured from unidentified callers.

c. Select **Save.**

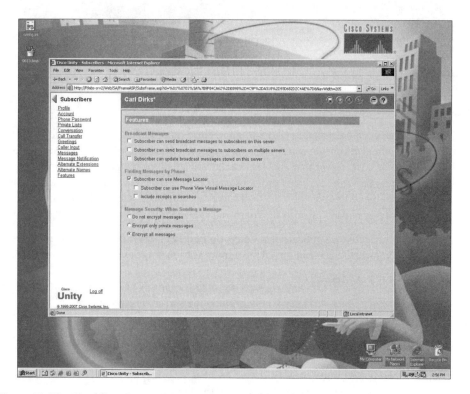

Figure 5-13 *Enabling Secure Messaging in Unity*

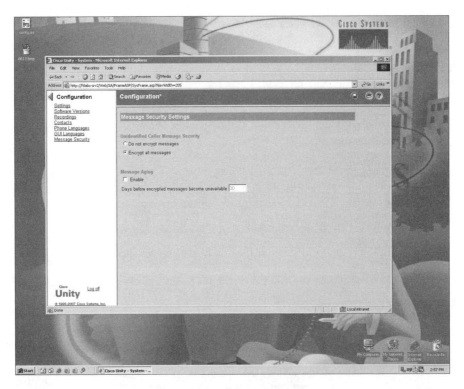

Figure 5-14   *Enabling Secure Messaging in Unity Continued*

Configuring Voicemail Servers in CUPS

Voicemail servers are defined in CUPS to allow for required interactions between CUPS and the specified voicemail server. Voice message web service (VMWS) is the service on a Cisco Unity or CUC server that enables deleted voicemails to be moved to their correct location in the mail store and also provides encryption service for secure messaging environments. The IP address of the voicemail server and the peer Microsoft Exchange server (if using Unity) is needed prior to the following steps:

Step 1.   Navigate to **Application > Cisco Unified Personal Communicator > Voicemail Server** in the CUPS administration page, as shown in Figure 5-15.

Step 2.   Click **Add New.**

Step 3.   Select **Unity** or **Unity Connection** in the server type menu.

Step 4.   Define the voicemail server name.

Step 5.   Define the FQDN hostname or IP address.

Step 6.   For Cisco Unity Servers, define **443** for Web Service Port. For Cisco Unity Connection Servers, define 143 for the Port.

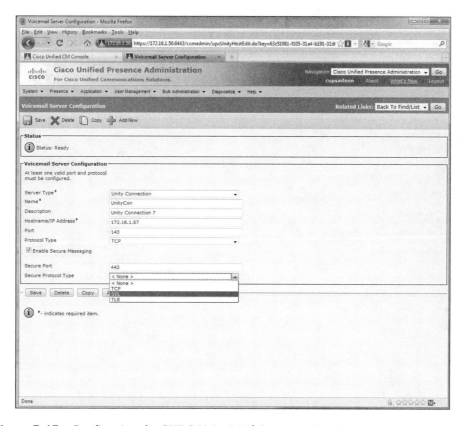

Figure 5-15   *Configuring the CUPC Voice Mail Server in CUPS*

Step 7.   For Cisco Unity Servers, select **HTTPS** for Web Service Protocol. For Cisco
Unity Connection Servers, select TCP, UDP, TLS, or SSL. The default is UDP.

Step 8.   If enabling Secure Messaging (optional), define the Secure Port and Secure
Protocol Type. For Cisco Unity Servers, choose HTTP or HTTPS for Protocol
Type. For Cisco Unity Connection Servers, choose TCP, SSL, or TLS as the
Protocol Type.

Step 9.   Click **Save**.

Configuring Mailstore Server in CUPS

Defining a mailstore in CUPS is required for the CUPC client to access the voicemail messages on the voicemail server. Figure 5-16 shows the CUPS Mailstore page. The FQDN
hostname or IP address of the mailstore server is necessary to complete the following
tasks.

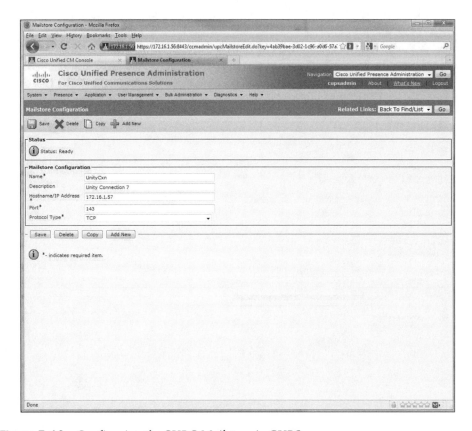

Figure 5-16   *Configuring the CUPC Mailstore in CUPS*

Step 1.   Navigate to **Application > Cisco Unified Personal Communicator > Mailstore** in the CUPS administration site.

Step 2.   Click **Add New**.

Step 3.   Define the mailstore server name.

Step 4.   Define the FQDN hostname or IP address.

Step 5.   Define the IMAP port number for CUPC to use in connecting to the mailstore server.

Unity Connection options follow:

- **TCP:** port 143

- **SSL:** port 993

- **TLS:** port 143 or 7993

Unity with Exchange options are the same as Unity Connection except TLS is supported only on port 143.

Step 6.   Click **Save**.

Configuring Voicemail Profiles in CUPS

The voicemail profile is required in CUPS to enable the CUPC client to access the correct voicemail resources for the end user. The following steps are necessary to configure the voicemail profile:

Step 1. Navigate to **Application > Cisco Unified Personal Communicator > Voicemail Profile** in the CUPS administration page, as shown in Figure 5-17.

Step 2. Click **Add New**.

Step 3. Define the profile name.

Step 4. Select the Voice Message Pilot number for the correct voicemail server of the CUPC end user.

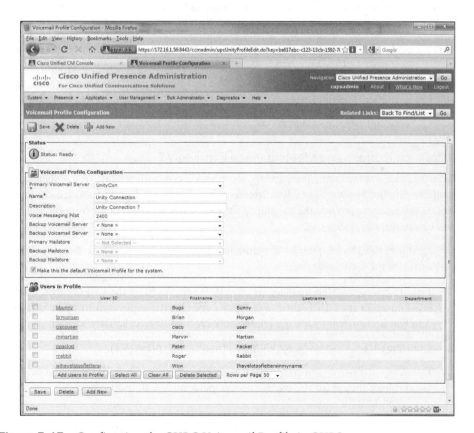

Figure 5-17 *Configuring the CUPC Voicemail Profile in CUPS*

Note Voicemail and mailstore server failover is not supported in CUPS 7.0(4).

When the voicemail profile configuration is complete, CUPC end users are now ready to log in and access the voicemail services through the desktop client.

Conferencing Configuration for CUPC

One of the major benefits of using the CUPS and the CUPC client is that application integrations allow for consolidated user functionality into other applications, such as video and conferencing. These integrations are at the touch of a button and easy to use from an end-user perspective. Initiating a conversation through an IM window and then escalating that conversation to an audio or video call at the touch of a button and then further enhancing that conversation into a collaboration conference is compelling for end users and has a dramatic effect on their productivity. This functionality begins to bring the true value of CUPS and the CUPC client to the user.

CUPC can be configured to support ad-hoc web conference sessions with the following products:

- Cisco Unified MeetingPlace

- Cisco Unified MeetingPlace Express

- Cisco Unified MeetingPlace VT

- Cisco Webex Meeting Center

MeetingPlace Express and Meeting Place Express VT

MeetingPlace Express and MeetingPlace Express VT can both provide web and audio conferencing functionality to CUPC. MeetingPlace Express VT provides video conferencing resources to provide the capability for CUPC to escalate a point-to-point video call to a multipoint video call.

Several things need to be completed before integrating the MeetingPlace Express (VT) platform into the CUPS solution:

1. Install a release of MeetingPlace Express (VT) supported by the CUPC client. The release notes for the CUPC client will specify the specific supported software versions. You can find current CUPC 7.x release notes at http://tinyurl.com/y9dephh.

2. Configure CUCM to integrate with MeetingPlace Express (VT).

3. Determine the number of web, audio, and video ports required for the solution. A good rule of thumb for the average user population is 1:40 (ports:client) for web and video and 1:20 for audio.

The next steps cover the necessary configuration to integrate MeetingPlace Express (VT) with CUPC:

Step 1.   Configure the MeetingPlace Express (VT) conferencing capabilities:

a. Install the following licenses:

- adhocsystemsoftware
- webconf
- maxadhoc
- maxweb

b. Configure MeetingPlace Express (VT) for adhoc conferencing. You can find detailed documentation for this feature at http://docwiki.cisco.com/wiki/Cisco_Unified_MeetingPlace_Express,_Release_2.x.

c. Configure MeetingPlace Express for the reservationless feature to support full web meetings initiated by MeetingPlace Express and the web meetings initiated by CUPC. You can find specific details on configuring user profiles, call control, and such on MeetingPlace Express at http://docwiki.cisco.com/wiki/Cisco_Unified_MeetingPlace_Express,_Release_2.x.

Step 2. Enable Secure Sockets Layer (SSL) encryption. This is optional; however, if it is not completed, passwords sent between CUPC and MeetingPlace Express will be sent in clear text, creating a potential security vulnerability.

Step 3. Configure a user profile for each CUPC user that is going to initiate web conferences from the CUPC client.

Note This is not required for *all* CUPC users and is needed only for the users that will initiate the web conferences.

Step 4. Ensure that the Presenter add-in is installed on each CUPC user's computer. This can be done remotely by downloading the install package from Cisco Connection Online, or the user can download it by navigating to the MeetingPlace Express server's main page using a web browser.

Step 5. Configure the voice network so that inbound calls from the PSTN to the CUPC user support RFC2388. This allows an inbound call from MeetingPlace Express to the CUPC user to use the CUPC key pad for DTMF instead of key press markup language (KPML). This is required only for DTMF support on inbound calls to CUPC, which supports both KPML and DTMF for outbound calls. This will be done on the CUCM configuration page for the SIP Trunk configured to CUPS (see Figure 5-18).

When these configurations are made, CUPS configuration will take place to define a conferencing server and profile. Those steps come later in this chapter, after the MeetingPlace and Webex configurations are covered.

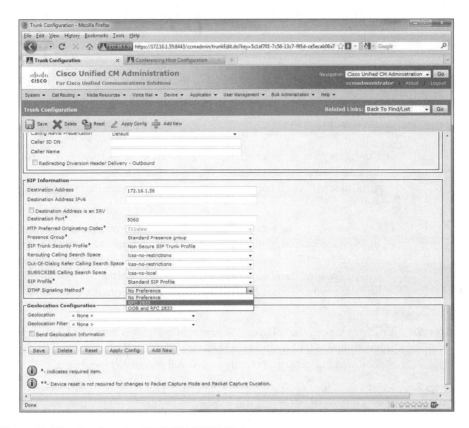

Figure 5-18   *Configuring RFC 2388 DTMF Support*

Configuring MeetingPlace

The following steps configure MeetingPlace to support the CUPC client:

Step 1.   Install the web and audio conferencing user licenses.

Step 2.   Enable SSL encryption. This is optional; however, if not completed, passwords sent between CUPC and MeetingPlace Express will be sent in clear text, creating a potential security vulnerability.

Step 3.   Configure user authentication on the web conference server. The following methods are supported:

- MeetingPlace

- LDAP

- HTTP Basic

- LDAP, then MeetingPlace

Step 4.   Configure user profiles for each CUPC user on the MeetingPlace server.

When these configurations are made, CUPS configuration takes place to define a conferencing server and profile. Those steps come later in this chapter, after the Webex configurations are covered.

Configuring WebEx Meeting Center

Integration for CUPC into WebEx Meeting Center is a new integration available with CUPS version 7.0(3) and CUPC version 7.0(2). The WebEx Meeting Center conferencing server must be installed prior to configuration. You can find documentation on how to set up this server on the provisioned WebEx site that is being integrated. Create a user profile on the WebEx Meeting Center for each CUPC user that needs access to initiate web conferencing meetings.

The previous three integration options outline the steps required to provision a CUPC user to have access to the conferencing features that the client provides. This provisioning, so far, has only taken place on the conferencing servers. The next section covers the steps to define these conferencing servers and the conferencing profiles in the CUPS for the CUPC client to leverage these resources.

Configuring Conference Servers in CUPS

This section covers the configuration of the conferencing server in CUPS so that the CUPC client can access the available resources. The configuration steps are done through the CUPS administration web pages.

Before beginning the configuration, you must complete the following prerequisite tasks:

- Get the IP address and the port number of the conferencing server.

- Integrating to a WebEx Meeting Center solution requires the Site ID and the Partner ID assigned to your WebEx site. If you do not know these IDs, you can get them from your WebEx administrator.

The following configuration steps are necessary to complete the integration:

Step 1. Go to **Application > Cisco Unified Personal Communicator > Conferencing Server** in the CUPS administration page, as shown in Figure 5-19.

Step 2. Click **Add New**.

Step 3. Define the Name of the conference server.

Step 4. Define an optional description of the conference server.

Step 5. Enter the IP address or a hostname of the conference server. The hostname needs to be a Full Qualified Domain Name (FQDN) that can be resolved by the DNS server used by CUPS.

Step 6. Define the port that the conference server is configured for. The options are for 80 (HTTP) or 443 (HTTPS).

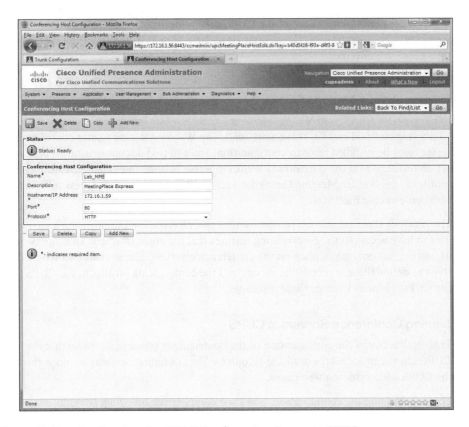

Figure 5-19   *Configuring the CUPC Conferencing Server in CUPS*

Step 7.   Select the protocol used when CUPS communicates with the conferencing server. The current supported protocols are HTTP and HTTPS.

Step 8.   Select the conferencing server being integrated.

Step 9.   If WebEx were selected, enter the Site ID and the Partner ID for the WebEx site being integrated.

Configuring Conferencing Profiles in CUPS

This section covers the final step for CUPC users accessing conferencing resources on the network. Prior to this section, the steps covered addressed the conferencing server provisioning of the CUPC user and configuring the conference server in CUPS. There can be more than one conference server defined in CUPS as required by end-user feature/functionality, migration from one platform to another, increased capacity requirements, and so on. Conference profiles enable the capability to have different CUPC end users configured for different conferencing server resources. The following steps are needed to configure conferencing profiles and assign CUPC users:

Step 1.   Navigate to **Application > Cisco Unified Personal Communicator >
Conferencing Profile** in the CUPS administration page, as shown in Figure
5-20.

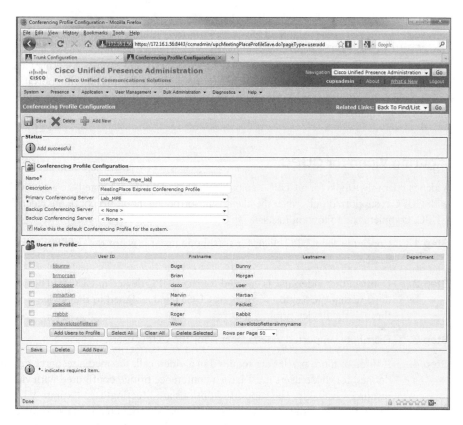

Figure 5-20   *Configuring the CUPC Conferencing Profile in CUPS*

Step 2.   Click **Add New**.

Step 3.   In the name section, define the name of the conferencing profile.

Step 4.   Select the **Primary Conferencing Server** as defined in the system.

Step 5.   You can add up to two backup conferencing servers defined in the system.

Step 6.   Check the **Make This the Default Conferencing Profile for the System** box
if this is the default system.

Step 7.   Click the **Add Users to Profile**.

Step 8.   Select the users for this voicemail profile.

Step 9.   Click **Add Selected**.

Step 10. Click Save.

> **Note** Conferencing server failover is not supported in CUPS 7.0(4).

This section completes the required tasks necessary to configure full conferencing features for CUPC users. This feature will allow for ad-hoc web conferencing leveraging Meeting Express, Meeting Place Express VT, MeetingPlace, and WebEx Meeting Center. Conferencing can be a conversation escalated to a point-to-point web sharing portal or a full-service web conference with the ability to invite other users to the conference via a click to add, e-mail, or IM.

Configuring Video for CUPC

Video is relatively simple for a CUPC deployment. The main thing to note here is that video with CUPC is supported only when the client is in softphone mode. To configure video for CUPC, complete the following tasks:

Step 1. Configure the CUPC client for softphone use if it is not the user's primary device.

Step 2. Confirm that video use is enabled for the CUPC device in CUCM. This is done within the Region settings of CUCM and assigned to the device through the device pool.

Step 3. Distribute supported video cameras for the CUPC users.

Step 4. If three or more parties are required in a video call, the media resource group defined for those users must have a conference bridge configured with video resources available. The supported options are MeetingPlace Express VT, MeetingPlace with video, and Cisco Unified Videoconferencing solution that leverages the 3500 series Multipoint Control Units (MCU).

> **Note** Steps 1 through 3 are the only ones necessary for point-to-point video.

Configure LDAP for CUPC

This section covers LDAP integration for the purposes of user lookup in the CUPC client. This enables CUPC users to search for and add contacts from a defined LDAP directory. The section does *not* cover LDAP directory integration for purposes of user provisioning and authentication with CUCM. Detailed LDAP integration for those purposes can be found in the "Configuring CUPC Users in CUCM" section of this chapter. Cisco strongly recommends having CUCM integrated to LDAP for user provisioning and authentication and configuring CUPC for LDAP integration on CUPS for user lookup functionality.

The first thing to understand before configuring LDAP servers in CUPS is the rules for how contacts are displayed in CUPC. This is important to understand because there will be attributes that need to be mapped for displaying names, and these rules determine how names are displayed:

- If a user edits a contact name retrieved from LDAP in CUPC, display that name. This is the Nickname attribute in CUPS.

- If the LDAP user field DisplayName is configured, display that name.

- If the LDAP user field Nickname is configured, display that name with the last name.

- If none of the preceding are configured, display the LDAP user field of the FirstName and LastName. If there is no last name, display only the first name. If there is no first name, display only the last name.

- If no LDAP user fields are configured, display the LDAP UserID or the CUPS user ID.

- If a non-LDAP contact is added, the user can define the Display As name, first name, and last name.

The first thing you need to do is to configure an LDAP attribute map for the supported LDAP server and the CUPC client attributes. Several attribute mappings available enable you to manipulate information between the LDAP server and the CUPC client, but only one is required at the start to provide the functionality of adding users retrieved in an LDAP search to the CUPC client contact list. The following are the steps necessary to accomplish that task:

Step 1. Navigate to Application **> Cisco Unified Personal Communicator > Settings** in the CUPS administration page, as shown in Figure 5-21.

Step 2. Select the type of LDAP server you want to configure in the drop-down menu.

Step 3. Define the UserID field under the UPC User Fields to one of the following:

Microsoft Active Directory - sAMAccountName

Sun ONE - uid

Step 4. Click **Save.**

After you correctly set the attributes, you can configure the LDAP server. The steps necessary to configure an LDAP server in CUPS are as follows:

Step 1. Navigate to **Application > Cisco Unified Personal Communicator > LDAP Server,** as shown in Figure 5-22.

Step 2. Click **Add New.**

Step 3. Define the name of the LDAP server.

Step 4. Define the FQDN hostname or the IP address.

Step 5. Define the port number used by the LDAP server; 389 is the default.

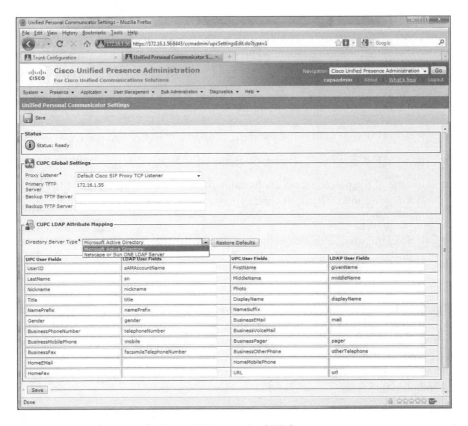

Figure 5-21   *Configuring the User ID Format in CUPS*

Step 6.   Select the protocol to use. The default is TCP.

Step 7.   Click **Save**.

> **Note**   More than one LDAP server can be defined in the CUPS system for purposes of failover. If this is done, all the defined LDAP servers must be of the same type.

The final required configuration is the LDAP Profile. The required steps to configure an LDAP profile in CUPS follows:

Step 1.   Navigate to **Application > Cisco Unified Personal Communicator > LDAP Profile** in the CUPS administration page, as shown in Figure 5-23.

Step 2.   Click **Add New**.

Step 3.   Define the name of the profile.

Step 4.   It is optional but recommended to define the Bind Distinguished Name field using an administrator-level account. Anonymous bind is available if wanted.

The syntax can vary depending on the LDAP server used. Table 5-2 provides a guide to the syntax for Microsoft Active Directory and Sun ONE.

Step 5.   Define the LDAP bind password.

Step 6.   Define the search context to be used for LDAP user searches by the CUPC client. A single OU search context is supported. For example (Microsoft AD):

CN=users,DC=cisco,DC=com

Step 7.   Check to perform a recursive search of the directory.

Step 8.   Select the primary LDAP server.

Step 9.   Select any backup LDAP servers.

Step 10.   Click **Add Users to Profile**.

Step 11.   Select the users for this voicemail profile.

Step 12.   Click **Add Selected**.

Step 13.   Click **Save**.

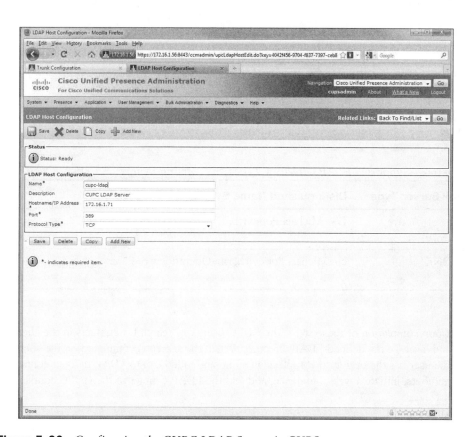

Figure 5-22   *Configuring the CUPC LDAP Server in CUPS*

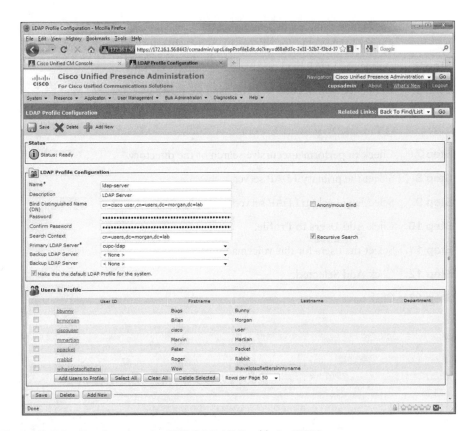

Figure 5-23 *Configuring the CUPC LDAP Profile in CUPS*

Table 5-2 *Supported LDAP Directory Types and Naming Syntax*

LDAP Server Type	Distinguished Name Syntax
Microsoft Active Directory	CN=Michael Popovich, CN=Users, DC=Contoso, DC=com
Sun ONE	cn=Michael Popovich, ou=Operations, o=Example Corp, st=CA, c=US

Upon completion of these steps, the CUPC users can search for contacts in the client and leverage the defined LDAP directory. When the search is completed on the client, the user has the option to IM, place an audio and video call to LDAP-defined contact numbers, initiate a web conference, and add the LDAP contact to the CUPC contact list.

CUPC Troubleshooting

The next few sections cover basic troubleshooting relative to the CUPC client. Some steps can be done by the end user and takes place on the client machine, and others are done by a system administrator or more experienced network administrator to narrow down possible root causes to an issue.

Basic CUPC Troubleshooting

If there is any service issues after a user has logged in, there are two basic things an end user can do to immediately confirm an issue and give administrators a good idea of what the problem is and how to resolve it follow:

- Look at the server health of the CUPC services. This is accomplished by navigating to **Help > Show Server Health** in the menu of the CUPC client (see Figure 5-24). There is an overall health status of all the available CUPC services that can be configured. Next to each process or service is a status indicator telling the user if the status is good with a green check or bad with a red octagon with an X in the middle. The end user can quickly tell an administrator what the initial problem might be. In the figure, there seems to be a couple of issues that need to be resolved.

- If the first option is not enough to adequately determine the potential problem, the end user can generate a more detailed dump of information that can be sent to the administrator. This is done by navigating to **Help > Create Problem Report** in the menu of the CUPC client, as shown in Figure 5-25. This starts a wizard in which the end users can quickly fill out the required information describing what they were attempting to do and what they were doing at the time of the problem. The tool then generates a log report and gathers necessary files that will be compiled into a zip file. This zip file will automatically be saved on the desktop. That file can be e-mailed to the administrator or appended to a Cisco TAC case for a more detailed review. One suggestion would be to enable detailed logging on the client and have the user log off and log back in to the client.

When the user and administrator have determined a specific problem, more troubleshooting will most likely be required. The following sections cover some initial troubleshooting steps for the various CUPC services, such as authentication, voicemail, conferencing, LDAP, and so on. Many of these topics are covered in more depth in Chapter 9. For more detailed information on using the diagnostic tools available for CUPC, go to http://tinyurl.com/ydhhfo9.

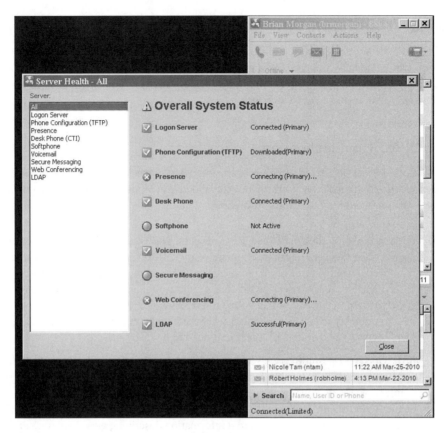

Figure 5-24 *CUPC Show Server Health Tool*

CUPS and CUCM Integration Troubleshooting

There could be issues with an end user not being able to log in to CUPC. This can be because of several issues and the following are some ideas on where to look:

■ Make sure the end user has network connectivity to the voice network. This can be through the enterprise network or VPN, but connectivity must first be confirmed. Pinging the IP address of the CUPS server is the easiest way to accomplish this.

■ LDAP integration with CUCM is the Cisco recommended way for deploying CUCM. CUPS authenticates users through CUCM, and if a user cannot authenticate using CUPC, verify LDAP is functional between CUCM and your LDAP server. This can be done by having the user authenticate to the CUCM end-user pages. If that is not allowed, an administrator can authenticate to CUCM admin pages using an LDAP account to verify connectivity.

- If this is a new user, it is possible that the user has not synced over to the CUPS cluster. Usually, the administrator would have verified this already because most deployments have some manual configuration of the CUPC user for voicemail and conferencing profiles. Deployments assign default profiles for all services, and when a user is synced and automatically assigned to a CUPS node, the user should be functional. If this is the case, make sure the Sync Agent and Proxy Service is running. If those services are not running, restart them manually and confirm the user is assigned on the cluster.

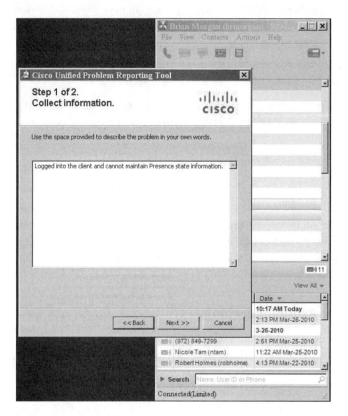

Figure 5-25 *CUPC Create Problem Report Tool*

Voicemail Troubleshooting

Most common voicemail issues from the CUPC client stem from a user not being able to log on, or voicemail messages are not downloading or don't appear in the recent pane. Here are some things to look at to address voicemail issues on CUPC:

- Make sure users enter their credentials correctly in the CUPC client. This is found under **File > Preferences > Account**. If the user can log in to CUPC but does not see any voicemail messages, this is most likely not configured correctly. Show Server Health will also reveal this issue.

- If voicemail messages are not downloading but authentication is working, there are a few things to consider:

  - Check the server configuration to make sure that IMAP is enabled on the mail-store and that the voicemail profile is accurate for the CUPC user.

  - (Cisco Unity Connection) If messages are still not being received and the credentials have been checked, make sure that port 7993 is configured on the server and that the CUPC client is listening on port 7993. If there are any firewalls between the client and server, make sure that traffic on port 7993 is allowed to pass through.

  - Clear the voicemail cache on the end-user machine. This is accomplished by deleting all the files in the following directories:

    For Windows XP: *drive*:\Documents and Settings*UserID*\\Local Settings\\Application Data\\Cisco\\Unified Personal Communicator\\VoiceMail

    For Windows Vista: *drive*:\Users*UserID*\\AppData\\Local\\Cisco\\Unified Personal Communicator\\VoiceMail

    For Mac OS: *home*/Library/Caches/Cisco/UnifiedPersonalCommunicator/VoiceMail

- If voicemails do not display in the recent pane of the CUPC client and server health shows that the server fails due to authentication failure, have the user re-enter their credentials in the CUPC client. If the client tried to reconnect but can't, it is most likely that the voicemail account is either locked or the password has expired.

Conferencing Troubleshooting

This section covers the basic troubleshooting steps focused on conferencing and covers MeetingPlace Express and MeetingPlace:

- If the user complains that the conferencing button is dimmed on the CUPC client, that is most likely due to the conferencing resources not being configured for the system, the conference profile has not been defined for the user, or the Web Conferencing Server credentials on the CUPC client are incorrect. Check the CUPS server and make sure that a conferencing server has been configured and that the correct conference profile has been identified for the CUPC client. When that is confirmed, make sure the CUPC user has configured the correct user information in the Web Conference Server setting of the client.

- If the user complains that he cannot escalate a call to a web conference when he clicks **Start Web Conference**, check the CUCM server and make sure that the directory lookup dial rules are configured correctly. This issue can occur when the CUPC client cannot match a calling party number with the correct person from LDAP via the CUCM server. Details on configuring directory lookup dial rules can be found at http://tinyurl.com/yd5pyd6.

> **Note** Advanced troubleshooting information for MeetingPlace express can be found at http://tinyurl.com/ychwbnw and for MeetingPlace at http://tinyurl.com/ya3s2os.

LDAP Troubleshooting

The following provide solutions to some common LDAP problems. For instance, if there are no results when a user does a query in the Search pane, there can be several reasons for this; here are some things to look at to resolve the issue:

■ If anonymous bind is configured in CUPS for the LDAP server, uncheck that check box and configure the Bind Distinguished Name information.

■ Check client connectivity to the LDAP server by having the user ping the IP address of the LDAP server or telnet to the LDAP port on the server. (The default is port 389.)

■ If using bind credentials in the LDAP server configuration on CUPS, double-check that those credentials are correct.

■ Verify the correct search space is defined in the LDAP server configuration on CUPS.

For more detailed LDAP troubleshooting information, go to http://tinyurl.com/yadqb4v.

Summary

The CUPC client is a feature-rich client that offers a lot of productivity enhancements to the end user. It is flexible for both the stationary and mobile workspace users with desk-phone CTI control and softphone. The collaboration features provided by the client cover Instant Messaging, audio/video calls, web conferencing—all at the click of a button. The idea of escalating a conversation as needed gives the end user the ability to get more done in a single interaction than has ever been provided before. The click-to-action functionality of CUPC gives the power of advanced collaboration features to end users with little to no knowledge of how to initiate them. This is especially evident with video and web conferencing because these two collaborative mediums have historically had low adoption rates because of complex scheduling and setup.

Chapter 6

Cisco Unified Presence Practical Applications

Businesses depend on their employees to make the most efficient use of work time as possible. In a world where modes of communication seem to be multiplying faster than our ability to manage them, there has to be a tool or feature that allows us to reach those whom we want to reach and, likewise, be reached how, when, or if we want to be reached. Presence defines a single focal point of availability. The concept of Derived Presence propagates an individual's current status in real time to multiple entities. So regardless of who is trying to reach you, they can know up front whether you can be reached and whether there are alternative possible methods to reach you. The curtain has thankfully fallen on the act of calling someone's office phone followed by a call to their cell phone, then home phone, and so on.

By far, the most common questions asked by those interested in Unified Communications (UC) solutions include, "Just what is Presence?" and "How can we use Presence as a tool in our environment?" The answer to the first question has been covered somewhat extensively throughout this book. The second question, however, constitutes the focus of this chapter. How can Presence be used in a varied array of environments by an even more varied array of users? To adequately set the stage for the user applications, a discussion of the UC components will be revisited with specific focus on the aspects relevant to each user and application of Presence capabilities.

Although we can't touch on every possibility, we can offer some basic user scenarios based on typical roles that seem to be rather standard in function throughout various corporations and enterprises. The focus is not solely placed on Presence use by these users, but on the user workspace as a whole. In each of these, Presence is a core element around which multiple facets of the UC revolve. These include

- Stationary users

- Mobile users

- Executives

- Teleworkers

- Call center agents

With Cisco Unified Presence 7.0, the concept of Derived Presence was introduced. This addition has had a significant impact on the user experience for all types of users. In exploring the overall experience for each user, a better understanding of both Presence and its versatility in the Cisco UC solution might be solidified.

Unified Communications Components

When viewed from the perspective of Presence, UC components can be separated into two categories:, Presence Source and Presence Consumer. Figure 6-1 illustrates the concept of Presence Sources and Consumers.

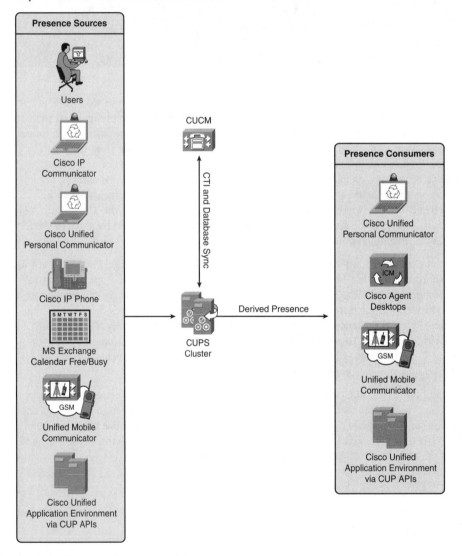

Figure 6-1   *Presence Sources and Consumers*

A Presence Source is simply a client or device on which Presence status can be set. A Presence Consumer is the recipient of that information and shares it with other clients and devices. As Figure 6-1 shows, a single entity can be both a source and a consumer.

The UC components most relevant to the user experience might not fill either the consumer or the source roles. However, that does not reduce their importance to the overall feature-set. The components to be discussed in the user application scenarios include

- Call control
- Voice messaging
- Presence
- Collaboration
- Mobility

There is not be a great deal of detail associated with each component. The goal is to merely properly direct your train of thought to possibilities enabled by Presence.

Call Control

The Cisco Unified Communications Manager (CUCM) is the core of the call control functionality. The essential underlying architecture of the CUCM cluster has already been discussed at various points throughout the book. Therefore, it is assumed that the various facets and features offered by the CUCM are known.

The focus here is on the overall user experience. With the advent of Cisco Unified Workspace Licensing (CUWL), the focus of Cisco UC solutions was shifted from phones and dial-tone to providing a rich user experience. Rather than being phone-centric, this new model changes the old paradigm from one focused on handsets to one focused on users. The concepts behind call control are still relatively unchanged; it simply takes on new responsibilities. Call control includes communication with other applications and services to communicate device states. The devices in question might be soft phones, physical handsets, conference phones, mobile phones/clients, video endpoints, and more. Any device via which someone is reachable for voice calling purposes falls under the call-control umbrella.

Voice Messaging

The user experience surrounding voice messaging has evolved greatly in recent years. No longer is voicemail accessible only via the desk phone. Feature enhancements have been introduced that enable users to retrieve voicemail from a graphical Telephony User Interface (TUI) on their desk phone, web access, CUPC desktop client, mobile smart phone, e-mail client, and of course the traditional call-in access method.

The stationary user might elect to scroll through voice messages via the TUI to see who has called and in what order to listen to each message. This is known as *Visual Voicemail*. Unity has call-screening capabilities that allow a user to listen to a voice message as it is being recorded. During the recording, the user has the ability to retrieve the call from the voice messaging system to speak to the caller immediately. This feature is known as Message Monitor.

The Live-Reply feature in both Unity Connection and Unity enables subscribers who are listening to their voicemail messages, by phone, to reply to a voice message by calling the message senders directly without having to hang up and dial the number.

If users want to have their voicemail at a glance, the CUPC client can show call logs and voice message counts. Messages can be played directly from the CUPC client.

Finally, a user can listen to messages and change preferences and other settings from a web interface known as the Cisco Unity Inbox Web Tool, which is a part of the Cisco Unity Personal Communications Assistant.

Available Cisco Voice Messaging Platforms include Cisco Unity, Cisco Unity Connection, and Cisco Unity Express. Each option has its place in the Cisco UC architecture. The various differences, benefits, and features of each are beyond the scope of this book. Regardless of which platform is chosen, the essential underlying functionality is the same. Each is a full-featured voice messaging platform.

There is, however, one notable difference in Cisco Unity. Cisco Unity Connection is based on the same Linux platform as CUCM. There are no underlying dependencies on Microsoft operating systems or applications. The message store is on-box. Cisco Unity Express is specifically built to integrate with a voice-capable router. As such, it is built in an IOS-like operating system. Cisco Unity, as always, is built on the Microsoft Windows Server platform with Microsoft SQL under the hood. The message store is maintained on a Microsoft Exchange server.

Unified Messaging and Integrated Messaging

Cisco Unity's reliance on Microsoft Exchange provides it a specific capability not available to Cisco Unity Connection and Cisco Unity Express. That capability is known as Unified Messaging. Unified Messaging is available with Microsoft Exchange and IBM Lotus Notes environments. For purposes of discussion and brevity, only Microsoft Exchange is addressed here.

Some discussion is in order to briefly compare and contrast Unified Messaging and Integrated Messaging. Both include the capability to send and receive voicemail from a Microsoft Outlook client. With Unified Messaging, the voice messages are delivered to the user Exchange inbox. That is, Cisco Unity–specific Active Directory (AD) extensions are irreversibly applied to the AD structure. When voice messages are received, they are stored as e-mail in the user's Exchange message store.

With Integrated Messaging, an Internet Message Access Protocol (IMAP) connection is utilized in delivering the voice messages to the e-mail client. The only difference from the user's perspective is that there is a separate inbox added to their e-mail client to which voice messages are delivered. As IMAP is a standardized protocol, the Integrated Messaging capabilities are not limited solely to Microsoft Outlook clients. Additionally, the voice messaging mail store is kept separate from the users' e-mail message store.

All three voice messaging platforms support Integrated Messaging. Only Cisco Unity supports true Unified Messaging because it can be integrated into the corporate AD infrastructure. The majority of voice messaging deployments are done via IMAP connectivity.

For further information about Cisco Voice Messaging products, check out the following links:

- **Cisco Unity:**
  www.cisco.com/en/US/docs/voice_ip_comm/unity/7x/roadmap/7xcudg.html

- **Cisco Unity Connection:**
  www.cisco.com/en/US/docs/voice_ip_comm/connection/7x/roadmap/7xcucdg.html

- **Cisco Unity Express:**
  www.cisco.com/cisco/web/solutions/small_business/products/voice_
  conferencing/unity_express/index.html

Presence

Presence provides a key functionality in showing availability of individuals in your contact list. If you need to track down someone quickly, the most effective manner of reaching that co-worker is easily visible in the CUPC client window. There is no need to play phone-tag or hide-and-seek calling one phone after another. I can easily see whether that user is available. If the user is on the phone at the current time, I can simply fire off an IM session and make contact. If the user is available, I can right-click and place a call rather easily.

For the user, this functionality avoids the need to call a user on multiple numbers and leave voice messages in multiple voicemail boxes. These users can keep their most frequently called contacts on their screen and know, at a glance, their availability. Additionally, the user look-up functionality in the CUPC client avoids the need to keep a printed (and updated) phone directory at hand.

Collaboration

The term *collaboration* is rapidly evolving. It has become a somewhat all-encompassing term used to describe a set (or subset) of UC applications and services in a single word. The concept of collaboration can be interpreted to infer a group of individuals coming together to discuss or solve a particular issue. Or more appropriate to our means, it can imply an instant sharing of resources and services across multiple media types without regard to geographic locale of those involved. The overall goal of collaborative technologies is to enable businesses to provide one experience for their users and customers regardless of the means by which they access the network.

The network is the platform on which all applications and services are constructed so that they can be offered in a consistent manner to all who access them. This means that a users accessing content via a desktop computer in the office can have a user experience identical to the user accessing applications via a laptop with a VPN connection sitting in an area covered by a public wireless hot spot. The same would also hold true for those users accessing the applications and services from a mobile device or smart phone.

Through the use of audio conferencing, web conferencing, and video conferencing, the idea of the office meeting has changed. Long has the ability to conduct simple audio conferences been a critical capability in many businesses. Video conferencing elicits sighs of expectant exasperation from even the most seasoned meeting coordinator and attendees. The experience of setting up even the simplest of video conferences has traditionally taken a team of individuals and unknown quantities of pain to initiate and maintain. Web conferencing is still a relatively new capability on the scene when compared to audio and video.

The evolution of collaborative platforms such as Cisco MeetingPlace and Cisco WebEx have revolutionized the idea of audio/video/web conferencing by providing a single interface through which all three can be scheduled and held in a pain-free manner. WebEx has further evolved the concept by instituting the one-click meeting along with the introduction of WebEx Connect.

WebEx Connect is an all-in-one collaborative platform providing Instant Messaging, softphone, video, and other services such as Connect Spaces. Connect Spaces provide a central repository for documents, discussions, meeting recordings, project timelines, contact lists, and more. These spaces are accessible by invitation only. The space admin issues invitations to specific individuals both internal and external to an organization.

In September 2008, Cisco acquired Jabber, which has traditionally been known as a large player in the Instant Messaging market. The Jabber client is renowned for being user-friendly, customizable and, most important, based on a highly programmable and customizable foundation known as the Jabber eXtensible Communications Platform (XCP). The version 6.x release of WebEx Connect is based on Cisco Jabber and is fully compatible with other Jabber clients. Federation capabilities exist with other IM services, such as AOL Instant Messenger Pro (AIMPro). Actually, AIMPro was the underlying platform for versions of WebEx Connect prior to 6.x.

Mobility

The advent of wireless Internet access on aircraft has opened a new realm for the mobile user. This might be good or bad depending on your perspective. Typically, air travel time has been a time for reading, rest, and sleep. Now that the ability to surf has been added to the list, a user need is not unreachable on travel days. Granted, voice calls over the network are still prohibited, but IM and other forms of collaboration are easily facilitated.

When the mobile user is away from traditional network connectivity, the typical smart phone has become the so-called electronic leash. If we can't be on our laptops, we can access the network and e-mail via the applications on our phones. With CUMC and Mobile Connect (also known as Single Number Reach [SNR]), your CUPC client functionality is essentially extended to your mobile phone. Presence status, messaging, IM (in the form of text messaging), phone logs (missed calls/received calls/placed calls), Corporate Directory, and Calendar functionality is enabled through the Mobile Communicator Client.

You can join meetings, look up contacts, send text messages, and listen to your corporate voicemail right from the client. All the interactions take place over the data channel and therefore do not use cellular minutes.

Mobility doesn't simply include the Mobile Communicator Client. There are also call control features that further enable ease of reaching individuals. These two key features are known as

- **Mobile Connect:** As mentioned, Mobile Connect is also known as Single Number Reach. This enables users to tie their cellular phone number to the desk phone and publish only the desk phone number. When the desk phone number is called, both the desk and mobile phones ring. Along with the need to publish only one number, this feature enables the users to track only one voicemail box. When a call comes in, both phones ring, but the system will pull the call back in-house when it goes to voicemail. So the need for a second voicemail box on the mobile device is mitigated or even eliminated. There is some value, however, in having the ability to keep a single mobile device that has the capability to keep corporate/business voicemail separate from the mobile device's voicemail. This enables a separation of business and personal mail boxes. All business-related messaging hits the corporate side whereas friends and family can leave messages on the mobile side. It makes for quite a nice delineation.

- **Mobile Voice Access:** This enables dialing via office functionality, which means that users can place calls from their mobile device via the corporate Unified Communications Manager cluster as if sitting in the office. This is especially valuable in cases where calls are missed and need to be returned. They can be returned from the mobile device but go out of the cluster with the users' desk phone caller identification information, thus keeping the mobile phone number private.

Stationary Users

In the typical enterprise environment, the overwhelming majority of users will be stationary; that is, they will be the traditional in-office users. Their overall work profile has them in the office during regular working hours and disconnected during off-hours. Overall, these users tend to be the ones most likely to take advantage of the most basic features in the workspace. The traditional workspace includes dial tone and voicemail. The expansive array of features available in a CUC solution might take them a short time to understand and fully utilize. After this learning curve is past, these users take their place among the most avid users in the enterprise.

This becomes even more the case if specific applications or features have been added with the express intent of providing a remedy for business obstacles or pain points identified during the planning and discovery phases of the UC solution deployment.

Call Control

Stationary users typically utilize a desk phone for most voice-related functions. However, they make significant use of the collaborative capabilities of the CUPC client. The CUPC client is a Session Initiation Protocol (SIP) endpoint that provides Presence, IM, control of the desk phone or softphone, and one click meeting escalation.

The primary use, however, will likely be directory lookups on the CUPC client followed by IM or click-to-dial. For click-to-dial, a simple right-click of the contact will provide a call function. With the CUPC client in Desk Phone mode, the desk phone goes off-hook and dial the selected phone number of the contact. Switching to softphone mode enables the use of desktop video using a webcam.

If the stationary users are in the role of an administrative assistant, Busy Lamp Fields (BLF) can be placed on the desk phone to monitor the phone status of their supervisor. The button can also act as a speed dial to reach the supervisor.

Messaging

Stationary users will find themselves fortunate to be the group who collectively receives the most overall benefit from messaging capabilities. This is primarily because the bulk of their working time is spent in their workspace where they have the most flexibility in receiving and responding to voice messages.

They can easily take advantage of features such as

- iDivert to immediately send a call to voicemail.
- Message Monitor (Unity only at this time) that enables the user to listen to the voice message as it is being recorded. During the recording, users have the option to retrieve the call if they decide to do so.
- Live-Reply enables a voicemail subscriber to place a call back to the individual who left the voice message being played.
- Visual Voicemail provides the ability to scroll through messages on the phone's LCD screen and selectively play/reply/save/delete messages.
- Unified/Integrated Messaging to manage voicemail from their e-mail client.

Presence

Presence plays an important role in reaching users in the manner in which they want to be reached. Having a clear indication of how to reach a contact immediately and on the first attempt is an incredible time saver and productivity enhancer over the course of a work day. When integrated with an Outlook calendar, Presence status can automatically change between *Available* and *In a Meeting* based on free/busy time specified over the course of the work day.

The essential intent behind Presence is to eliminate the dreaded games of phone tag. The capabilities added by the CUPC client in showing contacts, voice messaging, and a graphical directory in a single interface are invaluable.

Collaboration

Collaborative discussions don't always need to be planned as formal meeting events. Utilizing the CUPC client along with a collaborative platform, such as MeetingPlace, MeetingPlace Express, or WebEx, enables instant sharing of applications and entire desktops with the click of a mouse. Additional capabilities offered by WebEx Connect Spaces enables a centralized collaborative portal for groups of individuals based on projects or interests. An IM, phone call, or video call can be escalated to a collaborative session with a single click of the mouse in the Call Status window.

Stationary users can choose to collaborate with others both inside and outside of the office depending on job function and needs at a particular point in the day. The ability to immediately share a document, presentation, spreadsheet, or any combination of applications enables users to better coordinate time and resources. If changes are needed, all users in a collaborative session can make changes to a single document that can then be distributed. There is no longer a need for everyone to make their own changes and send them to one person to perform the merging of the changes followed by mass distribution.

Mobile Users

Mobile users tend to be the most versatile and demanding of the user types, from a functionality perspective. They make use of all the same technologies as stationary users, but they do so from a variety of devices. That is, they add mobility to the list of features in use as a part of their day-to-day activities. These individuals can have a workspace at the office, at home, and just about anywhere else they might happen to be at a given point. The idea is to provide one experience regardless of how the features and applications are accessed. Mobile users can be outdoors, indoors, or in transit between meetings, locations, or countries.

Mobile users can place and receive calls via softphone clients such as CUPC and IP Communicator (IPC). These users' offices can consist of any space with network connectivity (wired or wireless) that is large enough to hold a laptop and provide a modicum of comfort. The sight of users donning a USB or Bluetooth headset in preparation to place calls via their VPN-connected laptop is all too common. The workplace is no longer limited to an office building. Mobility features become the most valued of all with these users. This is especially true of the SNR feature.

Executives

In many aspects, corporate executives are a hybrid of the stationary and mobile users. They often utilize the same features; however, they likely have assistants who have the ability to answer calls, forward callers to voicemail, and such on their behalf. The assistants almost certainly use a BLF to see the status of their manager's phone. The assistants can also make use of an attendant console to manager interactions and line status of multiple managers and executives.

Executives are in a position to make the most use of the ability to provide Presence status regardless of whether they are in the office or making use of the various Mobility features available. In customer interactions, it is quite common for executives to want the ability to hide their mobile phone numbers from all but those who really need to know how to reach them. Physically, executives can be nearly anywhere on the planet and remain reachable via a single phone number. Presence status can indicate whether they want to be reached at all. In this case, the typical "find me/follow me" function provided by Presence can also become a "hide me" feature.

One of the lesser known features of Presence and, more specifically, the CUPC client, is the ability to build Presence groups and enable only certain individuals to view your Presence status. Executives tend to make great use of this feature, further insulating themselves from distractions to make the most use of productive time.

Federation capabilities expand this capability by enabling interaction and Presence status exchange with other CUP customers and Microsoft Office Communicator customers. This reachability can be easily utilized to keep track of peer executives of sister and customer entities.

Teleworkers

Teleworkers are a relatively new concept. Over the past decade or so, a shift has come about, largely due to rising costs and solutions offered by UC. This shift involves reducing the amount of real estate owned and maintained by the corporation and shifting employee workspaces to their homes. Working from home has yielded results that were previously unexpected. Companies have seen dramatic rises in productivity and general worker health and happiness. Along with this came increased job satisfaction and a propensity to remain with companies for a longer period of time.

True, it does take a significant amount of discipline to work from home. It also takes a dedicated workspace and per-user capital outlay for the necessary equipment.

The true teleworker space typically includes a broadband Internet connection, a router (for example, a Cisco 871), a computer, and a phone. The example of the Cisco 871 router is presented due to its all-in-one capability. It offers wired, wireless, and VPN capabilities to further enhance the flexibility of the teleworker network deployment.

These, of course, can vary. The phone can be a physical desk phone or a softphone. These users will be heavily reliant on Presence status of colleagues because they can't simply walk over to an office or cubicle to chat with a co-worker. The CUPC client, of course, provides the real-time Presence status, IM, and soft phone capabilities that they need to complete their daily job functions. If a webcam is present, they can also participate in video conferencing calls.

With the widespread move toward real estate reduction and the validation offered by the high percentage of companies offering teleworker solutions, the traditional call center has been redefined, and companies are beginning to use at-home agents to further reduce their facilities costs.

Note   Although Cisco does have a viable solution for emergency calling, it is not covered here. That said, careful consideration should be taken regarding how emergency calls will be placed by mobile and teleworker employees. Softphones and wireless phones might pose unforeseen (but not insurmountable) challenges.

Call Center Agents

Many companies with call centers are now pushing their call center agents out of the traditional call center and into the teleworker arena. Customer service agents can be located anywhere and still maintain real-time communications with a central call center to service customer calls. The Presence status can provide an indicator of whether the agent can accept calls at the current time.

In cases where a customer call requires escalation is required, an agent can know at a glance which individuals are available for escalation. Further expanding the Presence capability, integrations with other systems, such as Google Maps, corporate directories, and more, can enable the agent to perform a real-time search for globally available resources with the expertise to handle the escalation. The Google Maps integration with Presence can show individual Presence indicators on the map. Users provide keywords based on a standardized taxonomy that coincide with their various areas of expertise. As the call center agent performs the keyword search, the available resources can immediately be seen on the map. Figure 6-2 shows an example of just such an application.

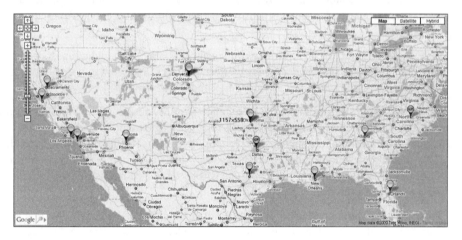

Figure 6-2 *Resource Location Application*

The figure shows available resources across the United States. It seems that resources are available in North Carolina and Texas based on a keyword search performed in bringing up the map.

Further capabilities might include the integration of Global Positioning Systems (GPS) capabilities with the Google Map, which tracks the location of a user based on a GPS-enabled smart phone. Presence status can be set by that user through the CUPC client (manually or via calendar free/busy time) or through the use of the Mobile Communicator Client.

When located, the escalation resource can be reached by clicking their Presence pointer. Contact information will be shown in a screen pop that includes phone number information. Alternatively, an IM session can be launched with the individual. Either way, immediate contact is made and the individual can be added to the call with the customer. Depending on the situation, the resource, call center agent, and customer can join an interactive WebEx session so that they can share resources in real time. This puts the right resource in contact with the customer with the least amount of time and frustration on the part of the customer. Presence allows the immediate contact with an available resource that can solve the customer's problem.

Summary

Hopefully, it has become somewhat clear as to the role played by Presence and that it isn't merely a simple side feature. It is a centerpiece that enables multiple facets of the overall UC solution. Presence is an enabler without which many of the key features and applications available to various types of users would be severely hindered and lost altogether.

The ability of the stationary user to locate co-workers (even if it's just to see where everyone wants to go for lunch) is key in providing a phone-tag free work day. How much of the lunch hour could be saved by simply collaborating with co-workers and getting out of the office faster? Granted, that isn't the intent with Presence, but it's certainly a side benefit.

The executive's ability to be anywhere and remain in contact with higher-ups, peers, the office administrative staff, and anyone else deemed necessary is key to not only productivity, but also to the success of the individual and the company.

Mobile users find that the added flexibility and versatility added by the Mobility features are highly valuable in not only providing customers a single point of contact, but also takes the elimination of phone-tag one step closer to reality. Having the ability to publicize a single phone number that can reach an individual in any number of places provides a high degree of flexibility not only to the few roles discussed in this chapter, but also to those in any customer-facing aspect of the business.

Teleworkers are those no longer bound to an office. In many cases, they're also no longer bound to specific office hours depending on their role, of course. They tend to have work moments that can occur at any time of the day or night. They can work just as well in pajamas as they can in the typical business garb of the office dweller.

Call center agents have begun to see the added benefit of Presence in communicating readiness to take the next customer call. Many companies have also merged the call center agent role with that of the teleworker to save costs associated with maintaining facilities and infrastructure necessary in the traditional call center.

Regardless of job role or function, Presence has provided a real-time, yet subtle, way of communicating with others how to reach you, when to reach you, and, well, whether they can reach you at all. One thing is certain, there will be no calling of phone number after phone number in vain attempts to reach colleagues. A simple glance at the Presence status of your colleague can accomplish the same function without wasting the time.

Chapter 7

Cisco Unified Presence Federation

The purpose of this chapter is to better understand what Presence Federation is and how to leverage it with a Cisco-to-Cisco Solution and Cisco-to-Microsoft.

Federation Within Presence

To understanding Federation, you first need to know what Presence is.

Presence provides the ability to detect the electronic presence of other users who are connected to the Internet through a PC or mobile device and what state of availability they are currently at in real time.

Presence services are commonly provided through applications such as Instant Messaging (IM) clients or through the web with Cisco Webex Connect or Facebook, or many others that have the same type of features.

In IM, federated IM networks are those that enable communications across different IM clients and platforms, similar to the way e-mail enables people to communicate regardless of which e-mail client they choose to use. Federated IM networks are those that maintain an open directory that enables other IM networks to message their users.

Many federated IM networks communicate using an open standard, such as Jabber, that leverages the Extensible Messaging and Presence Protocol (XMPP). Networks using XMPP provide open communications with other XMPP-based networks.

Derived Presence

Cisco Unified Presence Server (CUPS) maintains a database of presentities or *Presence objects*. These presentities are typically the users and devices but could be other entities, such as applications. The CUPS server maintains the Presence or availability state of the contacts being watched or monitored and contact lists for these presentities.

The server collects information from *Presence Sources* associated with a user and creates a derived Presence state. For example, sources could have a phone registered to a communications manager, desktop client, or mobile device, or all these.

The server then enables application services and devices to subscribe and consume Presence information. A consumer could be a desktop client showing whether a contact is available with a colored icon to more advanced uses, such as the Cisco Unified Expert Advisor, which uses Presence data from Unified Presence to locate expert knowledge workers.

Through Derived Presence, the confidence in Presence and the availability state being trusted or correct is increased because you're getting Presence information aggregated from multiple devices. The more sources of information available, the easier it becomes to communicate the availability status and what device is best to use for communication.

Federated Presence Configuration on the Cisco Presence Server

This section covers the setup and configuration of Federation between Cisco and Cisco CUP Servers. The setup for both a Cisco-to-Cisco and Cisco-to-Microsoft environment are the same with small differences. These small differences will be called out in the steps that follow. More information for Cisco Presence installation can be found in Chapter 3, "Installing Cisco Unified Presence Server 7."

Adding a New Federation Domain

When adding a Federation Domain entry in the CUPS, the Presence gateway and the incoming access control list (ACL) for the federated domain entry are automatically placed into the configuration.

Note that it is not possible to view the Presence gateway that is associated with a Federated Domain on the CUP GUI. Administratively, the incoming ACL associated with a Federated Domain can be seen on the CUP interface but cannot be modified or deleted. The incoming ACL can be deleted only after the deletion of the Federated Domain entry that is associated with the ACL.

To add a new Federated Domain, use Figure 7-1 in performing the following steps:

Step 1.   Select **Cisco Unified Presence Administration > Presence > Inter Domain Federation**.

Step 2.   Click **Add New**.

Step 3.   Enter the Federated Domain name in the Domain Name field.

Step 4.   Enter a description that identifies the Federated Domain in the Description field.

Step 5.   Select **CUP to CUP** from the Integration Type menu.

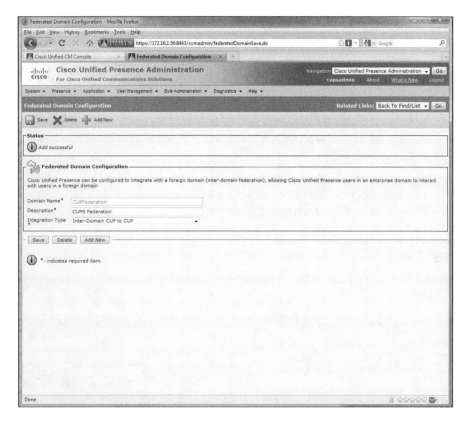

Figure 7-1   *Adding a New Cisco Unified Presence Federation*

Step 6.   Click Save.

> **Note**   The text string you enter in the Description field is displayed to the user in the CUPC privacy preferences available from the Manage Domains tab. The best practice is to enter a domain name that is easily recognized by the end user in this field.

E-mail Federation Enablement

When deploying CUP, the settings on both sides need to match up. If it requires e-mail address for federation, it will be necessary to enable the use of e-mail address because it is not on by default for interdomain federation.

The thing to note here is that CUP changes the SIP URI of each federated contact from userid@domain to the e-mail address of the contact.

Before enabling CUP to use the e-mail address for interdomain federation, it is important to note the following conditions:

■ If there has been no prior attempt to federate with the external domain, enable this setting *before* the end users begin to add any federated contacts.

■ It is important to alert the administrator of the external domain that you will be using e-mail addresses for purposes of federation. This is because the end users in the external domain must specify e-mail addresses when adding federated contacts to their contact lists.

■ If a federation is already in place with the external domain, it is important to inform the administrator of the external domain that users in that domain must remove any existing federated contacts from their contact lists and re-add them using e-mail addresses.

To verify or configure federation routing parameter, use Figure 7-2 in performing the following tasks:

Step 1. Select **Cisco Unified Presence Administration > Presence > Settings**.

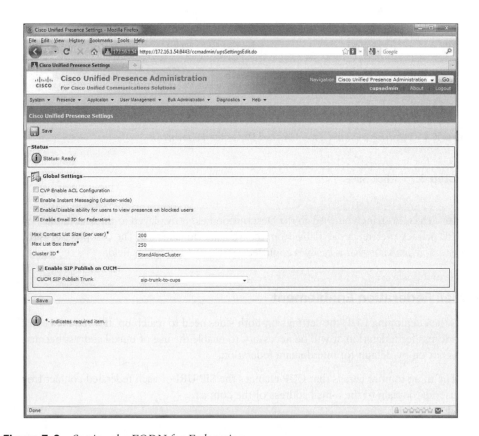

Figure 7-2 *Setting the FQDN for Federation*

Step 2.   Check the field for **Enable E-mail ID for Federation**.

Step 3.   If a warning message appears, read it and click **OK** to continue.

Step 4.   Click **Save** to finish.

Note   The FQDN value must match what was entered into the sip_federationtls entry in the public DNS for that CUP domain.

If the external FQDN (the hostname portion) is different than the internal FQDN, you need to specify the external FQDN in this field.

TLS Peer Subject Creation

As it is understood that the idea behind federation is the connecting of disparate networks to share features, some assumptions are made in this discussion. The first of these is that a Cisco Adaptive Security Appliance (ASA) will be performing firewall duties between these disparate networks.

The Cisco ASA acts as a TLS proxy between the CUP and the foreign server. This enables Cisco ASA to proxy TLS messages on behalf of the server (that initiates the TLS connection) and route the TLS messages from the proxy to the client. The TLS proxy decrypts, inspects, and modifies the TLS messages as required on the incoming leg, and then re-encrypts traffic on the return leg.

The Cisco ASA has a TLS Proxy feature that enables it to terminate TLS connections from the outside and pass necessary information on to their respective hosts, in this case the Presence Server. Within the internal CUP enterprise deployment, the Cisco ASA provides firewall, Port Address Translation (PAT), and TLS proxy functionality in the DMZ to terminate the incoming connections from the public Internet and permit traffic from specific federated domains.

Any CUP server can initiate a message to an external domain via the Cisco ASA. When the external domain sends replies to these messages, the replies are sent directly back to the CUP server that initiated the message via the Cisco ASA.

During the import of the Cisco ASA security certificate onto CUP, the Cisco ASA is automatically input as a TLS Peer Subject on CUP. This removes the need to manually add Cisco ASA as a TLS peer subject on CUP.

By adding the ASA security certificate, the administration overhead is alleviated of having to manually adjust the parameters. This enables the presence server and ASA to communicate securely.

To verify the TLS Peer Subject Creation, perform the following tasks:

Step 1.   Select **Cisco Unified Presence Administration > System > Security > TLS Peer Subjects**, as shown in Figure 7-3.

Step 2.   Click **Add New**.

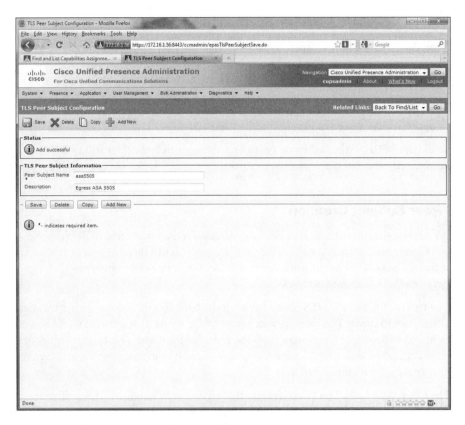

Figure 7-3 *Adding TLS Peer Subjects in CUPSs*

Step 3.   Enter the external FQDN of the Access Edge Server in the Peer Subject Name
field. This value must match the subject CN of the certificate that the
Microsoft Access Edge server presents.

Step 4.   Enter the name of the Access Edge or Access Proxy server in the
Description field.

Step 5.   Click **Save**.

When the creation of the new TLS peer subject is complete, you must restart the SIP
Proxy Service. Additionally, you will need the newly created TLS peer subject added to a
Peer Subject List. The following are the steps to take to put the Peer Subject into the Peer
Subject List:

Step 1.   Select **Cisco Unified Presence Administration > System > Security > TLS
Context Configuration**, as shown in Figure 7-4.

Step 2.   Click **Find**.

Step 3.   Click **Default_Cisco_UP_SIP_Proxy_Peer_Auth_TLS_Context**.

Step 4.   Select all ciphers from the list of available TLS ciphers.

Step 5.   Click the arrow to move these cipher selections to Selected TLS Ciphers.

Step 6.   From the list of available TLS peer subjects, click the TLS peer subject that you configured in the previous section.

Step 7.   Click the arrow to move the selected TLS peer subject to Selected TLS Peer Subjects.

Step 8.   Check **Disable Empty TLS Fragments** if you are federating with Microsoft OCS.

Step 9.   Click **Save**.

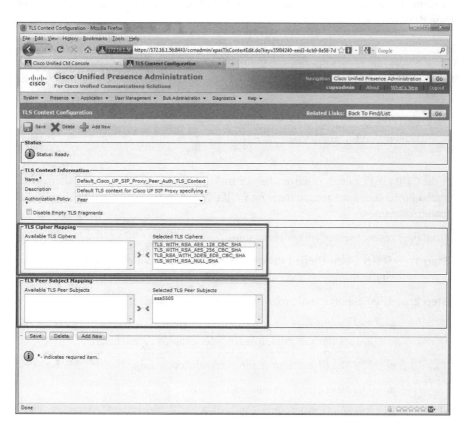

Figure 7-4   *Configuring TLS Peer Subject Lists in CUPS*

DNS Configuration

CUP must publish a DNS SRV record for the CUP domain to make it possible for other domains to discover the CUP server through DNS SRV. The Microsoft deployment requires CUP to publish a DNS SRV record for the CUP domain because the configuration of CUP is required so that it can act as a public IM provider on the Access Edge server.

CUP deployments need a DNS SRV record that points to _sipfederationtls._tcp.*CUP_domain*. Port 5061 is used and *CUP_domain* is the name of the CUP domain. This DNS SRV should point to the public FQDN of the routing CUP server.

For CUP to discover the foreign domain, a DNS SRV record must exist in the DNS server of the foreign domain that points to the FQDN of the external interface of the foreign domain.

Note   Use the following sequence of commands from a Windows command prompt to perform a DNS SRV lookup:

```
nslookup
set type=srv
_sipfederationtls._tcp.domain
```

If the CUP server cannot discover the external domain using DNS SRV, an alternative method is to configure a static route on CUP that points to the external interface of the foreign domain.

From the Presence server, follow these steps:

Step 1.   Select **Cisco Unified Presence Administration > Presence > Routing > Static Routes**, as shown in Figure 7-5.

Step 2.   Configure the static route parameters as follows:

- The Destination Pattern value needs to be reversed and must be in the following format: .com.*domain*.*, for example: .com.cisco.*.

- The Next Hop value is the external Access Edge FQDN or IP address.

- The Next Hop Port number is 5061.

- The Route Type value is domain.

- The Protocol Type is TLS.

Step 3.   Click **Save**.

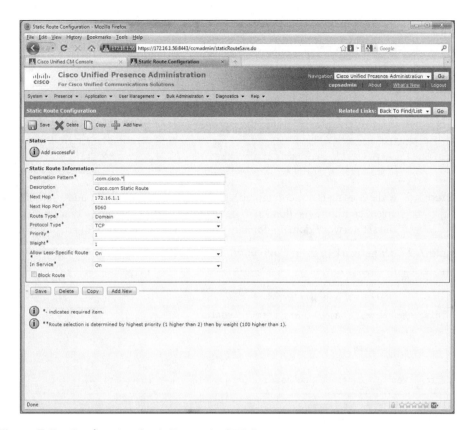

Figure 7-5 *Configuring Static Routes in CUPS*

Command-Line Interface Configuration of the Presence Domain

Because DHCP automatically assigns the domain, DNS, and IP address, this is not a necessary configuration unless DHCP has not been enabled.

If DHCP is not enabled, use the following procedure to configure the CUP domain from the CLI:

Step 1.   Log in to the administrator CLI on CUP.

Step 2.   Enter the **show network eth0** command to display the current network settings. Example 7-1 shows the output of this command.

Example 7-1   show network eth0 *Command*

```
admin:show network eth0
Ethernet 0
DHCP          : disabled        Status     : up
IP Address    : 172.16.1.56     IP Mask    : 255.255.000.000
Link Detected : yes             Mode       : Auto disabled, N/A, N/A
```

```
Duplicate IP : no

DNS
Primary        :                        Secondary  :
Options        :
Domain         :
Gateway        : 172.16.1.1 on Ethernet 0
admin:
```

Step 3. If the domain is not configured, as in the preceding example, and DHCP is disabled, configure the domain to be the same as the CUP proxy domain. Enter the **set network domain domain-name** command, as shown in Example 7-2.

Example 7-2 set network domain *Command*

```
admin:set network domain cisco.com
             ***    W A R N I N G    ***
This command will cause the system to restart.


            Do you want to continue ?


Enter "yes" to continue and restart or any other key to abort: yes
```

Step 4. Enter **y** at the prompt to confirm the changes.

Step 5. This server automatically restarts. This can take as long as 5 minutes.

Step 6. When the server has restarted, access the console again, and enter the **show network eth0** command to confirm you have configured the domain, as shown in Example 7-3.

Example 7-3 show network eth0 *Command*

```
admin:show network eth0
Ethernet 0
DHCP          : disabled          Status     : up
IP Address    : 172.16.1.56       IP Mask    : 255.255.000.000
Link Detected : yes               Mode       : Auto disabled, N/A, N/A
Duplicate IP  : no

DNS
Primary        :                        Secondary  :
Options        :
Domain         : cisco.com
Gateway        : 172.16.1.1 on Ethernet 0
admin:
```

Federated Presence Configuration on Microsoft OCS

The following sections describe the steps to configure Federated Presence on Microsoft OCS.

OCS Server Configuration

The Microsoft OCS server has several areas that need to be addressed to make federation possible between OCS and CUP. Note that the tasks herein are not highly detailed as has been the case throughout the rest of this book. It is not the authors' intent to focus on Microsoft OCS configuration tasks. They will, however, be outlined here so that the processes can be further researched.

The areas that will be covered in this section are all configuration tasks performed on the OCS server itself and are as follows:

- Global Federation setting enablement

- Access Edge server address configuration

- Front End Federation setting

- Enabled users for Microsoft Office Communicator (MOC) and Federation

Additionally, though not covered herein, you might want to configure security certificates on the OCS server because it will be required to properly communicate with the Access Edge Server. This requires a Certificate Authority to complete the task.

Global Federation Setting Enablement

To enable federation, perform the following tasks in the Microsoft OCS Configuration Utility on the OCS server, as shown in Figure 7-6:

Step 1. Launch the Microsoft OCS Configuration utility by clicking **Start > Administrative Tools > Microsoft Office Communications Server**.

Step 2. Right-click the Forest name and select **Properties > Global Properties > Federation** tab in the left pane.

Step 3. Check **Enable Federation** and **Public IM Connectivity**.

Step 4. Enter the FQDN and the port number for the internal interface of the Access Edge server.

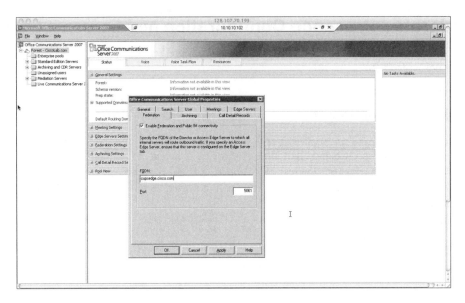

Figure 7-6 *Enabling Federation in OCS*

Access Edge Server Address Configuration

To enter the Access Edge Server address configuration, perform the following tasks in the Microsoft OCS Configuration Utility on the OCS server, as shown in Figure 7-7.

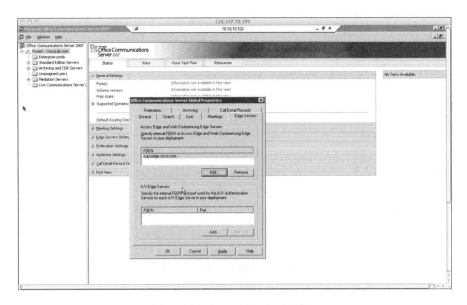

Figure 7-7 *Access Server Address Configuration in OCS*

Step 1. Launch the Microsoft OCS Configuration utility by clicking **Start > Administrative Tools > Microsoft Office Communications Server**.

Step 2. Select **Properties > Global Properties > Edge Servers** in the global forest branch in the left pane.

Step 3. Click **Add** in the Access Edge and Web Conferencing Edge Servers window.

Step 4. Enter the FQDN for the internal interface of the Access Edge server.

Front End Federation Setting

To configure the Front End Federation setting, perform the following tasks in the Microsoft OCS Configuration Utility on the OCS server, as shown in Figure 7-8.

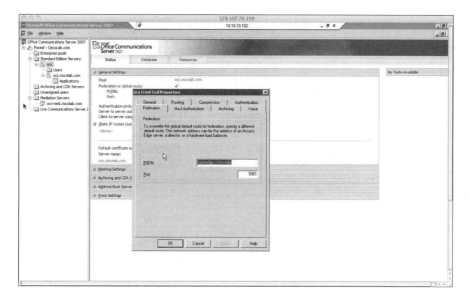

Figure 7-8 *Enabling Federation in OCS Front End Servers*

Step 1. Expand the **Standard Edition Servers** menu item, right-click **OCS** and select **Properties > Front End Properties > Federation Tab** in the front-end server branch in the left pane.

Step 2. Enter the FQDN of the Federation Server and, if available, Check **Enable Federation** and **Public IM Connectivity**.

Note For each front-end server that will be federating, the federation setting needs to be enabled.

Enable Users for MOC and Federation

To enable MOC user Federation, perform the following tasks in the Microsoft OCS Configuration Utility on the OCS server, as shown in Figure 7-9:

Step 1.   Click **Users** in the left pane of the Microsoft OCS Configuration Utility, and select the user in question from the right pane. Right-click the user and ensure that the required boxes are checked and are enabled for MOC (Enable Federation and Enable Public IM Connectivity).

Step 2.   If the user is not present in this list, enable the user for MOC in Microsoft Active Directory.

Step 3.   Enable the user for Public IM Connectivity in Microsoft AD. For single or multiple users, this can be done from the Configure Users Wizard. Launch the wizard by right-clicking the **Users** menu item in the left pane, and click **Configure Users**.

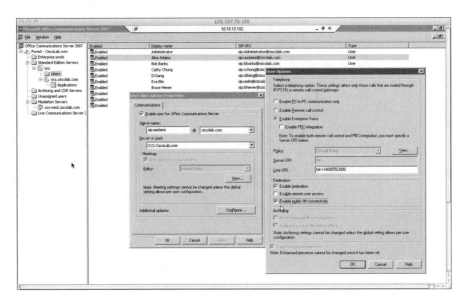

Figure 7-9   *Enabling MOC User Federation in OCS*

Access Edge Server Configuration

The Access Edge server, like the OCS server, requires configuration to ensure federation is enabled and will function. This section discusses the basic tasks necessary on the Access Edge server.

The configuration tasks in this section cover:

■   DNS configuration

■   CUPS configured as IM provider

- Verify access method settings

- Configure Access Edge server to use TLS

Additionally, though not covered here, you might want to configure security certificates on the Access Edge server because it will be required to properly communicate with the OCS server. This requires a Certificate Authority to complete the task.

DNS Configuration

For DNS servers, it is necessary to configure an external SRV record for all Access Edge servers that point to _sipfederationtls._tcp.*domain*, over port 5061, where *domain* is the name of the SIP domain of your organization. This SRV should point to the external FQDN of the Access Edge server.

CUPS Configured as IM Provider

To set the CUP server as IM provider, perform the following tasks:

Step 1.   Select **Start > Administrative Tools > Computer Management** on the external Access Edge server.

Step 2.   Expand the **Services and Applications** icon in the left pane. Right-click Microsoft Office Communications Server 2007 in the left pane, and then click **Properties**. Click the **IM Provider** tab.

Step 3.   Click **Add**.

Step 4.   Check **Allow the IM service provider**.

Step 5.   Define the IM service provider name, for example, the CUP server.

Step 6.   Define the network address of the IM service provider, in this case the public FQDN of the CUP server.

Step 7.   Ensure that the IM service provider is not marked as "public."

Step 8.   Click the filtering option **Allow all Communications from This Provider** option.

Step 9.   Click **OK**.

In the CUP deployment, it is a required to configure a DNS SRV record that points to _sipfederationtls._tcp.*CUP_domain*, where *CUP_domain* is the name of the CUP domain. This DNS SRV should point to the public FQDN of the CUP server.

Verify Access Method Settings

To verify the Access Method settings, perform the following tasks:

Step 1. Right-click Microsoft Office Communications Server 2007 in the console tree.

Step 2. Click **Properties > Access Methods**.

Step 3. Check **Federation**.

Step 4. Check **Allow discovery** if you are using DNS SRV.

Configure Access Edge Server to Use TLS

To enable the Access Edge Server to leverage TLS, perform the following tasks:

Step 1. Select **Start > Administrative Tools > Local Security Policy** to open the Local Security Policy.

> **Note** If you are configuring this on a domain controller, the path is **Start > Administrative Tools > Domain Controller Security Policy**.

Step 2. Click **Security Settings > Local Policies > Security Options** in the console tree.

Step 3. Double-click the FIPS security setting in the details pane.

Step 4. Enable the FIPS security setting.

Step 5. Click **OK**.

Summary

The configuration of Presence and Federation can be quite involved, so having a reference point of steps to use can help provide for a cleaner installation and smoother operation of the expected results.

This chapter defined Federation and Derived Presence, and provided configuration details of Cisco and Microsoft, which can assist in making for an easier deployment.

Chapter 8

Leveraging Cisco Unified Presence in Vertical Markets

The purpose of this chapter is to provide some real-world ideas of how the Cisco solution can offer enhanced productivity to specific vertical markets, such as healthcare, government, and retail. Basic Presence is mostly viewed as a "nice to have" when using applications such as Instant Messaging or chat, web conferencing, and so on, but is rarely viewed as a true productivity tool in an enterprise environment.

In the current economic condition, there needs to be solid return on investment for any solution being considered, and the Cisco Unified Communications (CUC) solution can provide this with some of that return in the form of increased productivity and not just "lower monthly payments." Keep in mind what was outlined in Chapter 2, "Cisco Unified Presence Overview," regarding the solution of Presence and that the productivity from Cisco Unified Presence Server (CUPS) extends beyond that of the ability to see the status of an individual but how to make communication decisions based on a person's projected status, time of day rules, calendar, desired interaction level, and so on. Leveraging all these parameters is what can increase productivity.

To illustrate these examples, this chapter describes solutions discussed in each vertical market with CUP as a core component of the solution. There are solutions that leverage partner applications from Cisco Technology Developer Program built on the development framework that Cisco has made available to partners and customers.

Basic Productivity Enhancements

Chapter 2 went through an overview of Cisco Unified Presence and touched on some of the benefits that end users can experience in everyday communication. This section reviews some of those to establish some baseline productivity enhancement users can attain in almost any work environment. We've seen how Presence enables the devices in the network to interact and to derive, as it were, a user's Presence status at a given moment. Figure 8-1 revisits the manner in which the roles of Presence sources and Presence Consumers meet in providing derived Presence.

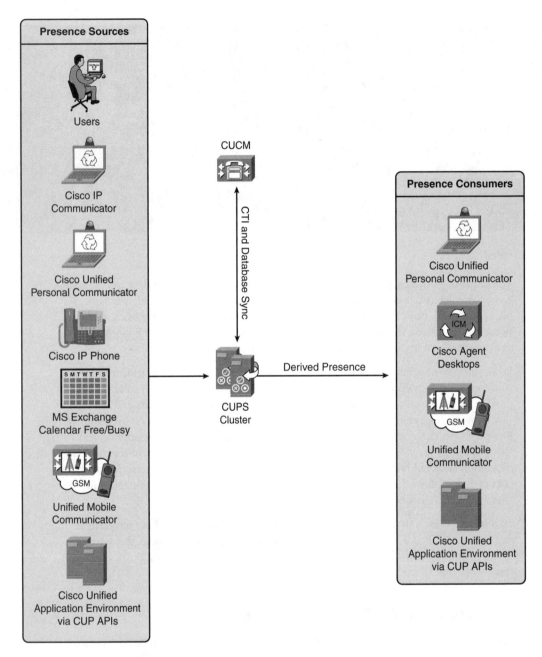

Figure 8-1   *Derived Presence*

The core component of the Cisco solution is the Cisco Unified Presence Server (CUPS).
This component is basically an aggregation of Presence information regarding specific
identities or presentities. The boundary placed on this is largely due to enterprise policy;

however, some limitations currently exist from a technological standpoint. Currently, the CUPS server can establish only interdomain federation relationships with Microsoft Office Communications Server (OCS) and IBM Sametime Server.

The next major release of the CUP solution will introduce new interdomain and intra-domain federation relationships. These federation capabilities will easily extend to interenterprise federation capabilities. Figure 8-2 shows a simplified vision of this connectivity.

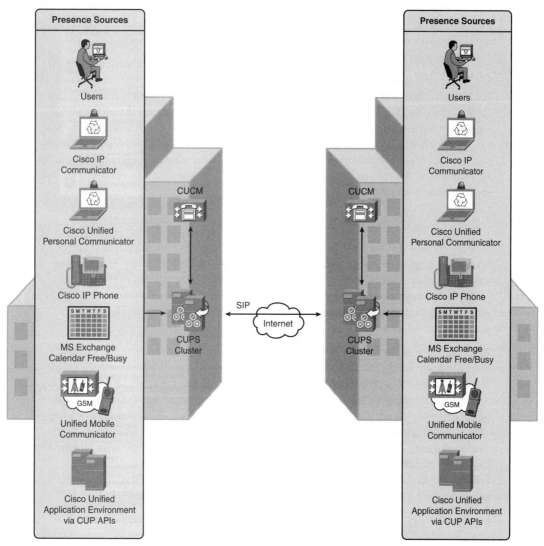

Figure 8-2 *Interdomain/Interenterprise Federation*

Corporations, hospitals, government agencies, and other entities wanting to share advanced collaborative capabilities have the option of creating secure connections between one another via the public Internet or via private, leased lines. SIP enables the two entities to share not only on-net calling, but features such as Presence, collaboration, and more. The features utilized day-to-day within an organization can now be extended to business partners.

This can greatly expand the potential boundaries for the Presence solution. The current Cisco Presence solution is more focused on the enterprise and business-to-business (B2B) interactions. The next few sections cover specific business vertical scenarios, but there are basic enhancements that are good to review first.

The simplest Presence integration is built in to Cisco Unified Communications Manager (CUCM), which does have a basic Presence server component that offers the ability to see Presence indicators focused on a user's line status. The main benefit here is that the Presence information attained in a corporate directory or missed calls list on the phone empowers the user to quickly make decisions on who they want to call based on the status of that person's line. A simple example is that of a callback scenario. A person comes back to the office from lunch and quickly sees on his phone that he missed three calls. He navigates to the missed calls directory and notices that the first two entries in the list show that the line is off-hook, so those users must be on a phone call. The user easily assesses that those two users cannot answer the callback, so the user first attempts the callback to the third person on the list.

How much time was saved in that one interaction? How many times does that type of scenario happen to each user every day? In determining the productivity enhancement that a user might experience with Presence, it is important to think about the normal communication steps taken every day. The easier or more intuitive communication decisions can be made, the more productivity can be realized, and the more flexible it is to each user.

Realizing more out of our conversations is the next step. In most environments today, there are many situations where two people are on a phone call and are discussing something that relates to a problem, future event, document, and so on. In those conversations, a significant amount of time is spent describing something to get a point or image across to the other person that could better understand if there were a visual component to it. These conversations are often initiated with some other goal in mind, and either are ended with each party not fully satisfied with the result or another meeting is scheduled that might include some conferencing resources such as video or web collaboration to enhance the visual experience. How much time is saved by having immediate ad-hoc access to these types of collaboration resources at the click of a button?

Leveraging Cisco Unified Personal Communicator (CUPC) with CUPS as the core Presence aggregator and integrator to network services such as web collaboration, audio and video conferencing, and so on allows for this initial audio conversation to be immediately escalated to a video call or a web collaboration session so that the on-demand nature of the conversation can be met, objectives fulfilled, and everyone leaving with the feeling that time wasn't wasted. How critical can that be in the business world today?

Many more scenarios exist and this section, along with the following sections, are here to provide some illustrations on how Presence and the associated applications that make up the CUC portfolio can actually be used in real-world environments. This certainly isn't a definitive chapter, but it is supposed to get the proverbial "wheels spinning."

Healthcare

Healthcare is a vertical market in desperate need of enhanced productivity at all levels. In industry terms, information technology in healthcare is labeled as Healthcare Information Technology (HIT), and it covers almost every facet of the healthcare information technology business. This is a unique market to operate in, with specific needs that Presence can help address. This section is solely focused on ideas around leveraging CUPS and the associated applications and in no way addresses standards, legal or otherwise, which might exist in implementing them. The following sections outline a few conversation flows that interact with CUPS. In doing so, it would be prudent to illustrate the basic components active in making these flows work, and Figure 8-3 does just that.

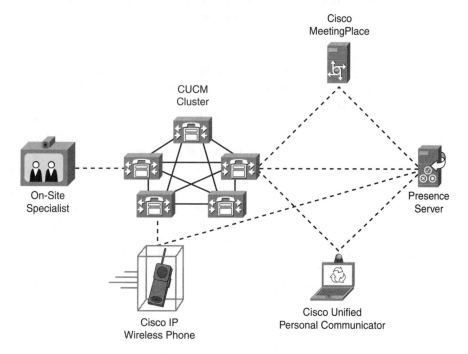

Figure 8-3 *Scenario Collaborative Components*

Nurse Communications

One of the focus areas in healthcare is that of nurses, who communicate with just about every person who could possibly be involved in a medical practice. They help with the patient and interact with the doctors, pharmacists, administration, and so on. The challenges associated in interacting with all these people can be helped with Cisco Presence solutions. Presence can be leveraged in ways that enable nurses to not only be more efficient in everyday processes, such as bed checks, but also enables them to be more responsive in emergency situations.

Application integration services provide nurse connectivity from common patient care platforms that monitor patient vitals and integrate them into the CUC platform. Nurses can go through their rounds, and as they complete itemized tasks, use network wireless phones that not only provide location services of where the nurse is in the building but also enable the nurse to mark a specific room as complete through the application on the phone. Should an emergency occur while the nurse is on rounds, notifications can be automatically sent out to all nurse phones for immediate response with the location of the emergency. This enables the nurse to be productive during normal business and responsive in an emergency without having to constantly move back and forth between tasks and the main desk.

Nurses might also have the task of confirming lab results or orders, answering patient questions regarding medication or results, and getting back to doctors for many reasons, all of which require many different communication interactions. This lends itself to being caught up in "phone tag," calling multiple numbers, and so on, all with periods of time eaten up in waiting. The ability to have contacts that are always being communicated with in a list on a desktop application and have features, such as an individual's current status, click to dial, click to collaborate, click to conference, and so forth, would not only greatly enhance the communication experience but also increase the speed of any result.

A nurse who needs to get results for the hospital lab can immediately look at the status of all the contacts in the lab and select the one that is marked available to initiate a quick Instant Message chat. Quickly into the chat, the lab technician realizes he needs to speak to the nurse and clicks the phone icon to immediately place an audio call. During the call, they realize they need to look at the lab results together and discuss in more detail, so the nurse clicks the collaboration button and a web collaboration immediately opens and they are both looking at the lab results together, with the ability to annotate the document and record the interaction for later review by them or someone else on the team. This is all done without multiple calls and rescheduling for advanced resources.

How would this impact the business of a healthcare facility? Keep in mind that some things such as interaction with patient care applications require third-party solutions or middleware that interacts with industry-standard applications and the CUC solutions.

Doctor Communications

Doctors are also spread thin, with their knowledge and expertise being needed in many places at once and having their own medical practices, specializing in specific areas of medicine, with the ability to communicate or consult across many cases with their practice peers is critical. Leveraging the services provided by CUPS and CUPC enables doctors to stay in constant communication with their peers, nurses, pharmacists, and so on so that they can communicate with necessary resources as quickly as possible and have available, easy access to advanced services such as voice, video, and web collaboration.

Doctors can leverage such tools as CUPC and high-definition video provided by the Cisco TelePresence solution integrated into to a CUC system that provides remote clinics or other hospitals with the capability to leverage a pool of doctors to do a consult without the travel requirements associated with those destinations. As additional resources become necessary because of complexity or responsibility, specialists (radiologist, anesthesiologist, neurologists, cardiologists, and so on) might need to be quickly brought into the conversation. The CUPC display might show which doctors for each specialty are available at this moment. They could then be reached and brought into the conversation via desktop video or via TelePresence. Even geography is no longer a barrier. Off-site specialists could be just as easily accessed as those on the premises.

Mobility is a key feature part of the CUCM solution that offers single-number reach functionality doctors find quite attractive. This provides the capability to reach a doctor on a single number and have multiple devices called at the same time, so the doctor can answer on the device that is readily accessible. These remote devices and the time of day this feature is enabled can be controlled entirely by the doctor. This not only increases doctor mobility, but also dramatically enhances the chances doctors can be reached on the first attempt.

To accomplish these types of interactions, the same core components are used as outlined in this book: CUCM, CUPS, CUPC, and Cisco TelePresence.

Public Sector

The public sector vertical has a rather large footprint and covers anything related to K-12 and higher education and state, county, and city governments all the way up to the federal government. Also falling within that realm are the departmental and institutional substructures of those governments. This includes all agencies (tax collectors, Department of Public Safety, tax offices, the IRS, and so on). Additionally, public utilities and healthcare facilities are included under the public sector classification. As you might imagine, there are more than a few needs to be addressed within such a diverse market space. The following sections outline some ideas associated with government and how CUPS and associated applications can help provide service enhancements, continuity, and so forth.

Emergency Services

Emergency services generally cover police, ambulance, and fire departments providing the services of security, safety, and rescue. Communication is extremely critical to these groups to provide the best emergency services available and do so with rapid response, accuracy, and real-time information. In emergency or disaster recovery situations, the ability to communicate is vital. Figure 8-4 shows an addition to the Cisco collaborative technology arsenal that facilitates communications in such situations; it's called Cisco IP Interoperability and Collaboration System (IPICS).

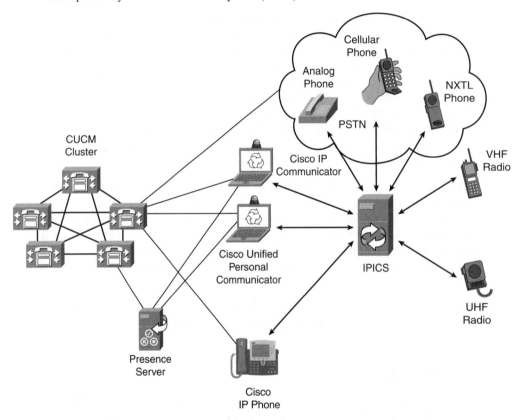

Figure 8-4   *Cisco IPICS*

It's sometimes easiest to think of IPICS as a conference bridge of sorts. CUCM still performs all the call control functions associated with call setup and teardown. IPICS merges radio signals from disparate radio systems, IP Phones, PSTN phones, and more into a single stream that is then sent to all devices. It provides full voice connectivity to nearly any device on any network. In emergency situations, everyone can communicate using the devices they have on hand.

Network services such as Presence offer the capability for emergency dispatchers to have police units respond to a potential robbery call and the network aware of police location during the response. The responding unit can have area cameras automatically direct video information to their unit as they approach the scene. This provides not only real-time information, but also is done automatically giving the responding police critical information about the scene they are approaching, and their focus can be on the task at hand rather than figuring out how to get the technology to work. It is this intelligent network that allows for services such as video to be easily or automatically accessed. Providing the ease of use is what is critical to adoption rate and realization of the benefits the services provide. It's one thing to provide video access to street cameras to police, but what would the adoption rate be if the process was manual and cumbersome? In this specific scenario, automatic transition is the best way to ensure not only adoption of the necessary technology but also the safety of the police. Intelligence in the network is key to this, and when considering this scenario and any other, remember that the easier the process can be made, the more accepted and used the process will become.

City and County

City and county governments deal with zoning and land deeds as an everyday part of business, and they can leverage many benefits offered by the CUC system. Land management is a critical piece to a city and county government that can easily benefit from enhanced speed and productivity offered by CUPS and CUPC. The basic interaction is similar to what has been covered already, but understanding the application of the technology helps to have it adopted.

A local development business is looking to expand its business and needs to buy some land. It needs to check the current plat and zoning information filed with the local county office to start its due diligence on the project. The time associated with this process is typically long and can consist of several trips to the municipal and county records offices to get everything that is required. From a local government perspective, when this type of request comes in, the person in the zoning offices can leverage the CUPC client to see who in the clerk's offices is available to find the plat information and either have it delivered or shared over a web collaboration session. The specific conversation path is similar to that of the nurse scenario, in which it can start with an Instant Message and be escalated to voice/video and web collaboration. This greatly increases the productivity of the government offices in addition to the satisfaction of the individual.

What are other areas in government where multiple interactions occur that are often frustrating for the local citizens? These are ideal areas to apply the ideas of CUC and intelligent networks to see where these interactions can be minimized and offer higher results to the customers.

Retail

Retail stores often have large groups of people travel all over the world to locate merchandise to sell. These groups of people are widely dispersed and need to collaborate with corporate offices at all times during their review and buying process of potential products. They need to discuss manufacturing capabilities with other companies, market analyses, and so on, and considering the challenges with communicating with a team scattered across the globe, CUPS has some unique ways in addressing these challenges.

Consider, for example, a jewelry or antiquities purchaser. Individual team members might be independently seeking the most marketable items. After an item is located, it might be prudent to call for a peer review to validate the find. Rather than purchasing the item and returning to a central location, items can be reviewed in real time by individuals or groups.

The CUPC client can be utilized in identifying immediately available team members with the required skill-set necessary to authenticate the find and assess its immediate and potential future value. When contact is made with the relevant expert, the communication can be escalated from Instant Messaging (IM) to voice call or, as is more likely the case, to a video call.

Video is necessary in this type of interaction to enable corporate members to look at the potential product. A typical webcam might provide enough of an initial viewing to make an initial field review that indicates that the item warrants further discussion and negotiation. High definition (HD)–capable video endpoints can augment communications in allowing for an in-depth viewing of potential product purchasing. If additional in-depth product review is necessary or additional models of a particular product need to be seen, Cisco TelePresence can be used to deliver the in-person, high-definition video required for individual and group review interaction. Figure 8-5 shows an example of a meeting that brings the necessary parties together regardless of their location or means of access.

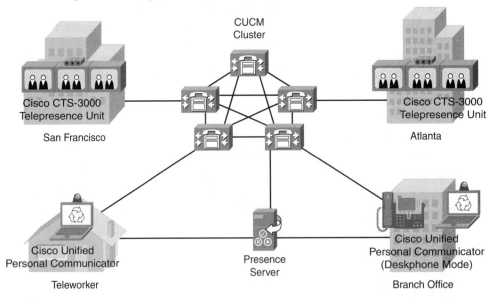

Figure 8-5 *Collaboration Removes Boundaries and Obstacles*

The initial review looks promising enough to order a market test order. During the market test phase, the extended team members can keep constant contact with each other with CUPS in order to address any immediate issues that arise. This type of interaction greatly increases the speed to market for retailers and gives them the edge needed to stay ahead of the competition.

Summary

There is an almost endless number of communication scenarios that Cisco Unified Communications (CUC) and Cisco Unified Presence (CUP) can impact in a positive way. This chapter outlined some of the basic productivity enhancements and provided some examples in major vertical markets. The idea is to look at common interactions with a different understanding of what is available in the network. The simpler it is to access advanced services, the more they will be adopted. This level of communication services requires that they be delivered by an advanced and intelligent network. Leveraging Cisco development partners to address vertical specific requirements is an advantage to customers to ensure the best possible service delivery. The healthcare integration is an excellent example of providing a communications foundation through CUC and industry applications, such as Emergin, for a comprehensive solution.

Chapter 9

Troubleshooting Cisco Unified Presence

Overall, the Cisco Unified Presence (CUP) components of a Unified Communications (UC) solution are relatively simple. That is not to say that things cannot go wrong; it simply means that a limited number of issues might arise. This chapter covers some of the more common issues arising within CUP deployments. This includes both Cisco Unified Presence Server (CUPS) and the Cisco Unified Personal Communicator (CUPC) portions of the solution.

To add some method to the potential madness, so to speak, this chapter is structured in a beginning-to-end manner. That is, the troubleshooting discussion covers installation and moves on to configuration of both CUPS and CUPC components. With that in mind, it might be prudent to discuss some of the tools and diagnostics utilities available specifically for troubleshooting.

CUPS Troubleshooting Tools

Certain tools are built in to the CUPS Administration page that are extremely useful in diagnosing issues and simply viewing system status. Launching the CUPS Administration Utility with your browser, log in to the system. The interface looks similar to the CUCM interface. When installed and integrated, the CUPS admin page is reachable via the Navigation bar in the top-right corner of the CUCM interface. The names of the CUPS servers appear in the list beneath the Serviceability and OS Administration options.

> **Note**   One of the most helpful tools in Cisco UC Components is the Help page. While in the Administration Utility for CUCM, CUPS, Unity Connection, and so on, click **Help > This Page** for a field-by-field description of the information needed to configure a particular page or feature. These Help pages provide what might be the best documentation and information on particular topics anywhere within each system or online. This is especially true in the Serviceability pages. If you're curious about a service and questioning whether to enable it, read the Help pages. Use them often.

When logged in to the CUPS Administration page, hover the mouse pointer over, or click, the Diagnostics tab. Figure 9-1 shows the options available under this tab.

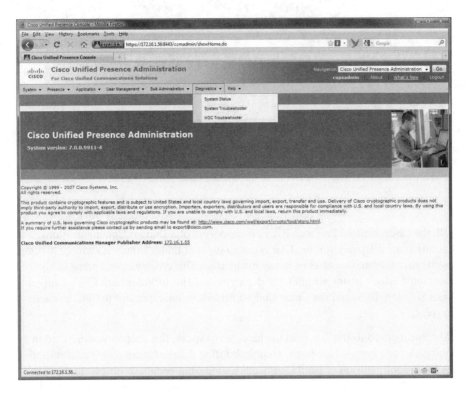

Figure 9-1   *CUPS Diagnostics Options*

The options available from the Diagnostics tab include utilities for System Status, System Troubleshooter, and MOC Troubleshooter.

System Status Page

The System Status page is purely informational. Figure 9-2 shows the System Status page.

As shown in the figure, the information on this page is fairly basic. All the fields are read-only. They are populated in a snapshot manner. That is, the information is gathered when the System Status page is clicked. They do not refresh without administrator intervention (that is, pressing F5 or clicking **Diagnostics > System Status** again).

As CUPS 7 introduced the concept of a Presence Cluster, the CUPS Publisher address is listed along with the Sync Status, including the time/date of the last successful sync, with the CUCM Publisher. In addition to the Sync Status, the following information is also included:

■   Number of end users

■   Number of phone devices

- Number of licensed Cisco Unified Presence (CUP) end users

- Number of licensed Cisco Unified Personal Communicator (CUPC) end users

- Number of assigned Microsoft Office Communicator (MOC) end users

- Number of end users associated with an inter-cluster peer

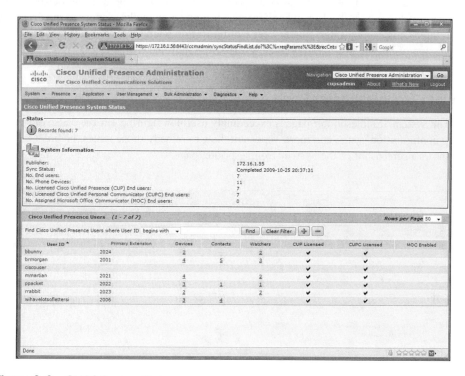

Figure 9-2 *CUPS System Status*

The number of phone devices is the count of phones associated with Presence users. This includes the physical desk phones and the CUPC clients associated with the Presence-enabled end users.

Note the user count breakdown. The first user count is the total number of users included in the sync from the CUCM Publisher. This is the count of users regardless of whether they have been licensed for Presence through the **CUCM System-> Licensing > Capabilities Assignment** page. Figure 9-2 shows that there are seven total users, yet only five have been assigned as CUP end users. One of those users is the LDAP user I created for all my LDAP synchronization services. The other is a new user I created specifically for this chapter. His name is Wow Ihavelotsoflettersinmyname. There will be a section discussing an increasingly common topic of how to deal with users with long names.

After the boxes are checked in the CUCM Capabilities Assignment page, the user count for licensed CUP end users increments. When a user is enabled for CUPC usage, the corresponding number increments as well. If there are Microsoft Office Communicator (MOC)–enabled users on the CUP cluster, the MOC user count will increment. Finally, the number of intercluster peer users is tracked.

Intercluster peering is a new capability in CUPS 7. It was discussed in some detail in Chapter 2, "Cisco Unified Presence Overview." The number of end users associated with an inter-cluster peer displays only after you configure an intercluster peer in the **Presence > Inter-Clustering > Inter-cluster Peer Configuration** window. This enables the transmission of instant messages/presence status across multiple CUP clusters.

System Troubleshooter Page

The System Troubleshooter page is exceedingly useful in figuring out the cause of specific configuration issues, and more important, how to remedy those issues. Figure 9-3 shows a screenshot of the System Troubleshooter page.

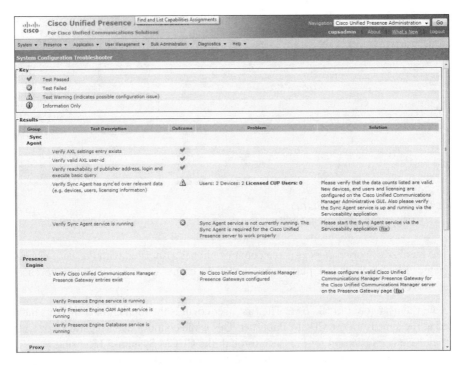

Figure 9-3 *CUPS System Troubleshooter*

Various critical components are arranged into groups according to their function. Each is tested for proper functionality (that is, configuration). There is a legend at the top of the page explaining the various symbols, but they're fairly self-explanatory. The difference between a green check and a red X are quite well known. If there is a misconfiguration, a red circle with an X appears next to that particular item. If it tests successfully, it gets the green check. The figure shows a couple of examples of failed features. Alongside each failure is an explanation and a link to the page where the failure can be remedied.

As an example of how to make use of the System Troubleshooter, let's walk through a real problem.

Notice that problems are in the configuration. It seems that our AXL Sync Agent is not happy. When a problem is presented, a solution is offered in the right column along with a **fix** link to the page where the changes need to be made. Figure 9-4 shows the CUCM Publisher page accessed by clicking the **fix** link.

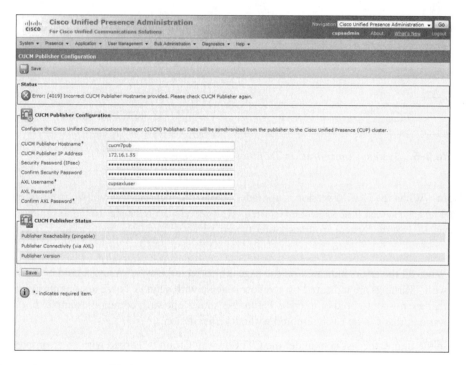

Figure 9-4 *CCM Publisher Page*

Evidently, it thinks I entered the publisher's name incorrectly as **cucm7pub**. Looking back at my documentation from the install of both the Presence server and the Communications Manager, I see that it is correct in that assertion. The name as entered during the install is **cm7pub**. Changing the name and saving the change provides the fix wanted by the System Troubleshooter page. Returning to it shows that one issue is corrected and the next one awaits. Figure 9-5 shows that we now have a green check by the Sync Agent entries.

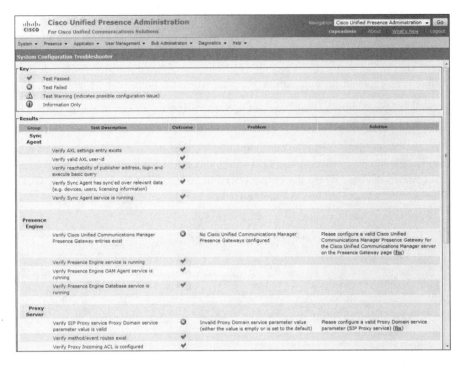

Figure 9-5 *System Configuration Troubleshooter Page*

Note When the CUCM version is upgraded, the Sync Agent Service will be stopped on the Presence server. It needs to be restarted on all servers in the cluster to begin functioning again. Use the System Troubleshooter to verify that all functions are working properly.

When all the errors indicated on the page are corrected, any warnings should be dealt with. Warnings are indicated by a yellow triangle with a ! in it. These are not always items that are misconfigured or in error. Figure 9-6 shows one such common example of a warning that can be easily ignored without repercussion.

In the figure, the last item under the CTI Gateway Group is marked with an error indicator. The item, **Verify If Any Users Are Currently MOC-Assigned**, is valid only when a Microsoft Office Communicator (MOC) integration has been configured on the CUPS server. In a typical CUP installation, this is not be the case. Therefore, you can ignore this warning. If an integration is to be configured, click the **fix** link. This takes you to the MOC User Assignment page. After users are assigned, the warning indicator changes to a green check mark, indicating successful test verification.

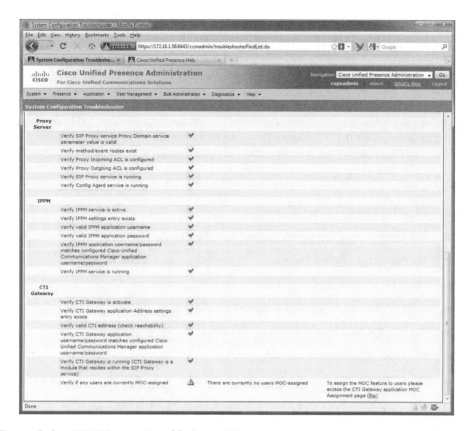

Figure 9-6 *CUPS System Troubleshooter Error*

MOC Troubleshooter Page

The intent behind the MOC Troubleshooter is to validate user configuration on the CUP side of the integration. Figure 9-7 shows a screenshot of the MOC Troubleshooter page.

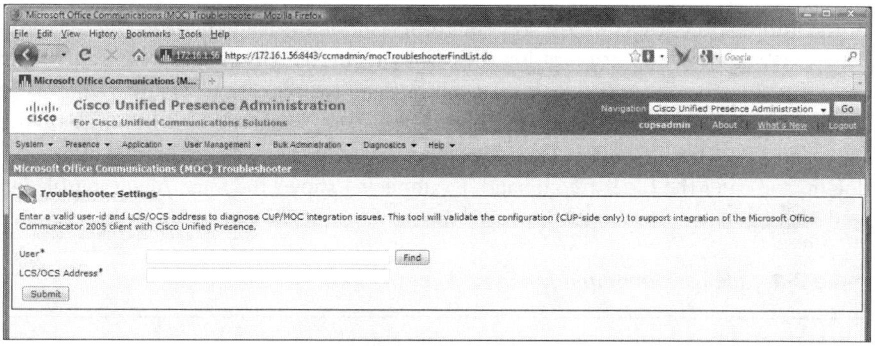

Figure 9-7 *CUPS MOC Troubleshooter Error*

Two fields are on the page, both of which require input. The user name must be a valid user configured in the system. The LCS/OCS Address is the address to which the integration has been configured. As with other queries on CUPS and the CUCM Admin pages, there is a **Find** button next to the User field. Clicking **Find** launches a pop-up window where you can enter a user query. Clicking **Find** in the pop-up window returns a list of all users. Click the one you want to query, and click **Add Selected**. Only one user at a time can be selected. The selected user's name will be entered into the User field automatically. At that point, enter the IP address of the Live Communication Server (LCS)/Office Communication Server (OCS) server, and then click **Submit** to initiate the validation test.

The test verifies the following:

- The CTI Gateway service is active.

- The Presence user is properly in sync with the CUCM.

- The user is licensed for Presence.

- The CTI Gateway Application user name and password are valid.

- The Preferred Proxy Listener transport type is not set to UDP.

- The LCS/OCS address is resolvable in DNS (if DNS is in use).

- The LCS/OCS address is reachable.

- The LCS/OCS address has a corresponding incoming access control list (ACL) entry.

- The LCS/OCS address has a corresponding outgoing ACL entry.

The MOC Troubleshooter functions in a fashion similar to the System Troubleshooter. If any of these tests fail, the results will be returned with a problem description and a suggested solution with supporting information. After implementing the suggested solution, rerun the MOC Troubleshooter until it returns no errors.

Trace Files

If the information offered in the System Troubleshooter is inadequate to find the problem, CUPS keeps a collection of log files. They might be requested by a Cisco TAC engineer if you open a case. The most relevant logs and their locations are the Sync Agent, SIP Proxy, and Presence Engine, which must be accessed via the CUPS Console directly or via an SSH Client. Connect to the Presence server through the chosen methodology, log in, and enter the **file list** command. Example 9-1 shows the Sync Agent log file list and location.

Example 9-1   file list *Command for Sync Agent Logs*

```
admin:file list activelog epas/trace/epassa/log4j
syncAgent.bin                          syncAgent00001.log
```

```
syncAgent00002.log                      syncAgent00003.log
syncAgent00004.log                      syncAgent00005.log
syncAgent00006.log                      syncAgent00007.log
syncagentStatus.log
dir count = 0, file count = 9
admin:
```

Example 9-2 shows the SIP Proxy log file list and location.

Example 9-2   file list *Command for SIP Proxy Logs*

```
admin:file list activelog epas/trace/esp/sdi
esp-sipdctl.txt                         esp00000001.txt
esp00000002.txt                         esp00000003.txt
esp00000004.txt                         esp00000005.txt
esp00000006.txt                         esp00000007.txt
esp00000008.txt                         esp00000009.txt
esp00000010.txt                         esp00000011.txt
esp00000012.txt                         esp-num.bin
dir count = 0, file count = 14
admin:
```

Example 9-3 shows the Presence Engine log file list and location.

Example 9-3   file list *Command for Presence Engine Logs*

```
admin:file list activelog epas/trace/epe/sdi
epe-dropReplication.script.txt          epe-dropReplication.txt
epe-executeSql.txt                      epe-pres-postinstall.txt
epe-repAgent.txt                        epe-setupReplication.script.txt
epe-setupReplication.txt                epe-startup.txt
epe00000001.txt                         epe00000002.txt
epe00000003.txt                         epe-num.bin
dir count = 0, file count = 12
admin:
```

It might well be that the command line is not for the faint of heart. If you are an administrator who prefers a graphical interface for troubleshooting and information gathering, Cisco has included the Real Time Monitoring Tool (RTMT) for CUPS. It can be installed from the **Application > Plugins** page. Figure 9-8 shows the Plugins page.

Download instructions and a description are included with each plugin entry listed on the page. When you first navigate to the page, like many others throughout the CUPS

Admin utility, it is blank. Click the **Find** button to list all available plug-ins. Unlike CUCM, in CUPS there are only three available plugins:

- **Cisco CallManager AXL SQL Toolkit:** A Java-based toolkit used in issuing and receiving SQL queries and receiving results. This utility communicates directly with the AXL interface built into the CUCM. The *.zip* file includes instructions and examples of how to utilize the tool.

- **Cisco Unified Real-Time Monitoring Tool for Linux:** Known as RTMT, this tool monitors real-time behavior of components within the CUPS Cluster. As noted, this is a Linux version of the tool.

- **Cisco Unified Real-Time Monitoring Tool for Windows:** Windows-based version of the RTMT.

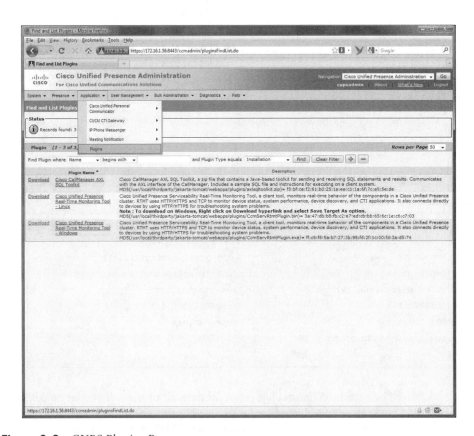

Figure 9-8 *CUPS Plugins Page*

Because this discussion is focused on troubleshooting, no more mention will be made of the AXL SQL Toolkit. The focus, from a troubleshooting perspective, falls squarely on the RTMT utility. This is the foremost tool in monitoring activity on the CUPS and

CUCM clusters in real time (as the name denotes). Figure 9-9 shows the Windows version of RTMT in use.

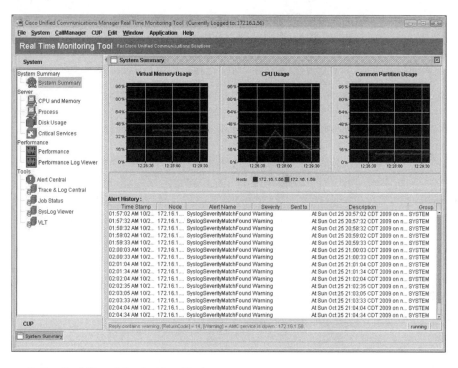

Figure 9-9 *Real-Time Monitoring Tool*

The figure shows just one of the many views and functions of the RTMT. Easily visible are real-time graphs of Virtual Memory Usage, CPU Usage, and Common Partition Usage. All CUPS servers in the cluster show on each of these three graphs. A legend below the three windows shows a colored box and Name/Address of each server in the cluster. At the point this screenshot was taken, the CUPS subscriber was inactive. Therefore, it is listed in the legend, but the RTMT is not showing any activity for it.

Below the graphical windows is an Alert history. Each alert contains a timestamp, associated CUPS node address, name, severity, description, and Group designation. At the bottom of the window, an alert can be seen complaining about the CUPS Subscriber, 172.16.1.58, AMC Service being down. You might think, instead, that it should be more worried about electrons flowing to the server because it was powered down at the time. Those alerts are, of course, there. They are simply scrolling along in the alert history.

By now, you might be asking what this tool, as pretty as it might be, has to do with a troubleshooting discussion. A few pages back, some discussion was put forth on trace files and their locations. Being somewhat less than motivated at times, I would prefer to have a tool gather those files, zip them up, and drop them somewhere easily accessible. The RTMT does just that. Figure 9-10 shows the RTMT trace file collection dialog page.

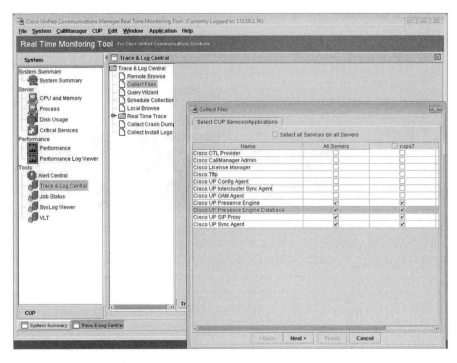

Figure 9-10   *Trace File Collection Dialog*

When RTMT is launched, click **Trace & Log Central** in the far left pane; then double-click **Collect Files** in the middle pane. The Collect Files dialog box pops up. Check the files you want to collect, and click **Next** at the bottom. Another page of files ready for collection is presented, but the files of interest for this discussion are all on the first page. Click **Next**. Figure 9-11 shows the final page in the Collect Files dialog.

It requests a time/date range and presents download options that enable you to specify the location of the files and whether to zip them. When all options are properly entered, click **Finish** to complete the file collection. You can view the files in the specified Download File Directory. If you are collecting them for upload to a case with Cisco TAC, go ahead and have it zip them so that you need to deal with only a single file when attaching the collected files to the case.

Troubleshooting CUCM/CUPS Dependencies

Like any installation, a number of things can be missed, mistyped, or simply just don't work. The goal of this section is to discuss some of the most common issues and their resolutions. Rather than go through specific scenarios, as will be done for other potential issues in this chapter, a summary of the specific dependencies on both the CUCM and CUPS servers is provided. This will allow a single source for not only troubleshooting but also configuration of future implementations with an at-a-glance capability.

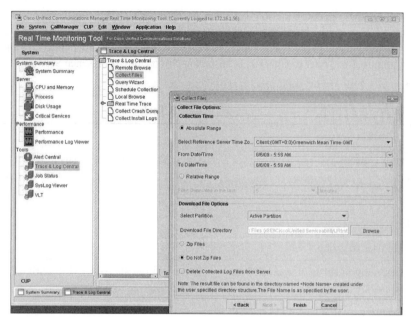

Figure 9-11   *Trace File Collection Dialog Continued*

Communications between the Presence servers and the CUCM Cluster depend on AXL, SIP, and CTI components. During the installation, you configured all these various components on both CUPS and CUCM. Figure 9-12 shows the interconnections between the CUCM cluster, CUPS, endpoints, and LDAP Directory server.

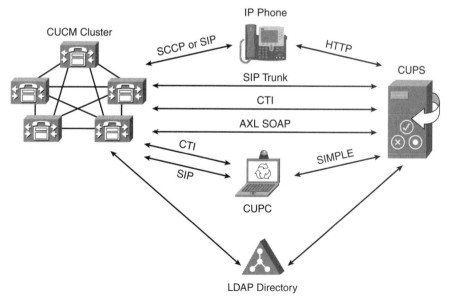

Figure 9-12   *CUPS/CUCM Connectivity*

Table 9-1 shows the configuration dependencies between CUCM and CUPS. The first step in troubleshooting the installation will be to verify that all of these dependencies are properly configured and in place. For a more in-depth discussion of the dependencies and how to configure them, refer to Chapter 3, "Installing Cisco Unified Presence Server 7."

Table 9-1 *CUCM-CUPS Dependencies*

CUCM Task	CUPS Task
Add Application Server: **a.** Add AXL group. **b.** Add Standard AXL API Access to group Roles. **c.** Add AXL user. **d.** Assign user to group.	Enter AXL User Credentials in Initial Install Wizard the first time CUPS Admin page is accessed.
Capabilities Assignment to enable CUP and CUPC for users.	Users will not show in CUPS until CUCM Capabilities Assignment is done.
Assign end users to Standard CTI Enabled group.	
Create SIP Trunk to CUPS (if multinode, need a SIP trunk to each node).	**a.** Select SIP Trunk in SIP Publish Trunk Settings. **b.** Enter CUCM Publisher Address as Presence GW in Presence Gateway Settings.
Create IPPM User: **a.** Create IPPM Phone Service. **b.** Subscribe phones to the service.	*Enter IPPM user credentials in IP PhoneMessenger Settings.*
Create CtiGW user and assign to Standard CTI-enabled group.	Enter CTI User Credentials and all CUCM addresses in CTI Gateway Settings.
	Set Proxy Domain in SIP Proxy Service Parameters.
	Load License files for CUPS nodes and users.
	Start Services ON Service Activation page.

CUCM Task	CUPS Task
Associate end users with their phones in Device Association section of End User Configuration: **a.** Select Primary User Device in Mobility Information section of End User Configuration. **b.** Configure Owner User ID at Phone Device level. **c.** Associate end users at Phone Line (DN) level.	

The tasks to be performed and information to be remembered is daunting. That said, it is important that you keep detailed notes of each step in the installation where input is required. There seems to be no shortage of opportunities to mistype user names, passwords, or IP addresses.

Troubleshooting CUPS User Problems

A number of issues can arise that affect the way users are shown in the CUP server. This section is meant to address a few of the more common issues surrounding the addition of users to the CUPS configuration.

Problem: Users Not Showing Up in CUPS

At times, users will be somewhat reluctant to show up in the CUPS user listing. These troublemakers can be brought to heel, often without a great deal of effort. The first issue to be addressed in the user discussion is the difficulty with one or more users showing up in the CUPS user list. Figure 9-13 shows a new screenshot from the System Troubleshooter.

After installing and configuring CUPS, this rather ambiguous screen can be a bit daunting. The System Troubleshooter shows it as a Warning. Warning denotes that it's not an error, yet there will be no logging into CUPC clients if this issue persists, so it might as well be one of the dreaded red circles.

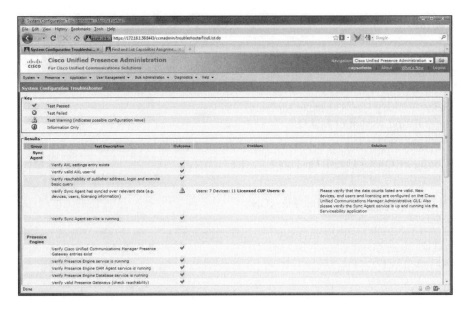

Figure 9-13   *CUPS User Count in System Troubleshooter*

Possible Cause: Capabilities Assignment in CUCM

Because the System Troubleshooter shows a warning rather than an error, that points to the first, and most likely, cause. Note also that there is no "fix" link. This is a good indicator that the problem might not lie within the CUPS server itself. The solution suggested hints at the problem. Point your browser to the CUCM CCMAdmin page, and check the Capabilities Assignment for your users. Click **System > Licensing > Capabilities Assignment**. If you see a picture similar to Figure 9-14, there's an easy fix.

Notice that the figure shows all the users, but none of them show the requisite check marks in the CUP Enabled and CUPC Enabled columns. Assign these capabilities to the desired users by clicking the box next to their names; then click the **Bulk Assignment** button. Check both boxes, as shown in Figure 9-15.

After you've checked both boxes, click the **Save** button. A prompt tells you to ensure that you have adequate Device License Units to perform the operation. Click **OK**, and you should see a more welcoming screen similar to that in Figure 9-16.

Note the message stating the assignment was successful. More important, note that the checks are properly showing in the CUP Enabled and CUPC Enabled columns.

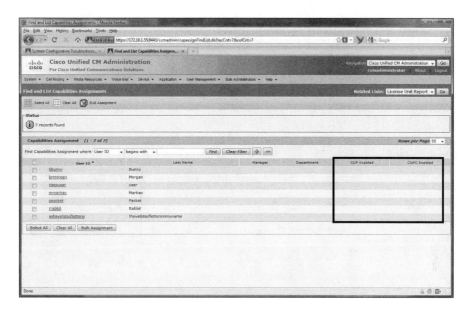

Figure 9-14   *CUCM Capabilities Assignment*

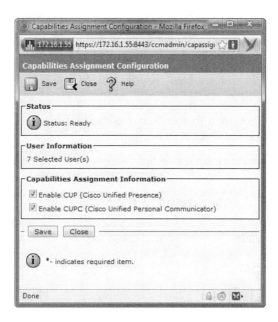

Figure 9-15   *Assigning CUP Capabilities*

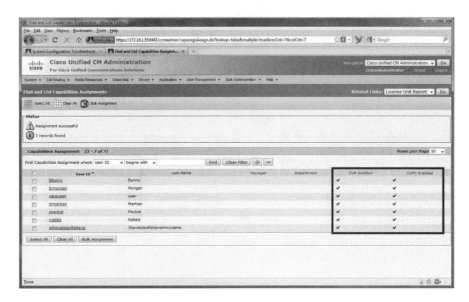

Figure 9-16   *Assigning CUP Capabilities Continued*

Note   For a user's Presence to be seen by others, they must have the CUP Enabled box assigned. Without this, their Presence status will neither be seen nor maintained by the server. They don't necessarily need to have CUPC enabled if all that is wanted is to allow others to see their Presence status.

Returning to the CUPS System Troubleshooter, as shown in Figure 9-17, you can see that it is happily returning green check marks again.

At this point, the users are available to assign to applications and profiles.

Possible Cause: LDAP Synchronization Failing

In cases where Lightweight Directory Access Protocol (LDAP) is in use for managing users, additional dependencies need to be checked should the restart of the Sync Agent not succeed in bringing the user into CUPS. There is a key question to consider in this circumstance: Was LDAP Sync working at one time and no longer seems to be doing so? The answer to that question somewhat determines the direction of your troubleshooting efforts.

The relationship of LDAP services and the CUCM/CUPS Clusters can be a bit confusing. Users won't show up in CUPS until the Capabilities Assignment is done in CUCM. That has been established. However, how did the user get into CUCM? If LDAP Synchronization has been enabled on the CUCM, all users must be added via the LDAP utilities, which can vary based on the type of LDAP service in use (either Microsoft Active Directory [AD] or Netscape/SunOne). If AD is in use, the users must be added via the Active Directory Users and Computers tool on the Domain Controller. When the user is added there, and assuming that the user was added to a container within the search scope defined, it is imported to the CUCM at the next scheduled sync.

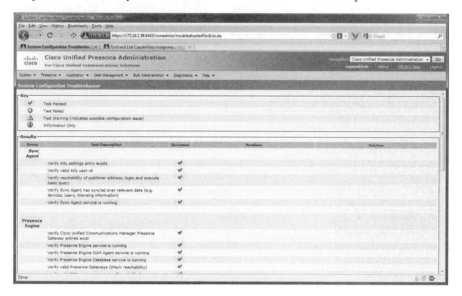

Figure 9-17   *CUPS System Troubleshooter*

If waiting for the next sync is not an option, because it might be quite a significant interval (that is, once per day, once per week, or more), a sync can be forced via the CUCM Admin page. Point a browser to the CUCM Admin page, and click on **System > LDAP > LDAP > LDAP Directory**. As usual, the blank query screen displays. Click **Find** and then click the LDAP profile you want to sync. Figure 9-18 shows the LDAP Directory screen.

There is a Perform Full Sync Now button at the top of the page, or you can scroll to the bottom of the page and click the **Perform Full Sync Now** button to begin the synchronization process immediately.

Note   The LDAP Sync could take a while and cause some service impact depending on the number of users in the LDAP search scope. Care should be taken to ensure that this is done during a maintenance window or during off-hours.

When the sync is complete, recheck the CUPS Admin page to see if the user in question has shown up in the list. If not, restart the Sync Agent on the CUPS server again.

If the simple resync doesn't do the trick or the sync has never worked (perhaps due to an entirely missing config), keep reading. The next discussion covers LDAP pitfalls.

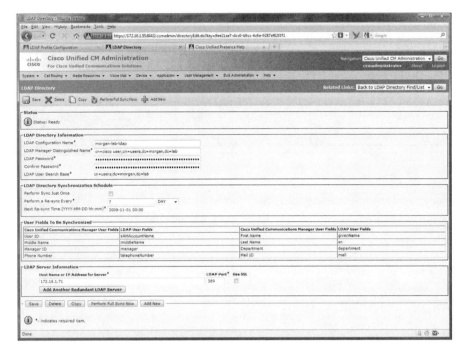

Figure 9-18   *CUCM LDAP Directory Sync*

Problem: LDAP Not Synchronizing

LDAP Synchronization is a relatively new feature for CUCM. Additionally, it seems that traditional telecom and network teams don't tend to have a full understanding of LDAP. This is especially true when it comes to an Active Directory infrastructure. LDAP sync is supported with AD and Netscape SunOne LDAP directory structures. The following sections explore a couple of the most common issues when the sync fails.

Possible Cause: Bind Distinguished Name Incorrectly Entered

To most of us who have been working with Cisco Unified Communications components for any significant length of time, a DN is a Directory Number. In LDAP terms, a DN is a Distinguished Name. This Distinguished Name is far from intuitive and it must be exactly correct.

An AD administrator creates a Cisco User specifically for purposes of LDAP Sync. All it really needs is visibility to the container where the users live. Along with the user name, the AD Administrator provides the DN and User Search Base. The User Search Base is a complicated means of saying, "where the users are located." For purposes of this discussion, I created a user named **Cisco User** in AD that provides the credentials to perform the LDAP Sync. Here's an example:

```
User Name: Cisco User
Password: cisco
LDAP Distinguished Name: cn=cisco user,cn=users,dc=morgan,dc=lab
LDAP User Search Base: cn=users,dc=morgan,dc=lab
```

Figure 9-19 shows the CUCM LDAP Directory page where the configuration was performed in the CUCM Admin utility.

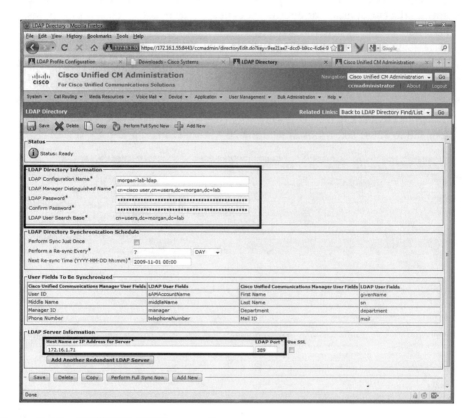

Figure 9-19 *CUCM LDAP Directory Page*

There are a few items of note aside from the info in Figure 9-19. You can see where all the information provided by the AD Administrator was entered. There is also an opportunity to set up a sync schedule. I run mine once per week, but then I don't have much in the way of user turnover in my lab. In production, you'll likely want to run it more frequently. Run it off-hours or during a maintenance window because it can take considerable time and resources.

Notice also the bottom of the figure. The hostname/IP address of the LDAP server needs to be entered. The default LDAP port is TCP 389. You can add additional LDAP servers for redundancy purposes.

There is a great deal of room for error when entering the Distinguished Name and the Search Base. I'm sure we're all aware of the dangers of mis-entering the password, so I'll bypass a lecture on that piece.

Possible Cause: LDAP Sync Going to Global Catalog Server

In AD, the Global Catalog Server keeps track of the directory structure and accounts. It provides the fastest means of directory lookups, authentication, and other functions. So, this is not necessarily an error; actually, it tends to be the recommended way to go. If you're going to be performing the sync to the Global Catalog Server, your sync will likely fail initially. This is true even if you somehow manage to type the entire Distinguished Name and User Search Base correctly on the first try.

The reason is simple. The Global Catalog Server likes to communicate on port TCP 3268. Click your way back to the LDAP Directory Page in the CUCM, and change the port from 389 to 3268. Take a look at Figure 9-20 where I've made just that change.

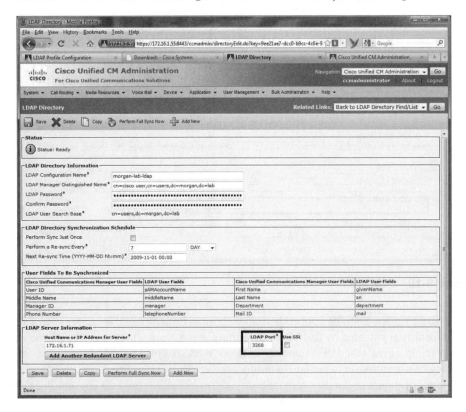

Figure 9-20   *LDAP Sync to a Global Catalog Server*

Make the change on your own configuration and click **Save**. Click the **Perform Full Sync Now** button to begin the sync. Again, be careful with LDAP sync during business hours.

In the CUPS Configuration, similar information is required and the same dangers exist; however, they're broken up a bit differently. Open the CUPS Admin utility and click **Application > Unified Personal Communicator > LDAP Server**. Click **Add New** and fill out the information (or edit an existing one). Figure 9-21 shows the LDAP server page.

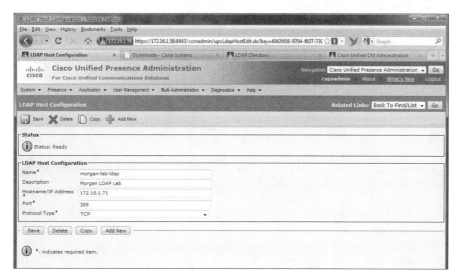

Figure 9-21 *CUPS LDAP Server Page*

Note that this is a fairly simple page. Of utmost interest are the Hostname/IP Address field and the Port field. Leave it defaulted to 389 if you're not synchronizing to a Global Catalog Server. Change it to 3268 if you are. Click **Save** and proceed to the next step.

While still in the CUPS Admin utility, click **Application > Unified Personal Communicator > LDAP Profile**. Click **Add New** or click an existing one to edit it. This page is where all the fun occurs. The prior page was just to give a false sense of comfort before dropping you into this one. The focus here is, of course, on the LDAP-related name and user credentials that specify the user container and the authentication information used in parsing that container. Figure 9-22 shows the LDAP Profile Configuration page.

This page presents you with yet another opportunity to mistype the Distinguished Name and User Search Base. Again, I believe that mistyping passwords will already be high on the priority list, so I'll avoid the topic.

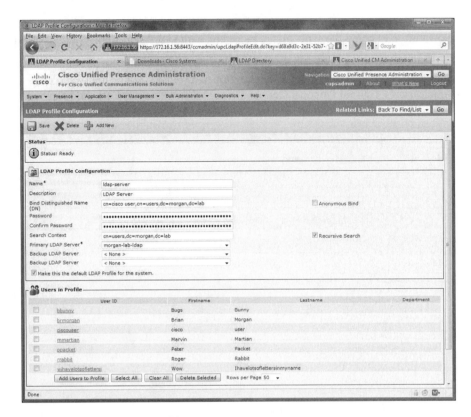

Figure 9-22 *CUPS LDAP Profile Page*

Problem: Newly Added Users Not Showing in CUPS

At various times, it will be necessary to add new users to the system. For the sake of discussion, assume that a new user has been added and the Capabilities Assignment properly performed. This, of course, assumes that said users do show up in the CUCM user listing. A check of the System Troubleshooter shows all green checks indicating that the CUP server thinks it's happy. That would be a definite formula for frustration. Thankfully, the likeliest fix is quite simple.

Possible Cause: Sync Agent Out of Sync

From time to time, the Sync Agent service decides to be difficult. Fire up a browser and wander over to the CUPS Serviceability page. It can be accessed directly by entering **https://***cups-ip-address*/**ccmservice**.

Alternatively, you can go directly to the CUPS Admin page; then use the navigation box to get to the Serviceability page. Regardless of how you get there, get there.

When there, click **Tools > Control Center-Feature Services**. You are presented with a drop-down box listing the servers in the CUPS cluster. Select the CUPS Publisher and click **Go**. Down the page a bit, you see the Cisco UP Sync Agent. Select the radio button adjacent to it; then click the **Restart** button at the top of the page. Figure 9-23 shows a screenshot of the Control Center-Feature Services page.

The Restart button is the green symbol composed of a Play and Stop symbol as would be seen on a CD or DVD player. It takes a moment to restart. When completed, go back to the user page in the CUPS admin utility and verify that the new user has indeed shown up.

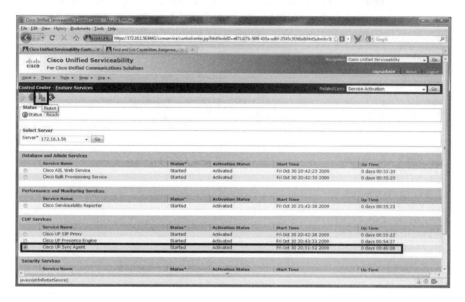

Figure 9-23   *Control Center-Feature Services Page*

Problem: Subcluster Defined but All Users Remaining Assigned to CUPS Publisher Node

Redundancy and High Availability are key features of CUPS 7. Users can be spread across multiple CUP servers in a clustered manner similar to IP Phones with CUCM. Adding a Subscriber node to a cluster is relatively simple. When the new node is up and in sync, users should be allocated to it in a balanced fashion by default so that they are evenly distributed across the cluster. On occasion, the situation arises in which they are not evenly distributed, but all remain assigned to the Publisher node.

Possible Cause: Cisco UP Sync Agent Service Parameter

The most likely cause is that an administrator was experimenting with Service Parameters and changed the parameter that deals specifically with user assignment. Open the CUPS

Admin page and click on **System > Service Parameters**. From the drop-down box, select the Publisher node. A new drop-down box appears from which you should select the Cisco UP Sync Agent service. The service should show a state of (Active) beside it.

When the service is selected, the screen automatically progresses to the Service Parameter Configuration page. There is only one configurable User Assignment Mode option on the page, as shown in Figure 9-24.

The User Assignment Mode sets the distribution algorithm of users across the cluster. The options are Balanced (default) and None. Because users are not spreading out across the cluster's nodes, it is most likely set to None. The None setting results in no assignment of users to the nodes in the cluster by the Sync Agent. Change the setting to **Balanced**, click **Save**, and then restart the Sync Agent service from the Serviceability page.

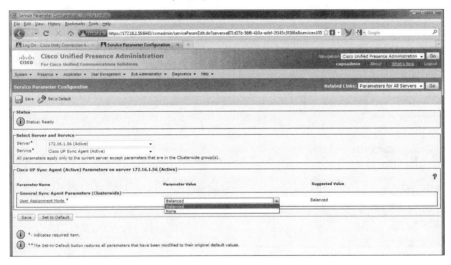

Figure 9-24   *CUPS Cluster User Assignment Mode*

Note   If you look at the help screen for this page (**Help > This Page**), it mentions a Round Robin Mode of User Assignment. Referring to the figure, the drop-down box is expanded. The only options are Balanced and None. Balanced is the setting that specifies the Round-Robin mode. It must be set before users can propagate to the subscriber node.

Given time, the users should start to be automatically reassigned to the subscriber nodes in the cluster. Verify this by clicking **System > Topology**. User counts are shown on this page in association with the node to which they are assigned. This page automatically refreshes periodically.

Troubleshooting CUPC Problems

CUPC has numerous potential issues associated with it. Many of the configuration issues will be due to server configuration problems initially. This is typical of new CUPS installations. This section focuses on a few issue surrounding initial installation and some of the more common issues not necessarily directly associated with configuration issues.

Problem: User's Name Contains Too Many Characters

This particular issue is relatively common and was previously mentioned in the chapter. In anticipation of dealing with this exact issue, a user was created in Active Directory. His name is Wow Ihavelotsoflettersinmyname, as shown in Figure 9-25.

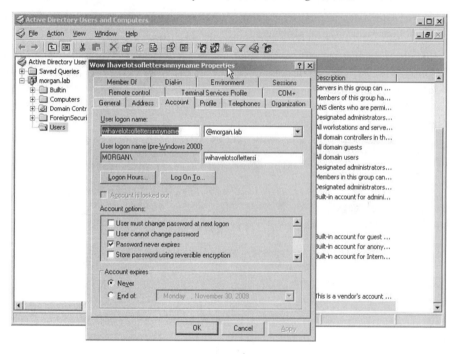

Figure 9-25   *Active Directory User Configuration*

The main source of confusion is in the varying character counts utilized by the interdependent systems that make up the solution. Consider the following:

- **Active Directory User Name:** Wow Ihavelotsoflettersinmyname

- **Active Directory User ID:** wihavelotsoflettersi

- **CUCM User ID (from AD):** wihavelotsoflettersi

Because we're importing the users via LDAP, one potential conflict is avoided. The CUCM user ID will match that in AD. The source of trouble comes in the configuration, or rather the creation, of the CUPC endpoint in CUCM. There is a requirement that dictates that the device name of an endpoint can contain only 15 characters. It's easy to see that, with wihavelotsoflettersi, we'll run out way before 15 characters. In fact, that user ID is 20 characters long.

Adding insult to injury, the CUPC device name rules state that UPC must be the first three characters of the device name. So, now, we're down to 12 available characters for the 20 characters we need to fit.

Possible Cause: Too Many Characters

I know, it's not a possible cause, it is *the* cause. But some sacrifices must be made in the name of consistency, right? Moving on.

The problem itself seems rather confusing, and it can well be just that on the surface. The solution, however, is not so difficult or confusing. Cisco anticipated such issues and has added a bit of intelligence into the system to deal with it. When you create the CUPC endpoint definition, go ahead and truncate the user ID to the first 12 characters, as shown in Figure 9-26.

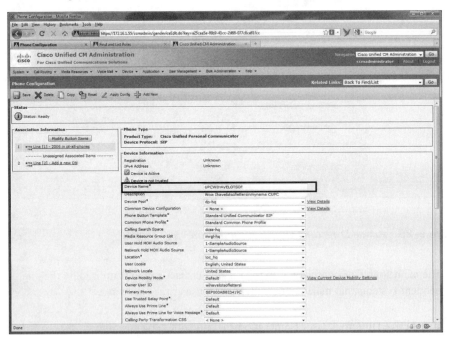

Figure 9-26 *CUPC Endpoint Creation in CUCM*

With the CUPC endpoint added as UCPIHAVELOTSOF as a device name, the user should be able to launch CUPC and log in. So our list now looks like this:

- **Active Directory User Name:** Wow Ihavelotsoflettersinmyname

- **Active Directory User ID:** wihavelotsoflettersi

- **CUCM User ID (from AD):** wihavelotsoflettersi

- **CUCM CUPC Device Name:** UCPIHAVELOTSOF

As you might have found by now, assuming you've already provisioned this user as completely as possible, and because this is a troubleshooting chapter, additional instances of the user ID will be needed for the Voicemail and Conferencing pieces of the User Profile puzzle. Luckily, CUPC provisioning seems to be the only place where the this poses a problem. In Unity and Unity Connection, for example, the user ID will match what is imported from AD.

So we're done, right? This user should be happily ready to go. I'm not quite done picking on him just yet. As we'll see in the next problem, all might not be ready for our problem-prone new user after all. Some other key points need to be made on the subject of adding users.

Problem: User Added but Will Not Fully Connect via CUPC

The scenario seemed simple—well, perhaps simple if you only consider the solution to the problem. When Wow launched CUPC, he did indeed get logged in, kind of. Take a look at Figure 9-27.

Figure 9-27 *CUPC with Limited Connection*

The status at the bottom of the CUPC client window shows Connected (Limited). This indicates a problem in the configuration, of course. But where? A number of places directly impact the CUPC functionality. All these eventually tie back to the user's profile in the CUPS configuration. We'll work our way to that point.

Possible Cause: User Device Associations

The first step is to validate all the places in which a user can be associated to a DN and a device. There are quite a few of these to check. Here's a quick list:

Step 1. **CUCM Admin Page > User Management > End User > Find:** Click the user's name and check that the Device Association has been made to both the physical desk phone and the CUCP client. While you're here, scroll down the page about halfway to the Directory Number Associations section. Use the drop-down box to select the user's primary DN. Click **Save.**

Figure 9-28 shows the End User Configuration page with Device Associations.

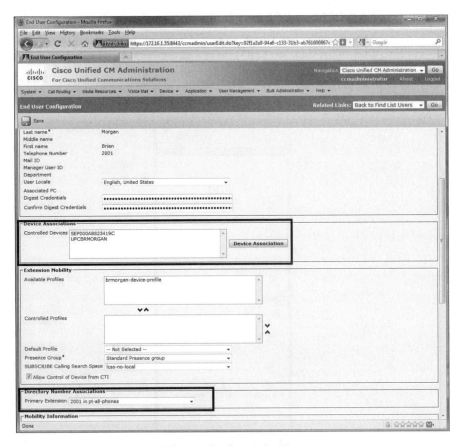

Figure 9-28 *End User Configuration Page*

Step 2.   **CUCM Admin Page > Device > Phone > Find:** Click the user's desk phone, and ensure that the proper Owner User ID is specified. Figure 9-29 shows the Phone Configuration page.

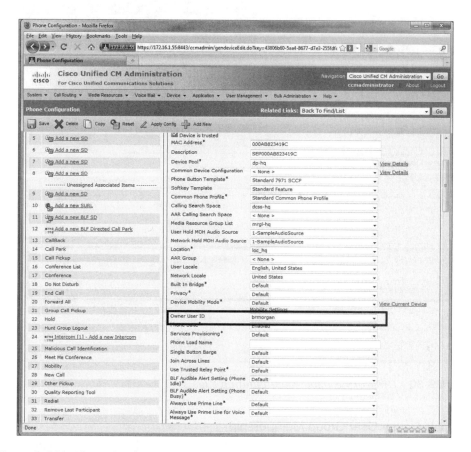

Figure 9-29   *Phone Configuration Page*

Step 3.   While checking the desk phone configuration, click the DN configuration link at the top-left portion. The Associated Devices box should show both endpoints. Scroll all the way to the bottom of the page, and click Associate End Users. A window pops up. Click **Find**; then check the box next to the user's ID. Click **Add Selected** to return to the DN Configuration page. Click **Save and Apply Config** (CUCM 7.1(3)+ feature). Figure 9-30 shows the Directory Number Configuration page.

Checking progress is as simple as having the user exit the CUPC client and relaunch it. Should our user's poor luck seem to be holding out, it's time to investigate the user's capabilities and permissions.

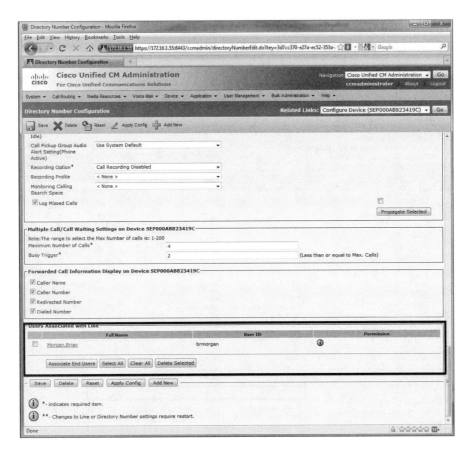

Figure 9-30   *Directory Number Configuration Page*

Possible Cause: User Group Membership

Because this is a new user, it would be prudent to compare the user's configuration to existing users. You know that all the necessary associations are there and properly made. The next piece to check is Group Membership in the CUCM. Fire up the CCMAdmin page and go to **User Management > End User**. Select a working user and check their group membership. Chapter 3, "Installing Cisco Unified Presence Server 7," includes discussions of group memberships and roles. Figure 9-31 shows a working user configuration.

Notice that a number of groups are selected. Make a note of these. Select Back to Find List Users in the Related Links box at the top-right portion and click **Go** to return to the user list. Select the user in question, in this case Wow. Figure 9-32 shows the user's existing group membership.

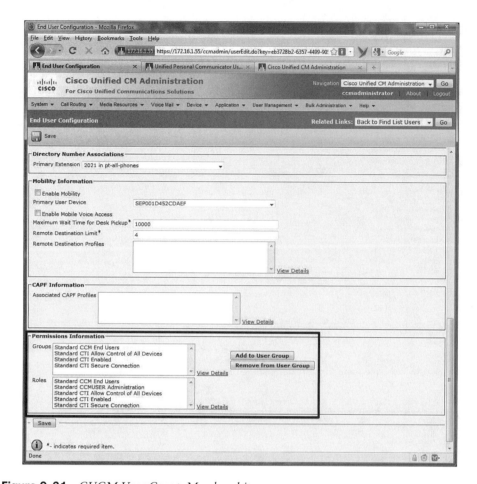

Figure 9-31   *CUCM User Group Membership*

Notice that the figure shows no group membership at all. Click on **Add to User Group** and select the following groups:

- Standard CCM End User

- Standard CTI Allow Control of All Devices

- Standard CTI Enabled

- Standard CTI Secure Connection

Click **Add Selected** to return to the user page. Click **Save**.

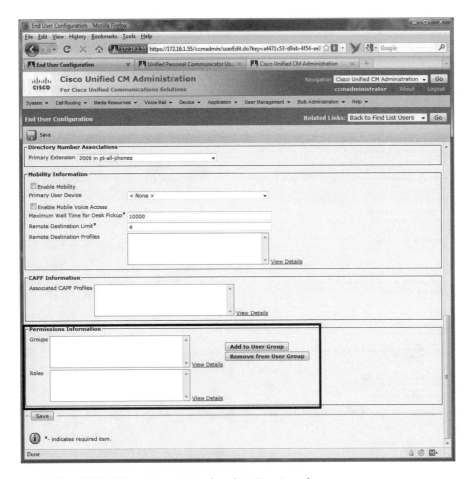

Figure 9-32　*CUCM User Group Membership Continued*

Note　Technically, all that is required for this particular function is the Standard CTI Enabled group. The Standard CCM End User group should have been added previously. That enables the end user to make use of additional CUCM capabilities.

If you scroll back down to the bottom of the page, you notice that the Roles have been populated automatically, as shown in Figure 9-33.

With the membership in place, there is one more thing left to check to ensure that the user configuration is complete. In the CUPS Admin utility, click **Application > Cisco Unified Personal Communicator > User Settings**. Click the **Find** button to bring up a list of users. Select the user in question. Figure 9-34 shows the Unified Personal Communicator User Settings page.

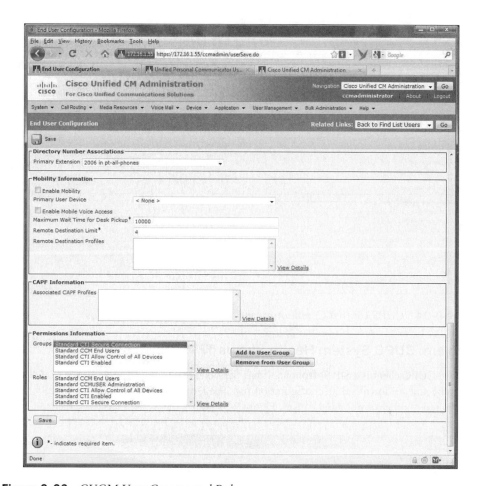

Figure 9-33 *CUCM User Groups and Roles*

This page provides the core functionality for users regarding their CUPC configuration. This screen specifies their voicemail profile, conferencing profile, CTI Gateway profile, and LDAP profile. If any of these components are left out of the configuration, that service will be inaccessible to the user. Take, for example, the conferencing profile in the figure. Because there is not a profile configured, this user will not be able to escalate communications into a collaborative conferencing session. You can see that the remaining items are selected. There might be multiple options for each profile. Ensure that each is properly selected based on the needs of the user in question.

With all things verified, let's check the user's login capabilities. Launch CUPC and login. The user should be able to log in and begin normal use of the CUPC client at this point.

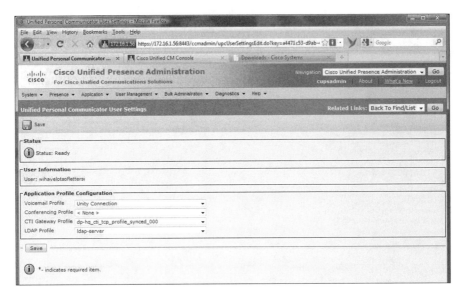

Figure 9-34 *CUPS Unified Communicator User Settings Page*

Problem: CUPC System Health Shows TFTP Download Failed

The CUPC client is a SIP Softphone. It has the same needs as any phone. That is, it needs to be able to download its configuration file. The Download Failed message usually has a limited number of potential causes. Figure 9-35 shows the System Health screen.

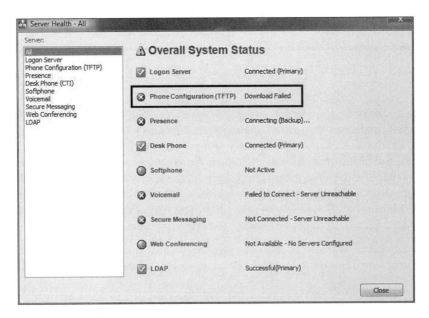

Figure 9-35 *CUPC Show System Health Showing TFTP Download Failed*

Possible Cause: TFTP Server Not Configured in CUPS

The first place to check is in the CUPS Admin utility. Launch a browser and navigate to it. Click **Application > Unified Personal Communicator > Settings.** Figure 9-36 shows the Unified Personal Communicator Settings page.

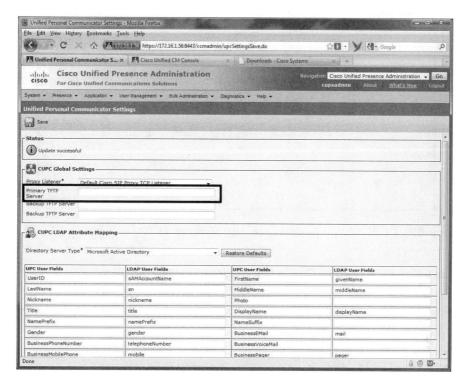

Figure 9-36   *CUPS Unified Personal Communicator Settings Page*

The issue should pretty well jump off the page at you. The Primary TFTP Server field is blank. Enter the TFTP server IP address in the Primary TFTP Server field. If redundant TFTP servers are in the network, add them as well; then click **Save.** Have the user exit and relaunch the CUPC Client to verify proper functionality, as shown in Figure 9-37.

Problem: Cannot Get Voicemail in CUPC

Voicemail integration has long been a source of mixed pain and pleasure. When it works, it works well. When it breaks, it seems to fall apart. Luckily, utilizing voicemail with CUPC is not so difficult. A few things need to be in place for it to function properly. We'll address them in order. CUPC works with either Cisco Unity or Cisco Unity Connection. In these examples, Cisco Unity Connection plays the leading role.

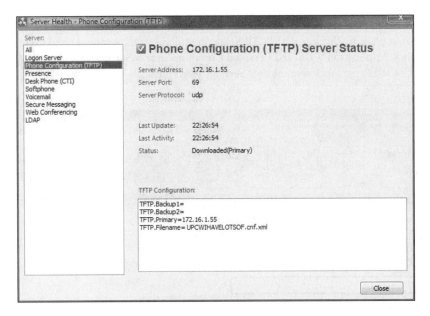

Figure 9-37   *CUPC Show System Health Page Showing TFTP Success*

Possible Cause: Voicemail Profile Not Selected in User Settings

In the CUPS Admin page, click **Application > Unified Personal Communicator > Voicemail Server**. If an entry has not already been created, click **Add New**. Figure 9-38 shows the Voicemail Server Configuration page.

Validate the information; that is, if you're not adding it for the first time. The port defaults to TCP 143. Don't change it unless you have a good reason.

Next up is the addition/validation of the Voicemail Profile. Click **Application > Unified Personal Communicator > Voicemail Profile**, and click **Find** to list existing profiles, or **Add New** to create one. Figure 9-39 shows the Voicemail Profile Configuration page.

This is the page where you set the voicemail pilot for CUPC users using this voicemail profile. The primary voicemail server at the top of the page is the one you just added on the last screen. You can add users to the profile here, or go back to **Applications > Unified Personal Communicator > User Settings**, and select each user to fill in their full profile. Figure 9-40 shows the User Settings page.

Notice that the user does not have a voicemail profile selected. That is the cause, in this case, of the inability to utilize voicemail. Select the appropriate voicemail profile from the drop-down box, and click **Save**.

Have the user exit CUPC and relaunch it to verify functionality.

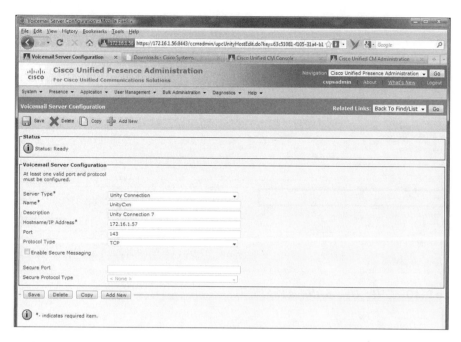

Figure 9-38   *CUPS Voicemail Server Configuration Page*

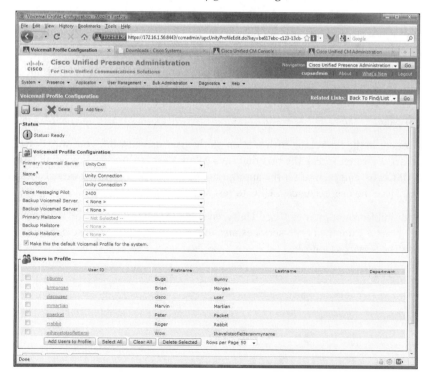

Figure 9-39   *CUPS Voicemail Profile Configuration Page*

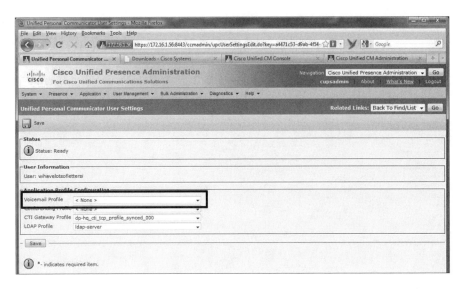

Figure 9-40   *CUPS User Settings Page*

Possible Cause: IMAP Not Enabled in Unity/Unity Connection

Although IMAP is part of the default licensing for both Unity and Unity Connection now, it is not enabled for users by default on the systems themselves. In Unity Connection, this is fairly easy to accomplish.

Launch the Cisco Unity Connection Admin page, and click **Class of Service** under the Class of Service header. It's the second one down in the list in the left column. Next, click the Voice Mail User COS. Figure 9-41 shows the Edit Class of Service (Voice Mail User COS) page.

As evident in the figure, the fifth section on the page as you work your way down is Licensed Features. Check the box that says **Allow Users to Access Voicemail Using an IMAP Client**, and then select the appropriate option below regarding user access to messages. Have the user relaunch CUPC to test Voicemail functionality.

If your implementation uses Cisco Unity, enabling IMAP is done on the Exchange Server. Click **Start > Run**; then type **services.msc** to get to the Services Console. Figure 9-42 shows the Services Console.

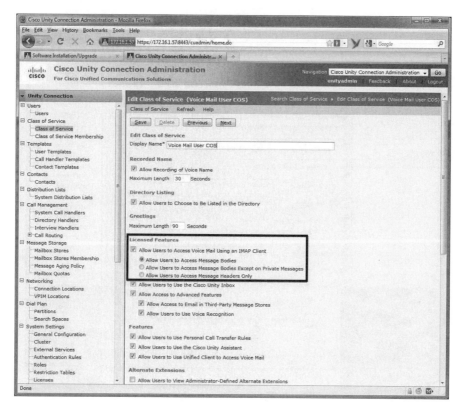

Figure 9-41   *Unity Connection Voice Mail Class of Service Page*

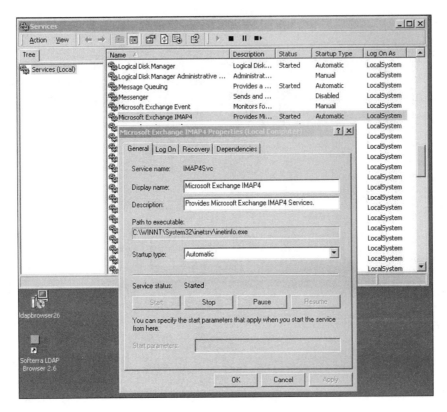

Figure 9-42   *Windows Services Console*

Scroll down to the Microsoft Exchange IMAP4 service and double-click it. Set it to Automatic, and then click **start.** When the service starts, click **OK.** At this point, you need to also ensure that the IMAP protocol has been added to the Exchange configuration.

To do this, open the Exchange System Manager. Click **Administrative Groups > First Administrative Group > Servers,** and select the appropriate Mailbox Server. Figure 9-43 shows the Exchange System Manager.

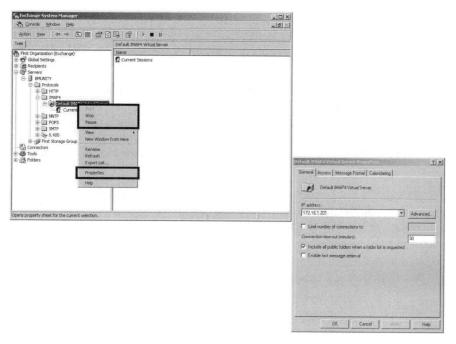

Figure 9-43 *Exchange System Manager*

Expand the Protocols entry and select **IMAP4.** Right-click the **Default IMAP4 Virtual Server.** Note in the figure that the options include Start, Stop, and Pause. Start is grayed out where Stop is available. This indicates that the service is already started. Select **Properties to** verify the settings and click **OK.**

Summary

Numerous dependencies are on both sides of the communications. For a list of dependencies on both the CUCM and CUPS servers, refer to Table 9-1.

At any point during the installation, the System Troubleshooter can be referenced as a general health check and next-steps tool. The System Troubleshooter indicates where errors exist in the configuration and offers suggestions and links to the page where you can fix those configuration errors.

If problems persist, the RTMT can be a powerful troubleshooting tool. RTMT is a graphical interface that pulls real-time information from the servers in the CUPS cluster. If a TAC case has been opened at any time, the RTMT can be used to gather trace files and zip them for download to your local machine so that they can be uploaded and attached to the TAC case for review by the engineer.

Outside of the RTMT, other tools are available for use in troubleshooting. The System Status Page, System Troubleshooter, and MOC Troubleshooter all provide significant information about their respective targets. By far, the most useful tool in troubleshooting a new installation is the System Troubleshooter; however, as this chapter discussed, there are no lack of interdependencies after the initial installation that can cause a headache or two.

The Cisco UC Components are all interconnected. This is both a blessing and a curse at times. They operate as a single solution from the standpoint of the user community. They are still individual components from an administration and maintenance standpoint. The manner and means by which these components interact must be understood. This includes LDAP integration, Voicemail integration, Conferencing integration, and of course telephony integration.

By no means has every potential possibility been touched upon in this chapter. In constructing the chapter, only the most common issues were addressed. Should additional information be required, check out these sites:

- **Cisco Unified Presence: Error/System Messages, Field Notices and Troubleshooting TechNotes:**
  www.cisco.com/en/US/products/ps6837/tsd_products_support_troubleshoot_and_alerts.html

- **Cisco Unified Presence: End User, Maintenance and Operation Guides:**
  www.cisco.com/en/US/products/ps6837/tsd_products_support_maintain_and_operate.html

- **Cisco Unified Presence: Configuration and Programming Guides:**
  www.cisco.com/en/US/products/ps6837/tsd_products_support_configure.html

- **Cisco Unified Presence: Install and Upgrade Guides:**
  www.cisco.com/en/US/products/ps6837/tsd_products_support_install_and_upgrade.html

If you cannot find the answers you seek within these pages, contact the Cisco Technical Assistance Center (TAC) at 1-800-553-2447 or open a case online (CCO ID required) at http://tools.cisco.com/ServiceRequestTool/create/. Severity one, network down emergency cases should be opened via the hotline at the preceding number. Severity two and three cases can be opened most efficiently utilizing the online creation tool.

Index

informIT.com — THE TRUSTED TECHNOLOGY LEARNING SOURCE

LearnIT at InformIT

Looking for a book, eBook, or training video on a new technology? Seeking timely and relevant information and tutorials? Looking for expert opinions, advice, and tips? **InformIT has the solution.**

- Learn about new releases and special promotions by subscribing to a wide variety of newsletters.
  Visit **informit.com/newsletters**.

- Access FREE podcasts from experts at **informit.com/podcasts**.

- Read the latest author articles and sample chapters at **informit.com/articles**.

- Access thousands of books and videos in the Safari Books Online digital library at **safari.informit.com**.

- Get tips from expert blogs at **informit.com/blogs**.

Visit **informit.com/learn** to discover all the ways you can access the hottest technology content.

Are You Part of the **IT** Crowd?

Connect with Pearson authors and editors via RSS feeds, Facebook, Twitter, YouTube, and more! Visit **informit.com/socialconnect**.

Cisco Unified Presence
Fundamentals

Learn how to use Cisco Unified Presence Server and
Client to streamline communication and
improve business agility

Brian Morgan, CCIE No. 4865 · Shane Lisenbea
ciscopress.com   Michael C. Popovich III, CCIE No. 9599

FREE Online Edition

Your purchase of **Cisco Unified Presence Fundamentals** includes access to a free online edition for 45 days through the Safari Books Online subscription service. Nearly every Cisco Press book is available online through Safari Books Online, along with more than 5,000 other technical books and videos from publishers such as Addison-Wesley Professional, Exam Cram, IBM Press, O'Reilly, Prentice Hall, Que, and Sams.

SAFARI BOOKS ONLINE allows you to search for a specific answer, cut and paste code, download chapters, and stay current with emerging technologies.

Activate your FREE Online Edition at www.informit.com/safarifree

> **STEP 1:** Enter the coupon code: XNDYYBI.

> **STEP 2:** New Safari users, complete the brief registration form.
> Safari subscribers, just log in.

If you have difficulty registering on Safari or accessing the online edition,
please e-mail customer-service@safaribooksonline.com